TRAVEL
To Free
The Soul

The seven-year journey of a girl's dream to be free . . .

A book by Natalie Ollivier

Travel to Free the Soul by Natalie Ollivier

ISBN 978-1-952027-20-8 (Paperback)
ISBN 978-1-952027-21-5 (Hardback)

This book is written to provide information and motivation to readers. Its purpose is not to render any type of psychological, legal, or professional advice of any kind. The content is the sole opinion and expression of the author, and not necessarily that of the publisher.

Copyright © 2020 by Natalie Ollivier

All rights reserved. No part of this book may be reproduced, transmitted, or distributed in any form by any means, including, but not limited to, recording, photocopying, or taking screenshots of parts of the book, without prior written permission from the author or the publisher. Brief quotations for noncommercial purposes, such as book reviews, permitted by Fair Use of the U.S. Copyright Law, are allowed without written permissions, as long as such quotations do not cause damage to the book's commercial value. For permissions, write to the publisher, whose address is stated below.

Printed in the United States of America.

New Leaf Media, LLC
175 S. 3rd Street, Suite 200
Columbus, OH 43215
www.thenewleafmedia.com

Contents

PART ONE: Spiritual Awakening 1
    A Seed in My Consciousness 3
    A Rebellious Teenager... 7
    Relationship vs. Freedom 15
    The Path to My Profession 19
    Travel for Growth 24
    A Great Adventure: Sayulita................................... 30
    Questions and Fears 55
PART TWO: Spiritual Journey 59
    Travel Diary 61
PART THREE: Becoming A Free Soul........................... 199
    The spiritual awakening of 2012 203
    2013: Travel, travel, and more travel 205
    Endings, movements, and beginnings in 2014.... 208
    Instability, financial crises, failed political career, a really hard 2015 213
    2+0+1+6 = year of infinite possibilities, reconstruction of the self, and a family battle for freedom 218
    Spirituality in the city and about my book 221
    Time for a soul rebirth, the 2017 transformational journey 223

2018 - Living the millennial dream 230
Time to confront reality, assume adulthood
and face Saturn return. A 2019 that changed
all directions. 238
Reshaping Natalie in the mountains. A 2020
of global lockdown and change of paradigm. 252
Reflections about spirituality, would I
recommend it? 257
Gallery 261

This book is based on a true story. However, in order to protect some individuals, names or descriptions of people, locations, and otherwise undisclosed situations not outlined here, have been changed. Any resemblance to any actual persons, living or dead, or locales is entirely coincidental.

Prelude

    This is the story of my life, a millennial girl with a millennial dream of achieving a life of freedom and true happiness. Like many others of my generation, I was touched at a young age by some revolutionary ideas of almost tearing down the present system in order to create a new world with equity, sustainability, and respect for all living creatures. Much has been said about millennials, and I can't deny many of those accusations. We are rebellious, unstable in work and relationships, addicted to our phones, and some permanently seeking that perfect Instagram life, where you are paid to travel and take photographs. We have inherited a world that has become really hard in so many ways; we work more and earn less, buying a house is almost impossible, and the environmental destruction is giving us a set of problems and uncertainties. That scenario, added to an open and global network that connects us all, showed the unsatisfied it could be another way of living. That's where all YouTubers, bloggers, and influencers started to appear. Their message; you can have a life of creativity, where doing what you love can become your full-time job.
    So basically all those factors touched me: I hated the system, I didn't want to work in an office, I wanted to travel the world and monetize with what I loved. I was convinced I could have the life I dreamt of if I worked hard enough. Since young I incorporated ideas from the New Age movement; I read Deepak Chopra, Eckhart Tole, Osho, and other masters

who became my leaders. I was convinced that pursuing a spiritual life was going to give me what I wanted. That through meditation, positive thinking, and five-year plans I would manifest my wildest dreams.

Results? Let me share about my current situation. I recently turned 30 years old, and while everyone is experiencing a global lockdown with the coronavirus pandemic, I'm living in a tiny home in Canadian wilderness. My partner and I have a beautiful life in the woods; we go skiing in the backcountry, we mountain bike around the house, and while he works in construction matters I use my time to write and do what I love. I'm happily away from my hometown Mexico City, a crowded and polluted place. And thanks to the decision of undertaking a spiritual journey in 2012, now I celebrate a lifestyle of health, freedom and connection to nature. I don't know what stress is, and overall I'm really satisfied with what I created for myself.

Although, the path I took came with consequences as well, renouncing to a material world and seeking a connection with the divine has its downsides. This book, being the third edition I publish has the mission to share a more realistic and down to earth exposure of what is to pursue "the life of your dreams" from my perspective and experience. This is to all those millennials and other generations that aim for something more with their lives; maybe a spiritual journey is calling, maybe you are already on it, maybe you are tired of the system and need a change, or maybe you just want to know about a wanderer's adventure around the world. Whatever your reason is, I hope my personal exploration of freedom, spirituality, and travel gives you some valuable ideas for your own journey.

My work through my seven years of experience seeks to create a pragmatic conversation around the New Age philosophies. The main difference that we find with this new book in regards to the "five-year journey" I published in 2018, is that back then my main objective was to demonstrate that the spiritual path was THE only way a human could attain true happiness and peace. Although, I have now realized that some things in my life turned out amazing, and others didn't. And with this book, I aim to share the two sides of the story, as I'm no longer trying a sell a lifestyle that will give you all the answers you are looking for. Does spirituality really work? Can we manifest what we truly want? Is it possible to be free? We'll respond to these questions along the way.

My book is composed of three parts; the first one is the spiritual awakening; where I come from and the incorporation of new spiritual philosophies. Then comes the second part, a travel diary where you will come along my adventure to Australia. These two parts are written by my 23-year-old self. For the third part, I resume my life experiences from the moment I finished my long trip, with a more mature perspective. All this to share what my life has been from the moment I decided to connect with my intuition and seek an alternative way of living. Something that has brought me so many blessings and adventures; since then I have lived in a beach in Mexico, in France, Australia, just returned from two months in India, now I live in Canada and soon in Portugal. Many from the outside see my life as something fascinating aiming to live the same way. Remember, the grass isn't greener on the other side. So here is who I am, and what I've done to live like this.

Hope you enjoy it,
xx

PART ONE

Spiritual Awakening

A Seed in My Consciousness

    In July 2012, I was driving with my ex-boyfriend through the State of Jalisco in Mexico, heading to Puerto Vallarta; a fight had left us in total silence, something recurrent in our relationship, consuming, and even boring. I was driving, focused on the highway, while my ex-boyfriend contemplated the landscape. At that moment, I began questioning different aspects of my life. Suddenly, I realized the upcoming end of my studies—I would get my college degree, in five months I would finally conclude my education, and I would never do homework again, no more 7:00 a.m. boring classes. A big change for my life was going to happen, and when I visualized it, suddenly a feeling of panic and suffocation invaded my whole body. I felt just like being on the tip of a mountain, watching a canyon under my feet, a moment where it is necessary to react for survival. I would no longer be a student, and I had to carve my financial independence. It was time to take things seriously. In a few months, I would enter the reign of adulthood and be alone, just as you come into this world. Then, I started dialoguing with myself in silence, and I asked, 'What is the first thing you want to do when you finish University?' And my answer was immediate: to leave.

    When that resolution came into my consciousness, I felt an anxious desire to leave, like a Friday before Easter, the last class of the day. I could not conceive the idea of staying in Mexico for the rest of my life. I knew about the speed of time;

in a blink of an eye, I was going to be working on formal a job and about to get married. I needed to break that bond, I wanted to fly before my conservative society and the system had cut my wings. A quick move was required, a magical escape from that world where I had been trapped my entire life.

This is how everything begins, like a small seed, an idea coming from the virtual world where the non-visible lives; something immaterial with strong mobilizing power. From that moment, my life experienced many changes. In just a few weeks, I decided to end my relationship, having a boyfriend was no longer part of my plans. I needed to solve my life and trace a new path.

A weekend shortly after the virtual seed was implanted in my conscious reality, I went to Chinconcuac, in the State of Morelos, with some old friends from high school, including my friend Leticia, a blonde girl with a nice body and very lucky with guys. She belonged to my group of friends in adolescence, and after finishing high school, she moved to Paris for studies, making our friendship something more of a memory, becoming absent from my everyday life. She came to Mexico for a vacation in the summer, so we went to a friend's house to spend a long weekend. Without knowing it then, it was a determining moment in my process of internal revolution.

My friend Leticia, who had a few years of very intense parties in the French capital, moved a semester to Sao Paolo for studies, a place where she transformed her life radically. She began to exercise regularly, she started to practice meditation, surf, yoga, and she left behind the vices related to party. On that trip, we had talks about nutrition of which I was really passionate about. I had just decided to stop eating red meat a few weeks before. Our discussion turned to meditation, health, exercise, and drug abuse in general, while our friends could not understand anything we were talking about. We quickly made a new friendship bond. For the first time, one of my friends was attracted to subjects similar to mine. I was tired of being the only one of my friends not interested in parties and drugs. I was fascinated to see Leticia veering away from that world too.

On the recent trip with my ex-boyfriend, in a hotel in Puerto Vallarta, I took a yoga class, the second in my life. Finishing the session, while facing the sea, I remember a feeling of inner happiness so great that it brought a smile to my face as I walked towards the restaurant. I never felt that good before. A strange energy enveloped my body, tickling my skin. Despite the conflicting vacation that I was having with my ex, the class made me feel great and I did not want to be pulled out of my blissful state. I realized while I was having breakfast in silence that I felt better than after a very long massage I had the night before. I remembered that moment in Chiconcuac. I could never forget that amazing feeling, and I wanted to explore further as to the reasons why. I would want to become a yoga teacher; it was not enough to take classes. I wanted to go deeper into it. I imagined the philosophical and spiritual wealth, and I wanted that wisdom.

I searched on the internet for courses I could take to be a yoga teacher. Within minutes, I found what I wanted—I would start in a month and it would cost 3,000 pesos per module (around 160 dollars).

Returning from Chiconcuac, I formally ended my relationship with my boyfriend. I had new plans in mind and I needed to be by myself. My parents were bewildered by my sudden decisions. My mother recommended that I take some classes first and see if I really liked it. I clearly didn't pay much attention and decided to take the course.

I felt great changes happening in my life. I wanted to be single and to focus on pursuing my dreams without the limitations of a demanding guy. I would finish my degree and I had to move the energy to escape as soon as possible from my house and the smog of Mexico City. One week after I made the major decisions about my future, I chose Australia as the place where I would go for several reasons: I wanted to improve my English, nature is very exotic, excellent weather, beautiful beaches, good surf, handsome guys, and very far from my parents' home—what more would you need in life? Besides that, on a trip through Europe, I was fortunate to meet young Australians and they caught my attention. Most of them were lighthearted, friendly, artistic, with a fashion sense expressing the freedom of being. Since then I felt intrigued. I wanted to know more about their country and their culture. I remembered that experience driving along the beautiful roads of Mexico; no further thinking was needed, it was the perfect place for me. Then I said to myself, 'Australia, here I come.'

A Rebellious Teenager

I was born in Mexico City on 26 December 1989. I come from a privileged family where I never lacked anything. I attended the French Mexican Lyceum from primary to high school, where I had a French education, something that has influenced my being and way of thinking. From my father's side, I have French roots; my grandparents speak half Spanish and half French, and they keep many of the traditions and kitchen recipes. For that reason, I was sent to the Lyceum. After high school, I continued my studies entering the University straight after, choosing a career in Political Science and Public Administration at the Universidad Iberoamericana. It took me four and a half years to complete it, and when I finished, I declared myself free from the academy and its forms of authority.

A lot of my personality comes from adolescence. I never really experienced any family problems as my parents are still together and in love. My mother took care of me and was very present, attending my affective needs from an early age. My father was the breadwinner, working in the family business, but never too busy to step away from family life. Later my sister Mariel was born. Our relationship wasn't the best but over time it improved, and now she is my best friend. As a child, no one could ever preview major complications in the future. I was not excellent at school but that wasn't an issue. My mother made me take ballet lessons (currently I thank her) and that was the only annoyance. When I was young, my father took us on different trips, educating us for the love of knowledge and interest in different cultures; however, when adolescence arrived, everything changed.

In the French Lyceum, I had the worst behavior; for two years in a row, I won the prize for 'greatest party girl', getting crowned as the queen of nightlife. I showed a deep rejection of authority, I always had problems with teachers, I was constantly skipping classes, and at the Director's office. My parents didn't know about my misdeeds because I learned my mother's signature and used it regularly. The school had a lot of patience because they were only interested in forming intellectual elite to pass the *Baccalauréat*, a French exam applied in all subjects during the last two years of high school, without it, studies in any French university was denied. Because my grades were reasonable, they tolerated my misbehavior.

That time, I questioned my parent's teachings. They asked me 'to study' and I preferred skipping school, talking in classes, doing the minimum tasks possible, and fighting with the teachers. I was told that 'exercise is fundamental to health' yet I left ballet and forgot about any physical activity. I was also told 'having a boyfriend is a beautiful thing' yet I had a destructive relationship where I tried everything except formality: 'frees', 'friends with benefits', 'boyfriends but no one knows', and many more. I was also told to 'never try drugs', but my school was based on liberal thinking (French education), so we were told to think for ourselves, causing an open-minded youth that started drugs really early. It was almost impossible for me to follow the rules. I never accepted the night time set—, if I needed to be home at one o'clock in the morning, I would arrive at two; if I had the chance to come back at two, then I would push it until five in the morning. I wanted to be free and restrictions made me really angry. It was an endless problem with my parents.

My rebellion was manifested in various ways. I was the most limited in permissions among my friends, but I partied the most and was the most extroverted one. I lived my life by doing nonsense and challenging the limits of authority. My only interest in life was parties, I lived for them. It was the only moment where I could forget about my reality, getting drunk, and having incredible times, living the experience to the maximum. It was a total escape, where any concern or problem was forgotten, where ecstasy and happiness opened the doors to adventure and the unexpected. During a party, I experienced moments where I could be who I was and free myself completely, without ties, do whatever I wanted. This is how I lived freedom and that feeling fascinated me.

So where did all this rebellion come from? That's what my parents couldn't understand, as they did everything 'right'. They got married very young—, my mother was 21 and my father 24. My mother comes from a family with Spanish roots, and unfortunately, she lost her father at the age of 12, leaving her mother alone with four children. My maternal grandmother worked for many years at the Canadian Embassy and managed to support the children on her own. They attended private schools from primary to high school, but my grandmother did not consider paying for my mother's higher education, so she found a way by getting a 100% scholarship at the *Universidad de las Americas* to study Psychology.

My mother Carmen is an active woman, of average height. She has light brunette-dyed blonde and permanently straightened hair. She is always well dressed and uses basic make-up. She likes to be well-groomed and presentable, only in our country house in Valle de Bravo will you see her in sweatpants. She created the world that feeds her with happiness—she goes to dance classes, takes care of her body, had groups where she taught tarot cards and astrology and is a student of mystic sciences. She also applies her Psychology degree to patients at home. She is a lady from the rich area in Mexico City, who has no worries in life; she lives very happily in her big house and her garden where she plays with the dogs. She is always happy; it's very rare to see her in a bad mood.

She was very dedicated to my sister and me. She had me at age 24 and my sister at age 28. She picked us up from school, attended to us for the rest of the day, and took us to ballet classes in the afternoon; she never had a formal job so as to be a full-time mother. When my sister and I grew up, she began to focus on her profession and began to study certain aspects of mysticism such as tarot, astrology, Buddhist philosophy, chakras, Kabbalah, and began to meditate regularly. She never wanted to impose her new beliefs, but little by little, all these began to attract my attention. Nevertheless, my interest came from elsewhere. The only subject I liked at the Lyceum was philosophy. I had class discussions with the teacher and I liked to talk about philosophical topics. One summer, I read *Sophie's World*, a book that puts together the history of philosophy over time, and this influenced me a lot. At that time, I was not very fond of my mother's new mystical interests, but I started my own path in the discovery of new spiritual theories.

My father Felipe comes from a family with parents born in Mexico but with French roots; he is the second of four brothers. As a young man, my father was well behaved and was pretty much an introvert. At the age of 20, he met my mother and they fell in love. He is a tall, handsome man with brown hair. We were always told that we were identical, as little some people used to call me *Philipita* because many people call him Phili. He is a man focused on family and work, an engineer with a pragmatic mind. He loves to travel, French culture, and collects wines. He wasn't someone to have deep conversations with, although he is a very good father, always taking care of the family. My dad has always been oriented to good finance and a lot of saving. He only spent money to travel but never on expensive clothes or luxury cars; he never really liked the pretension around money.

Despite coming from families very attached to religion, something that defines our Mexican society, my parents weren't very attracted to Catholicism. Therefore, unlike other people in our social environment, we stopped attending church when we were young. I love my family from both sides, especially my grandparents, and I enjoy being with them; however, I never identified myself with any religious group.

As an adolescent, I was very rebellious, a girl who drank alcohol, smoked cigarettes, and weed and liked to party until sunrise. My favorite club was a dark place with electronic music playing at maximum volume, where I enjoyed dancing by the side of the speakers. Despite being somewhat known for hippies and drug addicts, I always supported the Lyceum, unlike the private Catholic schools of Mexico, where they create conventional-minded people. My friends and I always chose to define ourselves, find out who we were, and stand up for our individuality.

I used to have a peculiar fashion that my parents never liked or supported. They have always had a classic and conventional look, therefore anything out of the normal wasn't very welcome. Of course, I rejected the world of brands to immerse myself in the freedom of expression manifested in clothing. My school was the only one in the social circle of my parents where there was no uniform; so since we were young, we were able to dress freely. In my school, men could have long hair, dreadlocks, dyed or colored hair, nails painted, and if you wanted you could go in pajamas. There were no restrictions or a dress code. The only thing that was unacceptable was to wear excessively torn trousers, or they would take you to the Director's office to get them stapled.

As a teenager, I enjoyed playing with clothes. In my final year in high school, coming back home from school, I went straight to my room to organize an outfit for the next day. For having a notorious motivation I was nominated the 'most fashionable' in our generation. However, this caused several criticisms in my house; my unconventional way of being feminine always created a topic of discussion at the table. My parents wouldn't let me dress as I wanted in family or social events, so I had to adapt to their conventional style. Saturday meals with my grandmother also required an extra effort to look 'presentable'. It was always a constant battle between exploring my individuality, and being part of a highly conservative family environment.

My social group, something very characteristic of Mexico, was really attached to parties and drugs. They all smoked weed, and later, pills and cocaine became part of their lifestyle. Fortunately, I started to party young; and when those strong drugs appeared, I managed to stay away. I had a couple of experiences with them but I didn't enjoy it at all. I felt anxious and scared the times I tried it.

Time passed and I was becoming less attracted to parties. I didn't like to see that experience and fun required the consumption of some drug or altering substance. I began to look for alternative plans, to carry out activities in the day, and, above all, to make my way in the world of travel. The happiness I was looking for at parties, that connection with the present, the fun and the freedom, I began to feel it while traveling. That way, I transferred that energy into something that brought better experiences with more positivity.

My life was a constant fight to become different. At least I appreciated my French education, where individuality is something to aim for. Under our system of education, each of us had the freedom to discover and express our own opinions—as long as we wrote or said a good argument, we could think freely. In my final year in high school, I chose my career and I really felt it was my true vocation. I wanted to do something to change the system, I truly wanted to 'change the world' that's why I chose Political Science at the Universidad Iberoamericana, and I graduated in December 2012.

By that time I had become a vegetarian, regularly practiced meditation, took a course to certify myself as a yoga teacher, and began a life change that I now consider as my spiritual awakening. In May 2013, I decided to leave my country to travel the world. I wanted a time off; I wanted to be away from my family and friends, to explore myself deeply, and to live the practice of spiritual theories.

For quite some time then, I was attracted to the New Age books, as well as watching movies and reading various articles about it. Despite the lack of interest in my family and acquaintances on these topics, I decided to explore the philosophies and apply them in my everyday life. Something that strongly determined my personality is that I would not believe anything that was told to me until I saw and understood the result for myself. Of course, my parents were really mad with this, because all their prohibitions became invitations to disobey—nothing was valid until I could prove it for myself. The same thing happened in my career with theory subjects. While my colleagues were talking for hours of positive and negative freedom, Lacan's topological relations, Nietzsche's negativity, creating debates to brag about incomprehensible concepts, I'd better take the cell phone and lose myself in it. For me it was very simple: if philosophy cannot be applied in practical life, it doesn't make any sense. My readings were closer to topics related to Buddhism, positive thinking, the power of attraction, and I love authors like Deepak Chopra and Eckhart Tolle. For me, their teachings are very coherent and seek to help us achieve a harmonious and therefore a happy life.

    This is why I decided to write this book. I felt the need to record my experiences and through them, to find practicality in the teachings of our contemporary spiritual masters. I do not belong to any religion, I do not like dogmas or strict rules, nor do I require months in retirement of silence. There is a way to lead a spiritual life without the need of a complete renunciation of the material; it's something that not only the Buddhist monks can reach. There is a way to apply these theories in our everyday life in order to improve, grow, and become the best version of oneself. That is why I write this book so that all the readers can accompany me in the discovery, and more importantly, the application of different spiritual theories to obtain what we truly desire, something that resides in the bottom of our hearts.

    Much is said about following one's dreams or listening to our hearts, and probably for me, it is the most important and the main reason why I decided to leave my life in Mexico without any promise or guarantee of a better life abroad. I had an inner calling, activated by incomprehensible instincts. Perhaps I needed to let go of life's comforts that I was used to, to get away from the circle of friends, family, parties, blowouts, drugs, projects initiated, and studies that no longer inspired me. To have distance in order to pursue a self-discovery journey, alone, with my own resources, and to define myself with my experiences, among strangers, new locations, and perhaps, find my own place in the world. Thus, began the journey to Australia with scales and doses of uncertainty, new friends and reunited ones; fears, solidarity, courage, doubts . . . and love.

Relationship vs. Freedom

When I started attending the University at the age of 18, I decided to start a therapeutic work to understand the background of my destructive relationships during courtship. I wanted to understand what part of me, was attracting that particular type of guy. I needed to explore the reason behind it, I knew it wasn't their fault, something inside me needed to be fixed if I wanted healthier relationships for the future.

This was a very delicate topic for me since I was a teenager. It was too hard for me to have a normal boyfriend. I had a deep fear of compromise and loss of freedom. In high school I had a very destructive relationship with a guy with whom I tried every possible form of relationship; it never worked and I suffered a lot. It lasted two years, and for that reason, I decided to attend psychological treatment—I needed to quit. Thanks to my therapeutic work, a few months later I was able to liberate myself, I stopped loving him as before and I was able to break the chain that tied me to a destructive relationship. With that experience, I considered myself a graduate from the school of 'womanizers', understanding at the same time that I had chosen him as a reflection of my multiple fears to commitment. In the end, I didn't want a sweet boyfriend with me all the time. In addition to a major understanding of things, I devoted myself to study the behavior of my ex-boyfriend, knowing the suffering this type of man causes to women. I used all bibliography in order to understand the reason for their behavior. The most useful was Molière's, *Dom Juan*. I could see that men with the archetype of Dom Juan see women as trophies, an extension of their ego, and always seeking challenges. They love the conquest and that's what they want from women. In the end, they don't love them and that is a cause of a narcissistic wounds acquired at birth when their mothers didn't want them. I studied that ex-boyfriend for a long time, and with that, I never again fell into the spell of a womanizer. However, not all of my friends had the ability to detect them. I saw over and over again how they repeated the pattern.

From then on, I started to improve my relationships. I was with several guys but it was never anything formal. I always had them hidden from my parents. I never talked about them. I saw them a couple of days a week and I invented my whereabouts. Little by little I gained stability. I was calm in relationships and I stopped suffering. The estimated time was between four and six months and only 'went out' with them, there was never a real commitment. And that's what I did during my university time; deep down I did not want anything serious; I was still afraid of losing my freedom. I didn't want a man limiting my social life, something that was very important to me. I attended many parties with different people, and I liked doing whatever I wanted. However, I have always liked the idea of being with someone, getting to know him better, and learning from him, that's why I was with various guys and from each, I learned something different and valuable. In every relationship, I was breaking many barriers. For example in high school, I had a phobia of dating, which made me really nervous, and I always avoided going out with guys. I could only see them at parties. In my first year at the university, I broke that phobia and so on with other fears.

Returning from my backpacking trip to Europe at 21, I remember having a revelation of great importance. I realized and became aware of the reason why I had never started a serious relationship with someone: I had an Oedipus complex with my dad that wasn't resolved. In the case of women, it is called the Electra Complex. I realized that I avoided bringing men into the house for him. I never liked talking about love affairs with anyone in my family, and it was because somehow I could not stand the eyes of my dad knowing about his daughter with a boyfriend. When I realized that, I could heal myself, and a few months later I would begin my first semi-formal relationship with someone. I say semi because it lasted for about eight months.

In my seventh semester, in October 2011, I started to date a guy who was my same age. He was a friend from high school and suddenly, there was something more between us. With him I broke down the family barriers—I introduced him to my family, brought him to our home, and took him to various meals and social events. I was able to learn how a relationship worked and I had a good time. Unfortunately in a few months, I ran out of enchantment, I would not aim for something serious for various contextual reasons and personality issues. In my summer of the eighth semester, I was still with him, although everything was fights and conflicts. Therefore, I decided to end the relationship entering the following semester in August 2012. He was the unfortunate one that happened to be with me during my existential crisis, the beginning of my vegetarianism, and the urge to travel the world. So for quite selfish reasons, I broke up with him.

A few months after that breakup, I met someone very special. A guy that caught my attention a couple of years back, which I met in a concert in 2011. Since that moment I really liked him, although he got back to his girlfriend. I had a relationship as well, and we only followed our existence through Facebook. Ending my relationship of eighth months, single again, I turned on my radars and looked for options. I had heard from a friend that Coco was single, so I wanted to find him, his music and artist profile caught my attention once again. One night when I decided to go out, in September 2012, a time when I was back into parties, I 'casually' found him at a club (I put quotation marks because I do not believe in coincidences), which neither of us frequented. That night we talked a lot. However, I was very drunk and I think I frightened him a little. In the end, we exchanged phone numbers but we didn't plan anything. I was fascinated by how we found each other. A few weeks ago I was doing my research about his recent stops, moving influences, and trying to get information on Facebook. I wanted to see him, then one day when I definitely didn't expect it, we met; I felt fulfilled.

Despite having had an exchange of cell phones and a message from him to know if I had arrived well at my friend's house, time passed and Coco would not invite me out. Occasionally we spoke on Facebook, I was excited but it was just that. I really wanted to see him and go out with him, and in December he finally did, he invited me to do something. I jumped on the excitement and died on nerves at the same time. We saw each other at his house, we talked for hours about music and we had an incredible time, from there, our love affair began. I was a bit dismayed that a month later I would be going to the beach with my friend Leticia, I didn't think about having a relationship because it was detrimental to my freedom, but that was what happened. In a very short time, it became a relationship of great intensity and passion. I was completely in love with him. I saw him as the perfect man—a young musician, living alone, and able to make his passions a career, a sensitive artist. We had too much in common: we liked good movies, music, literature, arts and museums, travelling, and surfing. Through my eyes, he was the perfect man. I couldn't believe how this situation was happening to me when I was so close to my little beach adventure, but I accepted my fate and enjoyed the passionate relationship.

That way I was progressing in my relationships, nevertheless, I could never open myself completely because the flame of freedom existed in me. I wanted to leave Mexico—that was my deepest longing. In those moments, despite being very in love with Coco, I had just like Artemis, a drawn target with my bow and arrow and there was no way to stop me: I had to make it to Australia.

The Path to My Profession

Searching for my true vocation goes back to high school. I had planned to study Marketing because I liked to sell things since I was a little girl. I sold bracelets to my mother's friends, created magazines with my friend Andrea, sold junk food with my cousins outside my home in Valle de Bravo, even rented school supplies to the most unorganized kids of the Lyceum. However, my professional future changed when I was in the Economics class of my senior year of high school. We started reading an article on inequality of opportunity, an example of which is that a child from a family with insufficient economic solvency does not have the same opportunity for success than a child of a well-off family. One of my colleagues, with extreme right thinking, who currently graduated from ITAM University in Economics, began to argue until we created an environment of screams and fights in the classroom. Of course, I supported the idea that there was inequality of opportunity, but my conservative-minded classmate supported the idea that 'being poor is a personal election'. I left the room furiously and from that moment, I decided not to study Marketing. I needed a social career that would help me fight the present capitalist system.

Shortly after that episode, I began to look for Careers in the *Universidad Iberoamericana*, that institution attracted me for some reason. I found its location convenient. It was also famous for having a very social environment with a lower academic load, unlike other private universities in Mexico. I easily found the degree for Political Science and Public Administration. I read the curriculum and the profile of the student. I immediately identified myself and chose that academic training.

I felt a driving force inside me, Mexico worried me and I wanted to help my country in some way. That was how I chose the career that contributed so well in my formation. Some class subjects weren't as interesting, but I loved the background in general: reading, questioning, arguing, and writing; and I did that for four and a half years.

I loved to analyze societies, and in my essays, there were always strong but well-founded criticisms. I liked to sit down to write and develop my ideas, also to have intense debates in class. My favorite subject was social movements; I loved the French Revolution, and I was fascinated by leaders who had changed history like Gandhi, Martin Luther King, Obama, among others. I have always maintained a left-wing position, understanding this as the theory of socialism in the European style. State intervention to guarantee human rights in the population, decent housing, education, health, and food. I was also interested in the subject of democracy and citizen participation.

At 20 years of age, a great interest arose in me to participate in student movements, something that ignited an internal flame. I remember perfectly: I was in my Theory of Organizations class when one of my classmates interrupted by being extremely late—he was at a meeting with the Director of my university. I heard very little of his message to the teacher but he drew my attention very hard, and I went to ask about the subject. He talked about an ITAM project carrying out some mobilizations to support the students of the University 'TEC de Monterrey' who died in a shootout, a consequence of the war against drug trafficking. The movement was called *Ni 1 Estudiante Más* (not one more student) and sought to reorient the security strategy of the government of Felipe Calderon. I was immediately passionate about the words of my friend. I felt a burst of tickling emanating from the depths of my body, and I asked for my inclusion in the project. I worked with them during my fourth semester and part of the summer; that's when I met a new world, with young people who wanted to do something for Mexico. They began to be my role models because my social circle was only interested in parties and drugs.

It was in September 2010 when I started a project that was really important in my life. It all happened at my friend's car, we were only women. I remember we entered into a very intense conversation touching different issues related to politics, the capitalist economic system, the emergence of women as leaders, and the apathetic youth of Mexico. A few days later, a friend sent a common message to several women through Facebook, in which she explained the importance of a sudden meeting to keep talking about those issues and try to do something about it. It was time to stop being conformists and propose viable solutions to the problems that afflicted our country. One Saturday, we had our first meeting. We talked about several topics but we agreed on the lack of political involvement by the young people. We come from a privileged student environment, where our colleagues only care about their well-being and do not realize the responsibility that a bachelor's degree means in this uneducated poor country. Less than 30 percent of the population in Mexico has access to higher education. Most of our universities are private and extremely expensive. Only rich families can pay for their children's degrees. For these and other reasons, we decided to create awareness in society in order to achieve participation in different areas. I had several ideas in mind because I was the only one with experience in the field of organized civil society. However, it was important to have that debate among the girls to bring the concept down to earth.

That week we held other meetings. This time we approached a very creative young group of men who were working for NADA magazine. In their offices was where I proposed the name Mexiro (meaning 'I turn') a concept centered on the importance of conscious change in our country. 'I turn', 'Mexico needs to take a turn'. The goal was to seek the involvement of society and especially of young people. We realized the situation of environmental deterioration— our world was being shaken by social inequality, poverty, human and animal abuse, with innumerable injustices. We were young, in a privileged economic situation, and so were our friends. We knew about our great responsibility and we decided to act.

That is how my organization was born. From September to December 2010 we went to several reforestation journeys and organized a collection center for the victims of Hurricane Karl at our university. We created our profile in social networks and started to work with passion. We continued with our enthusiasm and more than that, we achieved institutionalization. On 5 May 2011, five members signed the creation of the youth organization Mexiro A.C.; I kept the position of President.

Mexiro made me fully happy and opened a space where I could channel my excessive energy and leadership, previously used in organizing parties at my house. Weekends arrived and I was exhausted. Between school, ballet, Mexiro, and the guy I was dating, it was enough to deal with. My grades at that time weren't the greatest. I was interested in school, but I couldn't devote much of my time to it. If there was something I needed to do for Mexiro, I abandoned some of my school responsibilities.

While in the university, politics was the most important and exciting thing in my life, where I dared to feel the flame of youth and wanted to eat the world without thinking of any kind of limit. In 2012, I experienced the birth of the *#yosoy132* (I am the 132) movement, a historical event that was born in my university. We as young people, in an act of collective consciousness, got together to show our discontent for the presidential candidate of the most corrupt political party in Mexico: PRI. Enrique Peña Nieto was envisioned as the new President of the Republic and that made the young people mad. Social networks for months were filled with criticism towards the candidate. Enrique Peña Nieto appeared like the living image of a highly corrupt political system, with the media as an ally, mainly press and television, that easily manipulated a poor and ignorant society. We netizens had real information, and it infuriated us to see the media lying in the news.

My life turned around politics, and I was so excited to be part of such an important student protest. During university, I had a period of six months working with *Ni 1 Estudiante Más,* then I had my NGO Mexiro where I could channel my longings to change the world, then I strongly participated with *Yo Soy 132*, and wrote my thesis about the subject. It was an extremely passionate time of my life, and while the majority of my friends just cared about parties and the everyday matters, I was attracted to subjects bigger than myself.

Travel for Growth

During childhood, I learnt the value of travelling as an inheritance from my father. We were never very spoiled, my sister and I, but our dad always saved money to take us travelling. Thanks to him I was able to know several places in the United States, Canada, Italy, France, Spain, and some countries in South America. We also made several trips around Mexico. So far I have been in all its states with the exception of Tlaxcala.

I know Mexico very well and I am in love with it. We have all the resources to be one of the best countries in the world. However, there is a lot of poverty, corruption, and social problems to solve. I am amazed by the natural wealth and the Mexican landscapes. I am fascinated to inhabit one of the twelve megadiverse countries of the world, a reason why we have a great responsibility for climate change actions. Mexico has tradition, gastronomy, color, folklore, nature, two oceans, more than 10,000 waterholes, diverse ecosystems, and the vestiges of one of the most emblematic cultures of all times: the Mayans.

Mexico is a beautiful country, I love it and I want to contribute to the change that it so badly needs. To understand this I had to travel a lot, to know different places, to try different flavors and see many cultures. I have gone to as many museums as I could and have tried to enrich myself with

Mexican culture and folklore. With my family, I travelled a lot, but I also did it with my friends.

I really got obsessed about travelling during the summer of my second semester. My father, during the early semesters at the university, was still very strict with my weekend outings. I wasn't able to spend the night in homes where there was no adult supervision because he thought the worst of us young people. And indeed, every opportunity I had, I did crazy things until early in the morning, and for that reason, my father had me under several restrictions. They never left me in the house alone, and it was very difficult to obtain a permit to go to sleep with a friend. I had to invent a pajama party or something, but I got used to always come back to my house afterwards. Several years I had an unbridled lifestyle, being at the age of 18 and 19, I probably had my most intense parties. Because of that, I was obliged to get a job during my summer of 2009. My parents didn't want to see me going out every night and doing nothing during the day. So they asked me to get a job and assume some seriousness in my life.

I knew my father's firmness, so I decided to save some money and prepare for summer. At first, I looked for work, it wasn't anything new. I previously worked two summers in a kindergarten and then in a department store in the area of toys. I looked for work in different kindergartens and summer courses but found nothing. The main problem was the future trip of my mother, my sister, and I to Puerto Vallarta for a week that interrupted certain summer jobs, for that reason I left my search aside. Then I calmly went on vacation to the beach with my family and forgot about any work. I came back from Puerto Vallarta on a Saturday. On that day I saw my best friend Chloe and she told me 'we are going camping on Monday at six in the morning'. Literally, I was forced to extend my beach clothes on the railing and redo my suitcase on Sunday. My father almost got a heart attack. He thought we were irresponsible to go to the state of Michoacan because of the high presence of organized crime in the area. He didn't support the camping idea, or the twelve hours' drive, even if we were accompanied by several friends. My father didn't agree and didn't give me any money; however, that didn't stop me from going. He wasn't able to control me with financial restrictions. That way, with 500 pesos, Chloe and my friends from the Lyceum went to Michoacan for a camping trip. It was an incredible journey—we connected in a very communitarian way and we had deep philosophical talks.

When I returned from this trip, I had a great idea and shared it quickly with Chloe: lining and selling lighters. That week we went to the center of Mexico City, where you can find the unimaginable and we bought several packages of lighters, one peso each. We also bought papers to cover and decorate them, the final price was 20 pesos. With this business, I was able to travel during the summer. We went a few days to Valle de Bravo, then to Cuernavaca, to Tepoztlan, back to Cuernavaca, and in the end, I went to Acapulco with other friends. I spent the whole summer travelling. When I came back to the city, I stayed a couple of days and then departed again. My father didn't agree but couldn't restrict me. I no longer needed his financial support to leave the city. It was the best summer I had experienced so far.

That's how my desire to travel was triggered and that of going out to party with friends decreased. During the third and fourth university semesters, I left the city several times for long weekends. In the summer of 2010, I went on a road trip with Chloe, a friend from the university, and her boyfriend. We toured Campeche, the Mayan Riviera, and finally returned through Chiapas and Veracruz. It was fifteen days in total. I had never gone so far with friends and neither did my car. On that trip, I felt a very strong connection with Bacalar, a magical place—a lagoon with seven shades of blue where I found a very eccentric character, Carlos, but that everyone knew as E.T. Around 60 years of age, he drove a dark green combi with a Buddha in front of the windshield. He had been living in Bacalar for several years; he made shoes, sold bread, painted murals. He had an intense obsession for aliens and told us several stories of them. He made me question various aspects of my life. There, I started to draft a book. I had the idea of starting to write in the city and return to Bacalar, detach myself from the material world, and live otherwise. I wanted to learn from him, to be with nature. I thought that our humanity was lacking that connection. I needed an adventure, to separate myself from money and luxuries, to go into the jungle and experience that wild part. Returning from the trip, I considered dropping out of University in order to do that project and write my book. However, a few months later, I lost that need to return to Bacalar.

That trip marked me deeply and created an inner crisis. I began to question in depth the subject of consuming animal meat, life in the city, and contact with Mother Earth, among other things. In my travels I felt incredible, I was happy all the time, but returning to reality was really hard—many times I cried and acquired the worst character.

Travelling had become an obsession, returning from any place made me plan the following adventure. I had acquired a healthy vice, which brought me learning, culture, personal growth, and a space to meet people out of the ordinary. Every time I was looking for more adventures and more outings. My dad didn't support it very much, but I almost never asked extra money for my travels; I saved as much as possible. To achieve what I wanted, it was necessary to reduce expenses in parties, concerts, and clothes. And like that, every time I could, I left.

During the sixth semester, summer of 2011, my partner from Mexiro, and I decided to make a trip through Europe together. Neither she nor I had had the usual backpacking trip as it was a tradition among our Mexican elite society; to celebrate the high school diploma, teens would get a sponsored trip to travel Europe accompanied by their best friends. For this reason, we spoke with our respective parents to obtain their permission and economic support. That is the only time I asked for money to travel. At that time I didn't have the resources to do it on my own. I had a great desire to discover Europe without the adult supervision and the strict itineraries of my family trips. It would be my fifth trip to the Old Continent, three with my parents, and one with my ballet classmates to England, where I took an intensive dance course one week and another to travel, that at age 13.

Finally, the trip was authorized, we quickly bought the plane tickets, and with that, we made something official. Time passed and Majo asked me to get together and organize the trip. I avoided her because I didn't believe in planning. A few weeks before leaving, my partner was hysterical because of the lack of itinerary; however, I did not believe in that style of travel and therefore I was not going to spend my time doing hotel reservations and other matters. I tried to make her understand my way, in the end, she managed to relax and only booked the first hostel in Madrid. And that is how we left, nothing planned. I was not worried because I have many high school friends living in Europe. I talked to them and asked them in advance to stay in their homes. So Majo and I travelled in Europe for two and a half months; in some places, we stayed in hostels: San Sebastian, Madrid, Milan, Amsterdam, and Berlin; but while in Barcelona, Toulouse, Montpelier, Paris, Rome, and London, we were welcomed by friends. It was an incredible trip! However, Majo and I had had a couple of arguments therefore we separated. I went from Rome to Paris and she went to Barcelona. Later we crossed paths again in Paris. We settled our conflict and we left for Berlin and Amsterdam where we had reservations.

Returning from our trip, she and I created some distance. We got tired of each other and left our friendship behind. We continued working with Mexiro but for the first time we started to divide tasks, each focused on something different and we stopped doing so many activities together. Ultimately it wasn't very serious, a few months later, we recovered our friendship and improved our work in Mexiro. The following semesters I kept travelling when I could, and in my summer of 8th semester, July 2012, I did my social service with a civil association called *Iluméxico*. Our job was to put solar photovoltaic systems in rural communities that have no access to electricity. I spent that summer travelling with them to several states of the Republic. Then I made a trip of two weeks with friends to the states of Michoacan and Jalisco, and we camped again in Carrecitos.

I am a very fortunate person to have a great track record in this area. It's a gift from my family and something I've been creating by myself. I feel a huge need to travel and I love adventure. I have found in it a space where I can express my freedom, feel a connection, forget thoughts and worries, to just live the moment and feel alive.

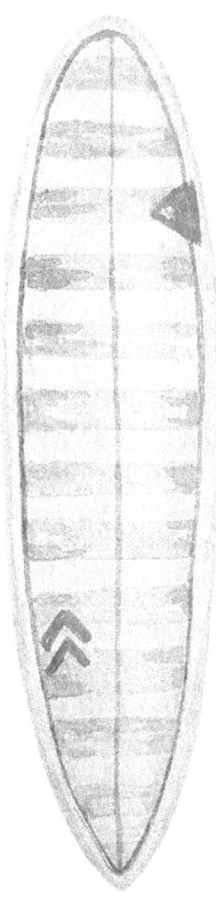

A Great Adventure: Sayulita

One day I was in my house, lying with my cousin talking in my sister's room, just spending a Saturday night away from parties and nightlife. Suddenly, my surprise could not be greater when I saw Leticia enter through the door. I instantly ran to hug her and cried with emotion. She was back in the city after five years living in Paris, so she explained her reasons for leaving and some new ideas for the future arose. I suggested including her in Mexiro and carrying out projects together.

That night we were very excited about her return; Leticia no longer found her place in Paris and everything opened up to come to Mexico. One of the main reasons for the sudden return of my friend was her infatuation with a surfer from Sayulita. She wanted to live on the beach and seek her love. One possible plan was to find work in universities in Puerto Vallarta, Jalisco, as she was a historian by profession. I suggested to her the development of a 'Huichol' project because of the strong presence of that ethnic group in Nayarit. I would help in starting the project, later we would seek for government and private funds, allowing Leticia to have a decent life working for Mexiro from the beach. To achieve that, we would need a serious research paper, make a business plan, presentations, and get the data to apply for government support. So little by little, we were designing the project and consequently our trip.

In a few weeks, Leticia and I had designed the plan: on 4 January we would leave the city; we would go alone to Sayulita in my car to work on our project and live the adventure. My grandparents have a time-share in Nuevo Vallarta—some apartments where we used to vacation as a family. As they were available those days, I decided to take an apartment for three weeks, which resolved our accommodation. In other matters, I had to be in Mexico no later than 1 February for my yoga module that gave us a few extra days to stay in Sayulita if we wanted. The part of the lodging we had resolved it, nevertheless, there was another important subject: money. Neither Leticia nor I had a big budget. We then decided to line up lighters and sell them to survive there. We would take 3,000 pesos (around 170 USD), 1,500 pesos each to get there (booths, gasoline), and the rest to return. Before leaving, I put my savings into a separate account to make available only the amount mentioned, that way I would not touch my money for Europe and Australia. We also decided to try veganism—we would not eat anything that came from an animal, not dairy, cheese, and so on.

Leticia had learned to surf in Sao Paolo and wanted to do it in Sayulita. I was very excited to learn. I was too intrigued by the surfing lifestyle. I always considered surfing the coolest sport: the guys with their boards, coming out of the sea wet and exercised, are really sexy. I was born and raised in Mexico City, so life by the sea, far from pollution and stress, seemed extremely attractive. Our trip was done: we would develop the Huichol project, doing interviews, and visiting communities; we would be vegans; we would live with the money we made selling lighters, and we would surf. A great adventure at the door.

My family was pretty hysterical about my plans. My father was outraged to see Leticia and I making lighters in my house. He said, 'Look at this, the great graduates doing that crap.' We could not expect a different reaction, to be honest. We didn't care; we trusted in the efficiency of our business.

Another day I had a very strong confrontation. We were eating with my mom, my sister, and her best friend from Argentina. The three began to attack me—they couldn't conceive my 3,000 pesos budget, it was very little money for them. If something happened to my health, I wouldn't have money to get treatment. My sister said it would take a very short time for me to call my father, and ask desperately for a bank deposit. During the meal they attacked me and told me I was practically stupid; my sister told me, 'the world does not work like this', I could not walk through life trusting in my luck. I told them that during travels things happen differently, but they thought I was crazy. I had no support from anyone but I would show them the adventurous magic in travelling.

On several occasions, before my travels, my parents tried to stop me, alarmed by the danger and general insecurity in Mexico. I never listened to them, but it affected me in some ways, creating doubts and questions in my mind. This wasn't the case then. I had a good feeling about it, I was a bit scared and nervous as normal before a trip, but I trusted the Universe. I hoped that everything would always be all right.

Upon returning from Valle de Bravo after New Year's Eve, we had two days to carry out the preparations for the trip to Sayulita—packing suitcases, buying amaranth, a variety of seeds, nuts, dried fruits, lentils, oats, and vegan chocolate. We also decided to get a tent and see how we would tie Leticia's surfboard to my car, a big challenge for a two-door Seat Ibiza. On 4 January 2013 we left, the car full of things: kitchen utensils and some basic food for cooking in the apartment, a sleeping blanket in case of using the tent, two very comfortable folding chairs, 700 lighters, 300 made and the others in box, yoga mats, suitcases for a month, and cushions. The first day we drove 500 kilometers to Guadalajara to spend the night at my uncle's house. I had driven long routes but I wasn't the most experienced. Leticia wasn't very confident to drive on the highway, so in my hands was the responsibility. The time passed very quickly, in six and a half hours we arrived at Guadalajara. That night we had dinner with my uncle, and we slept early to leave the next day. We left without rush; it would be four hours to arrive, a quieter journey than the day before.

In the middle of the road, I began to have an incredible sense of freedom. I felt like an adult, with a college degree, and the ability to take my car and go wherever I wanted. I didn't depend on anything or anyone. At that time I had forgotten about Coco—nothing in the world mattered at that moment. With my hands on the wheel between mountains and Mexican landscapes, I was free as a bird. A few hours and several curves later, we arrived at our destination: a perfect apartment with a sea view for Leticia and me, half an hour from Sayulita. That day we decided to unpack and stay in Nuevo Vallarta.

Sunday was our first day in Sayulita. We got up early, meditated, had breakfast, and left. The mission would be to find a board and surf teacher. Leticia was really excited; she had been thinking about going to Sayulita for months to find her prince. When we arrived it was an incredible feeling. We spent some time walking along the little streets so that Leticia saw the magical little town. After that, we went to several surf schools on the beach with the following premise, 'Hello, I want to learn to surf. I will be here for a month and I basically have no money. What can we do?' For me, it was very easy. Sayulita had an abundance of surfboards and I could have one. However, the schools did not seem to cooperate. Renting a board would be very expensive; the locals advised me to buy one and resell it at the end, using my remaining 1,500 pesos, but I did not want to make a hasty decision. Leticia and I kept walking, hoping to miraculously meet someone with a board for me. We arrived at a much more distant school where we met the owner. His school was different, didn't have many boards, and had no name on the outside, with a palm structure held together by a miracle. We quickly became friends with Pepe, a man over 40, long hair, and smooth dark skin. Within minutes his charm, sense of humor, and intelligence hooked us. He considered himself a poet, a walker of life without plans and without thinking about the future. If it weren't for parenthood obligations, this man wouldn't have any restrictions in his life. Through him the energy flowed; however, I could perceive a tormented being, perhaps because of that reason he defined himself as a poet.

Chatting with him, Leticia and I shared our situation without much response either. After some time sitting on the sand for a pleasant time, amid laughter and anecdotes, Pepe spontaneously told me, 'Hey, let's go to the water for your first surfing lesson.' I was astonished and explained my economic situation, but he didn't give much importance to that, I could pay later. That way Leticia, Pepe, and I went to the sea to surf, and without much theoretical explanation, madman Pepe got me into the water and threw me in small waves. Without knowing how I managed to stand on some occasions, others I was smashed along with the board. And that's how I had my first class, I was ecstatic. Pepe, Leticia, and I were laughing with full inner satisfaction. Pepe hugged us and felt fulfilled to see us so happy. There I proposed the following: I would give him 1,000 pesos, and he would let me use his board the month of my stay in Sayulita. He accepted immediately. With that, we ended our first day successfully.

If I had had more money the situation would've been completely different. I would've bought a very expensive board or rented at the first surf school that I found. The fact of not having resources opened a door to something more special—we found Pepe, the most generous and eccentric person that I have met and finally I fulfilled my mission: to surf.

The first weeks in Sayulita were spent surveying the Huichols, meditating, selling lighters on the Puerto Vallarta boardwalk, eating lots of vegetables, fruits, and seeds, and of course surfing. In a short time, the sport began to fascinate me. Every day was a new adventure in the ocean and I constantly noticed my progress. It was very difficult and my body was full of bruises; however, my desire to learn was greater. With practice and discipline, I would be able to surf. In yoga, I learned something very important: if I can see it in my mind, I can do it. That way I was able to achieve several very complicated postures quickly, using the power of visualization.

The third week, our girlfriends from high school came, gathering our old group self-named 'Fantastic Five'. It was beautiful because the last reunion took place two years back. We had never been, the five of us, at the beach, and we had an excellent time. That week Leticia and I met the manager of the apartments where we stayed, held a conversation, and told him about our projects related to Mexiro and the Huichols. The man was marveled at our independence and the impetus shown towards a professional search other than the conventional. Meetings with him were repeated; he wanted to know more details. The idea of Leticia and I was to promote the Huichol culture and philosophy to bring Mexican society closer to its pre-Columbian roots, a very noble project with an entertaining and youthful approach. We would make videos, create a brand with its embroidery, revalue its jewelry, and give it its deserved importance. The hotel manager found the idea formidable and thought it would be a good business to open a Huichol art shop in Mexico City. He started talking about numbers and asked us to make a contract to be signed among the three of us. We would create a store and the profits would be distributed equally between the partners—Leticia, the manager, and myself. We were fascinated; it seemed to us a miraculous act of the Universe to bring a new partner in the way. At the same time, we were somewhat skeptical. Once the money was on the account, everything would change for the two, but we could not anticipate the facts.

Our return was coming soon; we would be signing the contract a couple of days before leaving our comfortable apartment, then stay a few days in Sayulita with our friend Mariel before going back home. As the manager was going to deposit the money for us, Leticia and I had resolved our return. We would take the necessary amount to get to the city, for that reason we used our last reserves and stopped selling lighters, besides we were already tired of doing so. The deposit had to be on Monday. However, something happened to the bank and the manager informed us about the problem. Leticia and I were quite nervous, we said 'or we put an altar to this man or we send him directly to the asylum'. We didn't know whether to trust him or not. I no longer had balance after checking the ATM; the amount in my card was around 6 pesos, we could hardly afford to eat. The anguish was beginning to become noticeable. We could not continue waiting for that deposit. We went to the ATM to see if there was already the amount in my account, but nothing.

One afternoon in those complicated days, I went for a horseback ride because I was invited by one of my surf teachers. When we returned to Pepe's school, I realized that I had lost my debit card! A few minutes later I recovered it, an American found it on the beach and gave it to my teacher who was riding farther behind me. I was very scared, however, I wondered the meaning of the event, without having an immediate response. Later in the night, the sense came to me. I told Leticia the need to stop referring to the card as our ticket back home. It was necessary to look for other options. To top it all, in addition, our last 200 pesos were stolen at Mariel's house. We did not have a penny and the promise of becoming businesswomen with the partner who appeared out of nowhere, collapsed. There were two options: 1) easy way: talk to Dad and ask for money to return, 2) difficult road: get a job and save to go back to home.

Leticia and I faced each other and affirmed that we were not the women who opted for the easy way. We chose the second option.

The day after the big resolutions, on a Friday morning, we went out to look for work. Because it was very early in the morning many restaurants and bars were closed, we decided to return later in the evening. In between time, we went surfing. With a darker sky, we decided to continue the search.

There was a place where Leticia had asked in the morning, which seemed to have vacancies for waitresses. I preferred something around cooking. I had been eager to learn how to cook, one of my new centers of interest that arose shortly before finishing University. Walking down the streets we arrived at a small restaurant, the owner was closing and we went to ask if she was looking for someone. She had an assistant but on Wednesday she would probably leave. She asked me to come back a few days later. Then we went to the main square and Leticia complained of being thirsty, but for us to spend money for a bottle of water was a luxury. So we decided to go back to the restaurant and ask for a glass of water from the owner. When we arrived the owner was happy and said, 'How nice that you come back. I can't believe I didn't ask for your phone number. My assistant is not going to be able to come tomorrow, can you come?' I quickly replied yes. Leticia and I were both surprised and impressed with how fast we had found jobs. I was happy that my work was in the kitchen, that's what I wanted. If it hadn't been for the thirst of my friend and our 3 pesos in the bag, we wouldn't have returned to the restaurant and probably would never have that job.

That way we started our new life in Sayulita. I went in the mornings to work and my hours were changing a bit every time. It was a new place and we were adapting to the owner's schedules. For me, any time was fine as long as I could surf at some point in the day. On the other hand, things in the city were not so cool; my parents were hysterical with my decision to stay a few months, probably until after Easter when it's very high season and more people are needed in the restaurants. My father offered to deposit money for me in my bank account, but I replied, 'You told me that ending my studies, I would be an adult, and you would only offer me roof and food. I take responsibility for my actions and I will not ask for money.' Coco also offered to deposit money for me. In addition, he lived the progression of events related to the crazy manager of the hotel, he was desolate with my decision to stay, however, he supported my projects and understood my reasons. My yoga courses were no longer possible due to an unexpected change of dates and also it would be very difficult for me to pay the modules, that for the completion of my monthly payments. I had good savings for having worked in a hospital/foundation; however, that money was strictly for Europe. I sent an email to my boss to communicate my decision to stay. He was always very easy going, so without any disappointment, he wished me good luck.

My Mexiro partners were already questioning about my long absence, so I sent them an email to inform about my introspective projects of travelling the world and finding myself. It was a complicated process of detachment. No one expected the postponement of my return to the city. I had my grandmothers talking to me on the phone and friends asking about my whereabouts. I had decided to cut off the ties with the city and my past life, all but one: Coco. The first month of the trip, I talked daily with him on Whatsapp. When I decided to stay, we stopped talking every day, but I was still very attached. I always thought about him. I thought he was the man of my life and that I would never find anyone like him. I had no eyes for other men, beautiful foreign surfers passing by in Sayulita, but none interested me. In my mind was Coco, Coco, and only Coco.

The work went very well, when I chopped vegetables in the morning and I was alone with my music, I rejoiced in peaceful solitude. The owner also liked my music. If we didn't listen to it, we talked to each other; she was very friendly and made me laugh. The restaurant was serving oriental food. I had an area of works. I made dishes like vegetables with noodles and soy sauce, orange chicken, fried rice, and more. The place was very small and had a view of the main street where the surfers paraded daily. Being in a village, the faces quickly became very familiar. Leticia and I described Sayulita as the school's recess, daily you see Sayulita's inhabitants in the streets or the main square; going to the beach means greeting people around every corner. When I received my first payments, I felt the richest. Leticia and I lived a month with an average of 40 pesos a day; having 150 pesos after finishing my workday seemed a lot of money, I was the happiest. My life was going very well, I loved everything about it. My friends came to visit all the time. I could surf every day and I always felt happy.

Leticia and I were living then in a room that my friend Mariel from University rented; there were two double beds so our presence was not a problem. We knew of Karen's early arrival, she and Mariel planned to live in that place and pay rent between the two. Leticia and I thought we'd wait for Karen and see how we would fit in the room, then divide the rent among the four of us, so it would be a very cheap option to live in Sayulita.

Karen's arrival was very surprising. She appeared with a huge suitcase and a very snooty attitude from the city, while we were already accustomed to the beach rhythm. It felt like an electrical shock; she didn't have a very welcoming attitude towards us and it seemed like we were two invaders that occupied a bed in the room. Since the beginning, we knew that staying with Mariel wasn't a possibility anymore. The place was too small for the four of us. That night my friend Dani, an 18-year-old surf teacher, whom I saw every day, came and told him about the situation. So he kindly joined me in the search for an apartment or a room to rent.

The next day the search began. Leticia and I asked in some places without much success, then we went to the beach to look for Pepe, who could have something for us. We were resting on the beach while we thought about the unfortunate situation of being almost on the street, then suddenly Valentina passed through, a girl I met at Mariel's house once. I greeted her from a distance and she approached. We started to talk and I told her about our search for a new house, she told me that she was staying in a room for 1,500 pesos a month, and there was probably more for rent. As Leticia went to work, I stayed with Valentina to go see the rooms later. I had the day off from work and I could spend it looking for a place to stay. Valentina is Italian, as a custom in her country, she wanted an espresso from a very European café on the main street.

She drank her coffee while we were chatting. We quickly got along very well. Then we went to see the room where she lived. Valentina hated it, the mattress was deplorable, there was no door in the bathroom and the window was falling, also there were no other rooms for rent. Valentina accompanied me to ask in other places, and then we decided to look for something bigger where we could live the three, we were very excited because we could find a better option. We were looking for a good amount of time, then she went to work, and later I found a small apartment for rent on a second floor next to Mariel's house. I fell in love quickly and imagined myself living there with the girls. I talked to the owner to make an appointment at 9:00 a.m. the next day. The situation in the room wasn't great. Leticia and I wanted to escape as soon as possible, finding a place for us became the priority.

Early in the morning, we met Valentina and waited for the landlord to see the house. There were two apartments, one above the other. The second-floor tenants wanted to move downstairs for their little boy because there were dangerous stairs to go up and down. The landlord showed us the apartment below. It was still under construction. On the telephone, he told us the tenants were moving in a few days, but that was a long-term thing. We were perplexed by the landlord's lies. That apartment would not be in days like he said, it was months away! We needed something right away, moving as soon as possible and fleeing from the fearsome Karen who wanted so badly to get her bed back. Our moods declined. We had to repeat the search. That day I had to work, so Valentina would take care of the search. I tried to stay calm and think positively. I said to myself 'Everything happens for a reason. Something amazing is on the way.'

While I was working, Valentina came to tell me about the progress of the search. On one visit, she spoke to me about a promising place: 'It's like a loft, it has two rooms, a bathroom and a sea view, it's one block away from the main plaza'. A few hours later, I asked my boss for permission to go see it. It wouldn't take much time, it was very close. Outside it looked like a henhouse, just next to a beer shop, a dump with children running everywhere. American-looking houses surrounded the area, and that was the only one that looked like a Brazilian favela. The outside appearance didn't look good, although we decided to go in. We climbed a few stairs half-made without a railing, making it quite dangerous—a bad balance and you dropped 2.5 meters to the ground. At the top of the house, there were two rooms, our visit was in the first one on the left. When I entered I received a gust of air in the face. I instantly breathed peace and happiness. The place was getting the final details of paint, but from the moment I walked in, I received amazing vibes. Inside it was white with open yellow concrete windows. The bathroom door and the bedroom window to the kitchen were made of bamboo, and surprisingly had good taste in a few elements. You entered and there was the kitchen, which only had a refrigerator, a gas stove, and a sink, then (without a door) was the bedroom. At the back, there was a bathroom with a shower, without a sink. The space was perfect for three. From the kitchen, you could see the ocean and the whole bay of Sayulita, something that is priceless. It was incredibly central and the rent was very low, 2,500 pesos per month (around 140 USD). We immediately decided to live there, that same night we would move.

My boss gave me the afternoon free to arrange the move. So Valentina and I went to Puerto Vallarta to buy things for the house. Valentina paid the bill at Wall-Mart, bought plates, glasses, cutlery, trashcans, cleaning utensils, some groceries, and thin mattresses (more like thick quilts) to sleep on. We decided to remove the old mattress from the room, fill it with 'petates' (a sort of rug made by palm, very cheap), and put on the mattresses and sleep on the floor rustically. That night we made the move and started looking for objects in the street to furnish our house. We took several fruit wooden boxes to use as closets. We also took several curious things that we found in an abandoned warehouse; for example, an old skateboard with written words, one side 'peace' and the other 'love'. We hung it in the door separating the two rooms, the kitchen would be the part 'peace' and the second would be 'love'.

The following days we spent decorating and furnishing. I was the most motivated in the matter. I was fascinated with organizing what became the first apartment of my life. We put fabrics to cover the yellow windows of the kitchen and the room. We put more fabrics to divide the spaces. We got a table and chairs, which I painted later to cover the brands of soda and dirt, and I got more and more waste objects to give them a second life. In two days, our house was created, I just couldn't stop organizing it, and the space was beautiful, totally impregnated with our style. The rustic apartment met my needs. I was happy—finally, I had something of mine where I had full sovereignty, not as in my house in Mexico, where my voice is an opinion but never a decision. I was wondering about my family's possible opinion. I was living in a favela, without hot water, sleeping on the floor, with trash as decoration, and a shared sink for brushing my teeth and doing the dishes. They would probably get a heart attack to see my house, but for me, it was the perfect place where I felt fulfilled.

The first few weeks I was quite withdrawn at night. Leticia and my other friends were going out but I preferred not to. I wanted to go to bed early and make the most of my days. I lived for myself and totally enjoyed it, meditating as the first activity of the day, eating delicious fruits, going surfing, then to work, cooking healthy food, and being with my best friend. Dani was a blessing to my days in Sayulita, an 18 years old boy but with a special maturity that I could see through his penetrating and mysterious eyes. His skin was very dark, and his broad nose revealed African ancestry. He was 1.70 meters tall with a toned body as a result of surfing. He had been teaching for more than three years, his workdays were on the beach. If he was not in the water teaching, he was sitting on a chair watching the waves and waiting for the best time to go surfing. Maybe that much contact with water had created a wild boy with turbulent emotions, and I was very interested to know him more.

Dani practically couldn't read and his spelling was lamentable (as a result of really bad public education in Mexico). In spite of that, we got along really well; we could speak for hours of any subject, a good boy, chivalrous and attentive. The last two weeks of my stay in Sayulita, I had a slight affair with him. Clearly, for Dani, it was not a simple friendship and from the beginning, he wanted something more. I let myself go and enjoyed my peculiar relationship with this local boy.

At that stage I preferred not to go out at night, which meant getting up late and not feeling to the best; hence, I couldn't focus much in meditations and wouldn't make the most of my days. I was attuned to myself and that made me feel well like never before. Every day I smiled when I opened my kitchen window overlooking the sea. I was truly rested and any physical pain disappeared as a result of sleeping on the floor. My intestinal problems were remedied and I always felt light. I had never been so happy in my solitude, being in the house, organizing and cleaning gave me great pleasure. Sometimes I could stay in my comfortable chair brought from Mexico, looking at the ocean, submerged in my thoughts, feeling pure well-being. My body noticeably began to change; from two hours of surfing per day my back was broadened. I had stronger arms and the extra fat began to disappear. I felt healthy from head to toe, calm, relaxed, light, happy, and carefree; my days were a blessing and a different adventure, it never became a routine. Always at work, it was something new, the sea was different, I met people in the streets. My friend Dani arrived at unexpected moments and plans came out spontaneously. With none of my local friends I ever spoke on the phone, they came to see me at work or at my house, otherwise, I would go and find them. I lived in the present. I let myself be carried away and my days were always beautiful.

In those moments I was eternally grateful to the crazy manager for putting us in such a desperate situation that forced us to look for work. If it weren't for him, Leticia and I would've saved money to return to Mexico. I also appreciated Leticia's deep desire to come to Sayulita to find her surfer, although her romance didn't prosper because the guy showed no interest and practically never left his house. I also thanked infinitely the forces of the Universe for having put Valentina on my path, who was ultimately our angel. She paid 2,000 pesos for the furnishing plus the initial rent. Leticia had her 800 pesos to pay her, however, I had no more than 7 pesos with me. Valentina put my part and I agreed to liquidate as soon as possible. Suddenly, without money or anything, I found myself living in a beautiful place, with a great job and happier than ever in my life. Coincidence? Good luck? I don't believe in those terms; however, the concepts will be revealed little by little, a belief system and a quite different way of thinking have been governing me for some time. The best of my trip happened when I ran out of money—angels appeared and miracles were given. Now it's too early to share all my esoteric beliefs, but they will be shared through my journey around the world.

Sayulita filled me with blessings every day and several interesting events happened. The first is how I managed to get my own surfboard and the second how my return from Sayulita was. The surfboards were given to me either by Pepe or Dani. One day; after trying at least eight different boards throughout my stay in Sayulita, I used a new one from Pepe. When I got into the ocean and started to paddle, I noticed a good flotation and a perfect size. It was very easy to stand up and catch waves. I quickly felt a connection with the board. I was filled with euphoria and tickles in my body. I couldn't stay in the water for a long time because I wanted to see Pepe and talk to him. I left the ocean feeling very happy. I had fallen in love with the board, I wanted it to be mine. I walked along the beach feeling victorious with the board under my armpit. Pepe's school was pretty far away from the point, but I was already accustomed to walking that long distance. When I arrived I asked for Pepe but he was leaving, then I looked at the street and I saw him walking with his son in the distance. I was so euphoric that I ran barefoot and in my bathing suit while shouting to stop him. He listened to me and returned to see the reason why I looked for him with such madness. I said I was in love with his board. I wanted to adopt it at the time of my stay in Sayulita. Pepe was very skeptical and told me that I would take a board away to get more clients, but I begged him, at least to keep it now and in a few days we would negotiate, buy or rent it for longer. Pepe appreciated me a lot and therefore accepted my request. I was happy and I came back for the first time to my house with a personal board. The next day I took the board for a surf; however, the sea was impossible. There was a lot of wind and it was very choppy. I felt the hostility in the water, so I left. However everything would change after that, and the events happened on Valentine's Day.

Dani arrived at my house at 8:00 in the morning. He appeared with flowers in hand, gave one to Valentina, one to me, one to Leticia, and the others were for her boss and her friends. We had a plan to go surfing early in the morning, so I took Pepe's board and we went to his work to organize the beach stand for the surf school. Then he took his shortboard, I took mine, and we went into the ocean. Without realizing it and because I listened to Dani without questioning, we suddenly found ourselves in some pretty big waves, some of them scared me and others kept throwing the board towards the front. In one of my falls, the board was ferociously smashed by a wave, and when I took the leash of my foot to pull it back, I noticed a three-quarters break at the bottom. I was very frightened and I shouted to Dani in a rescue tone, but he didn't listen to me. So I took a wave and lay on top of the broken board and got out of the water. I set the board on the sand while waiting for Dani. I stayed there for a few minutes alone trying to digest the turmoil—I had broken Pepe's board. Dani didn't come out, but I saw a group of men near me, one of them was shirtless and making handstands, he had the most perfectly toned body, and he caught my attention. I decided, why not, to put my board next to them, hoping to start a conversation. They quickly came to see the board and to ask what happened. They were all surfers; the beautiful blonde came to speak to me and told me about his shaper friend Toño, who had been his travel companion for the last few months. After chatting with them and analyzing my options, I talked to Toño. I had to work at eleven but I was free from three to six in the afternoon. I asked him to take the board and at three we would meet to repair it. Toño was not from Sayulita. He just arrived the night before with the sexy blonde, nobody knew his work, therefore, Dani recommended me to go with a local shaper. I didn't listen to his opinion and as always (something not very good), I proceeded my way.

    I met with Toño at three o'clock outside my work. We took my car to go to Puerto Vallarta in order to buy the necessary materials and different paint sprays. The board had a light blue that I wasn't very fond of, so I decided to change the color. I chose a dark emerald green with a brown outline. At that moment, I had 700 pesos saved for my rent, but I decided to use them on the board. We returned to Sayulita and I went back to work. Once I finished, I went to my house and Pepe was there, waiting for me. He was told about the broken board and was quite dismayed. Then we went to the terrace to talk. I would pay for the repair, but I would keep it. I explained to him about the previous break that the board had. The night before the incident, my surfer friend Jairo came to my house. I showed him the board and in on second, with his eagle sight, he detected a line caused by a previous break; he marked it with his nails. I said that to Pepe, 'Your board has been broken before.' That gave me more credibility in the matter. I said the following, 'I keep the board and in return, I do the institutional marketing of your surf school—Facebook, content, photos, social networks, and so on.' For Pepe, I was speaking Mandarin, although he had an urge to employ digital strategies in order to improve his business. Basically I was not leaving another option to the good Pepe—his board was defective, and my money only reached to pay for the repair, and therefore I wouldn't return it. At first, Pepe didn't understand anything about the importance of my work. He said that the website role was already assigned to someone else, but the lack of content made it impossible. Pepe was in charge of that, but he didn't know how to work with digital media and that's how I could help. Pepe was a little annoyed, however his generosity, as always, was greater and accepted the deal. Later, I spoke with the German mother of his son and she thanked me for my proposal of work. She knew how important social media was to make a business grow, and then he was happier with the exchange. This is how my Valentine's Day ended, the best of my life when I got my first surfboard.

The days in Sayulita became perfect since the acquisition of a surfboard. I didn't depend on anyone to go surfing. Now I had the freedom to go to other beaches with my friends and we did it often. We would tie the boards on the roof of my Ibiza and we would leave. At that time, I was really happy with my surfing practice. My board and I understood each other perfectly and I started to improve a lot with it. I couldn't ask for anything more to be totally happy in Sayulita—I was complete. In a blink of an eye, my dreams come true. For a long time, I was tired of living with my parents and wanted to try my independence. I was also not pleased about my useless kitchen skills (for having domestic employees who since childhood made my meals, among other activities like housekeeping and cleaning). I wanted to develop myself in the kitchen. Living in Sayulita with Valentina, I learned Italian food and in the restaurant, Asian food. I had a strong desire to learn how to surf and I was doing it, improving day by day. My life had gone from routine, pollution, traffic, and stagnation to lucidity, health, total well-being, happiness, harmony, nature, balance, and self-knowledge. My life became a dream.

I was thinking of staying in Sayulita until May, then spend one month in Mexico City, and leave at the end of June to Europe with my parents and my sister for a family trip. I was committed to the restaurant with my boss for the upcoming high season. My parents were hysterical because there was a family trip to Easter, and I didn't show much desire to come back to the city. It would be a gathering of the Ollivier family, my grandparents, my four uncles, their wives, and my ten cousins. I had decided not to go; I had a job and a commitment in Sayulita. Easter would be a critical moment of the restaurant and I was being trained for it. My cousins were students, and as one of the oldest, I was in a different situation. 'When you grow, work doesn't give you many holidays', that was my argument with my parents. I didn't care if they didn't grant any seriousness to my life; for them I was lost somewhere, cooking and living like a hippie. I claimed to have mental clarity. I was settled in Sayulita, living my new life by the sea and making my own decisions, but soon after that, big changes happened.

My grandparents announced their visit to Sayulita at the end of March. I was afraid to think of their culture shock, but I tried not to overthink it. I wouldn't take them to my house. If my grandmother saw the favela I was living in, she would break down in tears. They came to stay at my uncle's home in Puerto Vallarta for a week. They would have an annual gathering with brothers and family. When my grandmother arrived in the hot lands of Jalisco, she called and invited me to the family meal. I agreed and I drove to the apartments where I stayed for the first few weeks. My grandparents picked me up and I followed them to my uncle's house. I was with the best attitude in the world, talking with the adults, of conservative thought, about my adventures in Sayulita. They laughed while they were perplexed by my extravagances. I had a good time with them. I was happy to see my relatives and to eat so many delicious things, then it was time to go and I said goodbye to everyone. I went to the bathroom in my grandparents' room and there was my grandfather waking up from a nap. He wanted to give me money for gasoline and I couldn't reject it, right? Without looking at the money, I only reached out to receive it and put it in the bag of my shorts. I thanked him, I hugged him, and I allowed myself to be spoiled by my grandfather who was worried about me. When I got to the car, I took the money out and I saw four 500-peso bills. I could not believe the amount of money in my hands. I was ecstatic. I didn't know how to invest that money, but I thought of saving it; the reason would come up later. I arrived in Sayulita and I told my friends about the magical help from my beloved grandfather. Something that would give me greater peace of mind.

Dynamics at work changed a few days before that, so I worked five hours a day and had the afternoon shift. My schedule was from six to eleven at night. I then had the morning free to go surfing to other beaches or enjoy it as if on vacation, and I was much calmer with three hours less of work. Consequently, my salary dropped to 100 pesos a day. The owner was adapting the schedules to have better productivity, so she decided to put someone in the morning to do the prepping. It was incredible because the responsibility no longer fell on me. If there was no rice, spring rolls, or chopped vegetables ready, it was not my problem anymore. I arrived in the afternoon and had to cook, the best part. At 9:30 p.m. the owner left and I stayed attending the bar, then I had to close, and organize everything. The truth is that the restaurant was a small place without many people, but times got busier, and we were gaining more customers, so I had to prepare more dishes and cook faster.

I really loved the place, and because it was pretty new, I was able to contribute many ideas: we put a sign outside saying 'VEGANS WELCOME' to attract vegans and vegetarian people feeling lost in the world, especially in Mexico where no one serves them as they deserve. When vegan costumers arrived, we offered them some delicious noodles with vegetables, totally free of animal products. Customers came out happy and tipped well too. I showed the owner my favorite drink in the world, mezcal with hibiscus water and chili powder with sugar. She loved it and decided to establish it as the drink of the house. I always had my music playing and really enjoyed my time there. My boss and I made a good team and we had fun talking and laughing. Every day I had a new adventure or funny story to talk about, and there was always a new topic of interest. However, the dynamics changed suddenly. One day I arrived at work promptly at 6:00 p.m., in good humor as always, and noticed the absence of the kitchen assistant on the morning shift. The kitchen was a tragedy, there were almost no chopped vegetables, everything was dirty, there was no rice and hardly anything cooked, no ginger or garlic, and it was a disaster! In addition to that, it was a long weekend vacation and there were many people in Sayulita. We had many orders and I was on the verge of an anxiety attack. We had too many things to do, the place was very small, and the panic was paralyzing me. I was constantly losing the utensils and I couldn't flow well. Mariel had asked me for fried rice, so when it was ready I would take it to her work, but there wasn't much rice left. Shortly afterwards, a couple of Americans arrived to order some takeaway woks. Those woks had white rice underneath and the stew on top. My boss was making the stews and I was heating the rice to put it in the boxes, there was very little left and I asked what to do, so she asked to distribute Mariel's rice among the other orders. My boss and I were quite hysterical. I couldn't believe the disorganization of my employer. To top it all she had a terrible practice (something quite typical within the Mexican society) of lying to customers 'in five minutes your order will be ready', when in fact it would take at least twenty. She should've warned the customers about the lack of rice; however, making money was more important than what she said. I was anxious, my poor friend had asked me for rice more than forty minutes ago, so I told Mariel the truth, there was no rice and therefore I would take her noodles with vegetables.

When I went to see her, it was a necessary escape. I was going mad in the restaurant—the lack of organization and inconsistency of my employer was making me crazy. Also, I had been four days without work because she decided to go to Guadalajara and closed the restaurant. If it hadn't been for my grandfather I would've been in red numbers then, at least I could survive for a few days. That month was complicated. I paid my board and I was forced to save again to pay my debts to Valentina and gather more money for the new rent. This left me with very little money for meals; living with the bare minimum to survive. With Mariel I shared all my work frustrations; the constant lies and the informality of my boss were not according to my principles, I couldn't accept that. Arriving at the restaurant, my boss wanted to have a talk, she told me she spent the day alone and could generate a lot of money. For that reason, she needed someone with the same impetus to carry out the restaurant, but I couldn't work like that. It was too much stress and for that, I would go back to

Mexico City. And like that, by a mutual agreement, we decided to end my work at Wok-Inn, then I decided to go with my friend Mariel and have a chat with some drinks.

From one day to the next, my life changed. The work for which I intended to stay the season was no longer mine. At the same time, I remembered my father's call to inform me about the flight to Europe on 30 May, a month earlier than contemplated. I was in the bar of Mariel's restaurant, tasting exotic drinks that she prepared for the clients, my head was spinning, and suddenly nothing was certain. The path to take was unclear. I needed to return sooner in order to arrange several unfinished businesses in the city. It was mid-March at that time, therefore I had April and May for the preparations. Suddenly in my head, my life was meaningless and at the same time, everything was being resolved. I had to make a decision fast. My family trip was approaching, and for several reasons, it would probably be the last one. I already had money to return thanks to my grandfather. I felt I had fulfilled my mission in Sayulita. At that moment the door opened and I told Mariel my verdict. She asked me to take it more calmly, to look for another job, or to think it more thoroughly, but my destiny was quite clear: to return to the city and to go with my family on the Easter trip.

I arrived at my house and I sent a message to Coco advising him of my decision to return. I didn't want to announce anything, however, those were my thoughts. He and I didn't talk very often anymore, but I still had thoughts about him and I wrote, 'You are one of my reasons for returning.' He didn't take it very well, being bewildered by my constant change of plans. I seemed to be playing with his feelings. He helped me to calm down, for once I didn't want to be impulsive and I waited a few days. My sister would arrive on Friday and this happened on a Saturday. In a week she would be with me to know more about my life in Sayulita. Suddenly I was on vacation and enjoying my days without much to do; they would be the last. My friends already knew about my decision to leave. They were sad but they understood and supported me. That week I surfed a lot, I had a good time, I went to several beaches, I smiled every morning opening my window overlooking the sea. I thought in retrospect of the incredible adventure I had experienced, seeing it as a journey and not like my daily life.

My sister Mariel came for a weekend; we had an amazing time and I was able to show her my wonderful lifestyle by the sea. Dani gave her a surfing lesson. She met my friends and tried some of my dishes, boasting of my new culinary skills. She left on Monday. Two days later I returned, on 20 March 2013 to be exact. I slept in Guadalajara and arrived Thursday in Mexico City. I had never driven alone for so long, a new challenge for myself. I did very well and enjoyed the road, the scenery, and the music. Arriving in the city I felt amazing, I fulfilled my mission and I made it back home; however, life in the city seemed like a dream. The day of my arrival was a shock; I took down my surfboard and put it in my room. It was difficult to adapt to the changes—I could not surf or see the ocean every day, I would be forced to breathe smog again, adapt to the rules and my house's cuisine. I didn't understand anything and just laughed. I felt like I was in a dream, surely the pollution made me dizzy and gave me a sensation of being high. That same day I saw Coco. I couldn't relive the passion as before because I wasn't acclimatized to the city, and my life was giving radical changes continuously. I had no expectations for our reunion. I thought to receive reproaches for leaving without the slightest regard for him. To my surprise, he was very relaxed and happy to see me. I was unprepared as a consequence of living too much in the present, and however, our date went well. And that's how we renewed our relationship, and our love flourished.

I arrived in the city on a Thursday, and on Saturday I went to Merida with the Ollivier's. I enjoyed that vacation as I have never done it before on a family trip. I had the best attitude, fresh and tanned from the beach. My relatives were constantly thanking me for my assistance; some knew about my plans to stay in Sayulita. I would've been the only one absent. As a custom in all Latin families, we were very close and we had several trips together, went to a cruise twice, every year to the beach, and we have shared countless weekends at my grandparents' house in Valle de Bravo. My grandmother on one of the cruises made shirts and hats with the name of each one, the back had cartoon characters of each member of the family, ridiculously sweet. My grandfather was getting older and the trip wasn't easy for him; he hardly walked or stayed up for long. We all said it would be the last family trip, my grandfather for his age and the grandchildren were growing; soon we would all have jobs or other forms of formality. I would probably be lost in the world and it would be almost impossible to get together the twenty-one of us. I was very happy with my cousins. I felt radiant and truly happy from within. My family noticed it as my attitude a few years ago wasn't so cheerful and positive. I wanted to talk to my cousins, know more about them, and share my story, urging them to follow their dreams and practice self-love. I wanted to make the most of each moment with them as if it were the last.

A few days after returning to the city, I went surfing with Coco and his friends to a beach in Guerrero called Saladita. I was then several months under the sun, living my best life. I had many things to solve in the city. I wanted to get my work back and finish some things, fix the papers of Mexiro not to hinder the projects with my absence. I needed to process the title of my degree, make the preparations for leaving, and to say goodbye appropriately to my relatives and friends. In fact, on the plane back from Merida, while sleeping, it was when I felt the need to write this book. I would use the two months here to start my writing project. I had it very clear in my mind and ideas began to come. I felt very confident about it. My inner voice asked me, I felt it as a call and I had to start working.

At the moment, I am two weeks away from leaving Mexico. I was already arranging matters regarding my luggage; buying clothes, a pair of snickers, and the necessary things for my trip. I have spent these two months unemployed, although my father offered to support me because starting my trip I would no longer have any resources from him. The Foundation hired another person therefore my work was no longer needed. They were receiving many donations, and they decided to put someone in my position. It made me feel good to hear that because when I arrived they had zero donations, so my work paid off in the hospital. That time I spent it with Coco, with my friends too, but not so often. I was a hermit, reading spiritual books, writing, and suffering the terrible knock on my ankle a few weeks back. I missed my surfboard a lot, so I decided to buy a skateboard. I was so excited that I abused; I fell and twisted my ankle horribly; I got a huge ball. I decided not to go to the doctor, I didn't want to be immobilized for three weeks. Tomorrow I will go. I want to be injected to end the discomfort and be able to go up and down the stairs normally. At the moment my life is going well. I will make a big farewell at my house this Friday. Next week I will sign an attorney's paper to give my partner in Mexiro Casio more power in the organization. I will have a family dinner to say goodbye, and I will take my portrait photos to my university and process my printed title of 8,000 pesos (such big money for a piece of paper). My life here has been fine, I feel on vacation from my next vacation. However my body lost form, my intestine broke down again, and parental limitations returned. I have been pretty quiet with my boyfriend. We make fun plans and enjoy our company. I haven't been drinking or partying much. I kept meditating daily and trying to maintain a Zen state; however, the city sooner or later catches up with you in its rhythms and stress. Now I feel the time is over, and I have several things to do and people to see. I'm just about to start my journey, where I'll have fifteen days with my family in Eastern Europe, then I'll stay in Paris to see my high school friends, then I'll look for a job somewhere while I let the winter pass in Australia.

    With money saved from work, I will go to the other side of the world, that longed-for country of my dreams: Australia. The dynamics will change. I will write more in the present with dates almost like titles. You will accompany me step by step in my adventure around the world.

Questions and Fears

My family and friends anticipated my plans to go to Australia when I returned to the city after Sayulita. My parents knew of my intentions, but adults don't always believe young people when they tell their plans that sound as crazy as mine. During those two months in Mexico, I faced several questions: How much time are you going for? How are you going to find work? Aren't you afraid to be alone and go so far? And to each question, I answered the same 'I don't know. The only thing I know is that I have to go to Australia.' In my mind that was the only thing. I felt a lot of security and determination. For me, it was a mission, a call, for some reason I had to go there. I never questioned it; it was something that I just declared as a fact and people thought it was a crazy thing, but for me, it was like saying, 'I will run a marathon.' It's an objective you set in your mind, and then you do everything you need to do in order to accomplish it.

The situation of my departure was not very easy for Coco. We were very much in love, and it took a lot of work for him to let me go. At the same time, he supported me. I explained how much I've wanted this trip my entire life, the absolute freedom to leave the country, to let myself go and be a citizen of the world. He admired my courage, how one day I dreamed of travelling to Australia, then suddenly, I was a month away to begin the adventure.

We spent some time fantasizing about our reencounter, although we both knew very well that I would leave without a ticket or a date of return. Therefore we decided to enjoy the present and have a great time together. I felt some guilt about leaving him, but at that moment I had really impregnated the archetype of the Goddess Artemis, with my bow and an arrow ready to shoot, a target in front of me and nothing or no one was going to stand in my way. This fidelity to my projects and my ideals helped me to put a layer of protection on my heart; that way it was easier to leave my summer love and keep my life plan firm.

I was leaving Mexico on very good terms with my family. I knew very well that if I ever needed them they would be there to support me. However, I never considered that as a valid option. I wanted to be independent, to take care of my resources, and to prove my adulthood. I have felt fear a few times, especially failure. I know very well that it is a mission and I have to get to Australia. The idea of not doing it, regretting it halfway, or staying for a very short time is what scared me the most; sometimes those thoughts took my sleep away. I didn't fear much about the resources or the job search. My trip was a spiritual experiment and I fully trusted the Universe. I repeated to myself a mantra, 'Everything is going to be fine.' I did doubt my strength to endure the loneliness and the difficult moments. I knew it could be hard sometimes but I was still excited and focused. I had to finish my chores and leave everything in order. I wanted to disappear feeling totally free and light.

I was at a perfect moment in my life, being 23 years old; I had little responsibilities and for that reason, I could permit myself to do something like that. I preferred to try the experience because I knew it very well, 'It's now or never.' My relatives agreed and some even envied me. I had everything on my side, also about 50 thousand pesos (around 3,000 USD) saved that I preferred not to spend in France and focusing on finding a job quickly. That is how the Universe lined up and allowed me an escape from Mexico. Me, a young soul eager to learn from the world, without fears (or at least not many), and with a clear objective in mind: Australia.

PART TWO

Spiritual Journey

Travel Diary

At this moment I am on the plane, high in the sky, still in Mexican territory, leaving so much behind, and thinking about everything there is ahead of me. A moment of limbo where I am neither here nor there, but flying between worlds, flying between the past and the future, without direction or road in front of me, leaving my whole life to do God knows what. It is a moment of confusion—what was an idea once suddenly becomes my reality. In the world of imagination, that idea lives for years, but in the tangible physical world, it is new and doesn't know how to behave. At this moment I'm on the plane to Paris. I'm sitting between my sister and my mom, my dad is behind us. After a few weeks with my family, there will be no turning back, there is no place for regret. My decision to undertake my own journey was taken, and I will face the consequences.

These last days have been one of the most difficult moments of my life. I had never before decided to go that far, with an uncertain itinerary and time, and I was forced to deal with a series of social and family pressures. The most difficult thing is leaving my boyfriend Coco behind. These days were filled with tears, sadness, and nostalgia. I have not been able to get excited about my trip, thinking about the terrible separation. It was a great desolation and now I'm not too happy. I really miss him horribly. In my imagination, I visualized myself in the airplane feeling complete freedom; I would've finished my chores and would be completely detached from the city. However, it is not so. I feel tired and very disoriented, first for several days of insomnia and sleep disorders; the second is that I don't know what course to take after my stay in Paris, once my parents return to Mexico. I want to spend a few weeks with my friends in the French capital, and then I will make some serious decisions. Living in the present requires a lot of practice, and only with enlightenment and a mastery of the mind you can be in the here and now with full peace and happiness. And because I am a human in the process of spiritual growth, forgetting about my boyfriend and enjoying ten hours of flight surrounded by French people was basically impossible. I was caught between the present and the future. I did not feel very happy. I repeat, being in a crowded and uncomfortable plane, eating horrible food was not exactly the biggest elixir.

At the farewell dinner with Coco, we talked about the process of detachment. The memories of my life in the city and my relationship with him were fresh—yesterday I was eating vegetarian dinner, holding his hand, and talking about how wonderful our encounter was, commemorating our history. Now I'm on the plane, separating myself with an ocean between us. I wish I could wake up from this dream and be with him again, even for a short moment. Despite the difficulty, the passage of days will create new stories and my memories of him will lose sharpness; new experiences will be presented and when I look back on my life in Mexico, it will be more distant and blurred. Coco and I talked about that, however, we knew how difficult it would be to recover our individual lives and go back to singleness.

I am grateful for the transition in my new life. My father has prepared the most productive trip with schedules and plans even at meals. So I won't have time to think about my boyfriend, finally, it is the only real difficulty in my separation from Mexico, besides my dog nothing else causes me conflict or nostalgia. I love my friends and family but I can live some time away from them. However, my dog and my boyfriend will be hard to forget. It will cost me a lot to let him go, but this is the only way Coco was going to make his life, and so do I. The Universe united us at a certain time, to learn and grow, but part of gaining maturity is to understand the cycles of life, and ours was a relationship destined to be short.

11 June 2013

I have been travelling with my family for eleven days. I am in Berlin and the day after tomorrow we are going to Paris. We will be there for a few days and then my parents will return to Mexico, while my sister and I will remain in Paris. It has been very strange to travel with my father. Last time we went to Europe as a family was five years ago, so I found it difficult to adapt and accept my father's travel arrangements. I am 23 years old now. I am an adult woman with my own ways, and to travel as a family was becoming very complicated for me, probably this would be the last one. My dad finds his greatest happiness when the four of us are together, that is when he feels really complete. On the other hand, I'm tired of being a spoiled child. I feel like an adolescent and I need a separation from them. My sister and I are completely different from my parents—in taste, in ideas, in food, and in ways to travel. My mom is still annoyed with my hairstyle and my arrangement; my dad can't calm down and leave the Michelin guide alone.

To date, I keep asking myself the correct relationship with the family. In the United States, teens leave their home at 18 years old and start to make their living. In Mexico, family togetherness is absolute; family is the most important value. I'm rather on balance, at 18 you're still an impulsive teenager, probably not the best age to go. However, in early adulthood, from my age to a maximum limit of 30 years old, it is inconceivable to continue living with your parents. In my case, I feel that way—tired of living every day with their ways. I am in the process of being a vegetarian, vegan, or something like that; they obviously don't understand it. It's so hard to be myself in such a conservative family. The way I dress is always an issue; the way I think is apparently from Mars, and they still don't know why I'm doing this journey to Australia. In my father's perfect form of education, I would've remained in Mexico City, met a boyfriend in University with a career in something technical, then got married, and lived five minutes away from his house. I understand my father's point of view because that's how society has worked for centuries, though our generation was born in a very different world—one that is overpopulated, exploited, highly damaged, where more and more of us are seeking a different way of living. I don't want the life my father wants for me. I see something different for myself, but of course, it's impossible to make him understand. For now, I just need my space, find my own way of seeing the world, and away from my parents for a while.

13 June 2013

We have been in Vienna, Salzburg, Prague, Budapest, Dresden, appreciating Eastern European landscapes travelling by car, and having beautiful family moments. The trip has been very touristy and little traveller, as was to be expected. My dad had everything planned from hotels and itinerary; however, the trip took an interesting turn one day when the road to Salzburg from Munich was flooded and closed. My father's perfect plans didn't work out, and we were forced to return to Munich. So we readjusted several elements of logistics that brought us some surprises, nothing too extraordinary either. On the one hand, it has been interesting to travel with my family in order to realize how opposed I am to the conventional style. In my opinion, the best experiences on a trip are presented when there is nothing planned, and suddenly you meet exceptional people or unique events happen. Many travellers say it's not the places you go to, it's the people you meet that make the difference. When you seldom travel, any place can marvel you, but if you have been travelling for many months, the best moments involve other people; local, eccentric characters, and plans arising out of nothing from knowing someone.

There is a saying in Spanish "preguntando se llega a Roma" (by asking you to get to Rome). To ask it is necessary to talk to people. Locals know very good tips and different places that may not be shared by your typical tourist guide. To travel well it's necessary to open up, to be willing to know other cultures, to seek to integrate as much as possible.

An example of this: my dad had a map tracing the best walk around Munich and specific places. My sister and I wanted to explore an interesting street; however, the wisdom of the map is 'superior' and we had to leave the street behind. In this way, the attachment to the plan doesn't allow intuition to do its work. The path is forced and limited; it comes from the rational mind with fear of the unknown.

Travelling with several people has its disadvantages. It is difficult to achieve a correct flow of energy when there are many; some will want to do one thing and others something different, and that's why I want to travel alone. To be in harmony, it is necessary that there is a good understanding, absence of quarrels and misunderstandings, everyone seeking to be happy and joyful at every moment. Travelling with other people has its advantages as well. If there is a good chemistry, where laughter and happiness predominate, energy flows well; that way positive results are achieved. The goal is to eliminate thoughts, stay in the present, and be open to explore. However, I believe that the energy flows better in a single person; finally you are completely free to go and do whatever you want. It is you and your soul around the world. The optimum journey is in solitude, but it takes a major mental control, to eradicate thoughts, and to feel complete and happy with oneself.

16 June 2013

At the moment I am not myself on this trip. Apart from some decisions regarding restaurants and other matters, plans and forms are from my dad, so I can't flow and connect with *me*. On the other hand, it has been a phase to restructure my person. I brought phosphorescent melon-colored snickers that I now hallucinate, people stare at me in the streets by the shine of my shoes. I can't take it anymore. Also, during hot days there is nothing worse than socks, so I bought a pair of black sandals in Prague that look quite peculiar, very comfortable though. To create the right style, I had to buy some new shorts and shirts. I also bought a hat and sunglasses to improve the looks. That way some clothes with similar colors than my tennis are no longer needed, neither my skateboard for not being recovered from the sprain. My suitcase is impractical because it carries a yoga mat and a skateboard. It's the worst idea that I could've had—trying to move that thing around the subway or any other transportation would be impossible; therefore I left it in the trunk of the car we rented.

My foolishness made me blind to the reality that you cannot travel with a heavy suitcase—primary rule. Now I will be forced to give my bag to my dad with much of my luggage. My sister and I decided to return her skateboard to Mexico, but I will keep mine for the moment. After having a slight crisis with my belongings, I need to detach myself and let go. To stay with the indispensable will be a challenge but I will achieve it. Using my horrible phosphorescent sneakers, I realized another very important rule for travelling: looking and feeling good. It has given me the worst embarrassment to walk with them. I feel the looks of the people and it makes me feel very uncomfortable, and that causes insecurity. Every day we must devote time to our arrangement, each one will have their way. The goal is to see ourselves in the mirror and be satisfied with our look. Love begins towards us, and once it's achieved it's important to show it and share it with all the people around us; giving smiles, hugs, and affection. These have been my days of travel—moving around Eastern Europe, seeing the mistakes of my suitcase, creating a style of clothing adapted to my new sandals, getting fed up with my parents, and progressively stop communicating with Coco. At first, I talked to him a lot, but now the communication has been spacing for several days. It is a natural process however painful. I remember him often and I get very nostalgic.

19 June 2013

I'm still very early in the journey, there is much ahead but uncertainty doesn't contribute to a peaceful state of mind. I try not to overthink but I find it difficult. I currently have some ideas: my former roommate from Sayulita, Valentina, returned to Rome yesterday. I want to go with her and spend some time in Italy. I have several reasons: first, I am attracted to southern Europe. The people in northern Europe are very cold. I want to be surrounded by people more akin to the Latin. Second, Valentina discovered a surfing beach an hour away from Rome. Third, I wouldn't spend on lodging and I could save to go to Australia. Fourth, Valentina returns to Mexico in September and coincides with the date when I want to go to Australia. I also understand Italian a lot and I speak a little. I love the language and I want to learn it, that way I would speak four languages. I spoke with Valentina and we agreed. It will be a short time in Paris, and soon I will go to Rome.

23 June 2013

Today is Super Moon day when the moon is 15 percent larger than normal. Paris is very cloudy and unfortunately, I couldn't see it tonight. Full moons cause me a bit of anxiety because the energy increases, the waves and the oceans take on greater forces, the hospitals have more work, there is more crime in the streets, and parties are crazier. During these days, things can turn out incredibly well or out of control at any moment. I prefer to take greater precautions on the full moon and do nothing in excess.

At the moment, I'm at my friend Victoria's house in 11ème arrondissement of Paris; she has been hosting my sister and me for a week. Before my night meditation a few moments ago, I did a Tarot reading using Victoria's cards. It was one for the past, one for the present, and one for the future. My question was regarding my trip. From the beginning, without knowing too much about the meaning and basic knowledge of Tarot, I was able to notice a really amazing combination, for the past, I had the arcane Strength, as present I had Emperor, and as future, Hierophant. To get a deeper understanding of the meaning, I took Jodorowski's book *The Way of Tarot* and began to read the meanings. I am still impressed with the accuracy and clarity of the message, and it fits perfectly with my experiences and aspirations of the future.

Strength opens the way for the inner voice. It indicates a beginning marked by instinct. This connection, this deep look, leads to hearing the voice of the Strength and would seem like an animal instinct because we don't know the reasons, but we must act upon it. The arcane also represents creativity, and that comes precisely from the creative source of the Universe. This is the card for my past, the moment where this instinctive force appeared indicating me to leave my house, to go away from my country and my family.

The second card referred to my present. I got the Emperor, which means material security. If you see the card with attention, the Emperor is half-way standing on his throne. It shows tranquility but is alert for any situation where it is required to take action. At this moment I'm like this and I want to trust this card. It's a moment of joy with my sister and my friends after my family separation. I have the Universe as my ally. However, according to Jodorowski, the Emperor can be evil if you don't obey, so I must hear my inner voice. This card is my inner warrior, knows my weaknesses, but is very strong in the end.

The last card, regarding my future the trip, is very positive and I hope at the bottom of my soul that is true. The main reason for my trip is quite ambitious, and I was very surprised to get this out, at the same time it gave me the certainty to be in the right place and doing the right thing. This card means a greater level of spirituality, through the Hierophant, divinity is manifested, his words and actions come from the supreme force of the Universe. His heart is immersed in love, abandoning the Ego's desires, a pure connection with God. He is a communicator of the Higher Force, unlike the High Priestess, he shares and has a social work of spiritual guidance. I was truly flattered to get such a great card for my future, causally coinciding with the deep reasons of my journey. I want to connect eternally with the force of the Universe and follow its voice that communicates with me through my intuition.

With this I would like to expose my spiritual knowledge learned from different books, the following are ideas of Deepak Chopra in *SynchroDestiny*, one of my favorite books. This is an essential philosophical baggage with which I will travel in the coming months.

There are three planes governing our human and suprahuman existence. The Physical Plane is the one perceptible to the eyes, objects that are within reach of our touch and that are around. The Quantum Plane is where our thoughts, dreams, and emotions reside. It is not something tangible, but you can't doubt its existence. The Virtual Plan is where the Universal Energy resides, the purest of existence, for some it is God, others will give it another name: the Cosmos, the Infinite Power, the Universe, among others. For me, it's pure love giving life to the beings and organisms of our world. In fact, during meditation, you can feel that energy flowing through the body. Humans carry a bit of the Virtual Plane that exists through their soul, where it resides the connection with the Universe, God, or whatever you want to call it.

To tune in with the frequency of the Divine or the Universe, the best tool is the present. The happier we are is when we enjoy the moment, when we think of nothing else, when we simply live and enjoy the moment. If we learn to live in the present, we can be happy in any circumstance, smile, and enjoy the simple fact of being alive and being healthy. If happiness is the ultimate goal of the human being and living in the present ensures happiness, the ultimate goal of the human being is learning to live in the present. It's a big challenge.

People live eternally burdened by the future or drag the past without letting go, that way stress is created and with stress a large number of diseases. With meditation we learn to silent the mind that is constantly overwhelming oneself; it doesn't let us be in the present moment because it transports us to the future and the past.

During my journey, the main key for success is to live in the present and listen to the voice of intuition. To trace the path that will lead me to my destiny, it's necessary to develop intuition; some call it 'the voice of the soul or the heart'. Intuition is the best power and the main tool to achieve our dreams. Intuition is the worm of our stomach, that sensation that gets activated in our gut. Often it is not rational but is very powerful and assists us in the decision-making process if we want to listen to it. The mind is unable to understand intuition, our Supreme Intelligence. Many people have repressed the worm for years, and their rational mind prevents them from understanding those feelings. Meditation opens doors and makes us much more sensitive to this inner voice. Hence, the famous saying 'follow your heart', and for what I've seen and I believe, it's always right.

Attaining this connection, I will be able to remain in a state of complete happiness and luminosity wherever I go, eliminating any trace of stress or restlessness.

25 June 2013

I've been to Victoria's house for a week with my sister not doing much. I've gone out in the evenings and I've spent good times in the French metropolis. Eight days ago, my parents returned back to Mexico, and it was strange saying goodbye to them without knowing exactly when I will see them again. I have been a few days quite sad. Luckily I said goodbye to my family to stay with another family, my friends from high school. I consider them my brothers and I have a great time with them. Somehow this could smoothen the separation from my parents.

I feel Paris as a transition to my real journey. Being with Victoria and my sister makes me not only depend on my decisions, so the Universal Energy does not flow directly through me but in a group way. With both girls, I have an awesome time. Victoria is a great friend, very friendly, nice, dresses cool, and likes to go out and have fun. Her company has been very pleasant, something very valuable at this stage of my trip. At the moment, I am concentrating on being with my friends and having fun with them. When I go to Australia and I'm completely alone, I will probably miss them a lot, so it's an incredible opportunity to enjoy them.

A few days ago I received an email with great news. It was from the Australian Government notifying the granting of my visa. Officially I can enter the country and legally work from one to two years if I renew it. A few days ago, I got nervous because I didn't know exactly how long the visa was going to take. I already knew thanks to some French friends about the forms online. From my iPad I was filling them in, entering data and passport numbers. They asked me if I had another nationality and I put Mexican. They made me fill information in another window respecting my Mexican nationality. I didn't know whether to lie or not. I thought it was a very strange case since I have a French passport. I had to put my birthplace in France, if I changed that, it would mark a mistake because this visa isn't allowed for Mexicans, only about fifteen very select countries. I proceeded with the form to the end, where you are asked for bank details to pay 365 Australian dollars. I had to do it, proceed without knowing if I would get it. After doing so, I took a shower, I was pretty nervous. I didn't know how long it would take to have the answer, but I had to stay calm. I couldn't avoid questioning whether I would get the visa or not. I was a very rare case because I'm French Mexican and that could be a factor for exclusion. Victoria's friends told me a few days ago that the Australian Government had limited the number of visas because the French were going in droves to make disasters in their territories. Several thoughts came to my mind: if for some reason I didn't get the visa my dream of the Promised Land would end here; nevertheless, I had to trust my destiny. Maybe Australia was not where I needed to be.

After my reflective shower and dressing up, I took the iPad to waste some time on the Internet. Suddenly I received a message from the Australian government and I started to read it quickly without paying much attention. It was probably about the request. However, a few paragraphs below the information something seemed strange. So I went back to the beginning and read paying more attention. I then understood that the mail was an official notice to grant the visa and details corresponding to it. Instantly I shouted with emotion and shared the news with my sister and Victoria; they were both happy for me. I felt a relaxed happiness. I had permission to enter Australia, all good related to my plans.

Already with the visa, I decided to browse some flight tickets to Australia. I want to arrive as soon as possible, although I highly prefer avoiding winter. So I opted for flights in mid-September. I searched for several dates and bought the cheapest day. I already have my ticket to leave; it is Wednesday, September 18. I decided to buy it in advance as a form of obligation. Whatever happens in this continent, Australia is where I must be. Europe doesn't convince me a bit and I refuse to stay a frozen winter here when I can enjoy the heat and the beaches.

These days in Paris I have confirmed my suspicions: there is a pretty negative vibe around, normal for being a city, but here it feels more. For some reason men in this city, find the freedom to speak to you and ask for cigarettes or any other random thing.

During my stay here, there have been some unpleasant situations with my friends. The first one, while we were walking in a group leaving a concert of the 'Music Festival' when turning to see where my friends where I realized that a young North African guy was taking Manuela's friend from the back and tried to kiss her neck, she said 'No' and tried to remove him. Then Manuela ran and hugged her to get rid of that person and fortunately nothing else happened. The second, my sister's friend returned alone by subway not very late at night, she was walking down the street only three minutes away from her house, when another North African man embraced and spoke with his wet breath to her ear, she tried to get rid of him peacefully telling him that she wanted to return home without his company. It is difficult to deal with them because if you are rude they could attack you, then it's best to be gentle and avoid them in the most peaceful way possible. The third, the American friend of Victoria came two months and yesterday decided to go to Barcelona a couple of days after a bad night.

Victoria's friend found herself pretty drunk in Paris, getting in an argument with an unknown man in the Seine that threw her cell phone into the river. Then she was attacked by men who were harassing her, and then she took three hours to come back to her house because she was too wasted and lost. She decided to escape from Paris for a while. From my point of view, the mismanagement of immigration by the French Government and the creation of an urban culture of vandalism, known here as *racaille*, results in an unfriendly city. My Parisian friends believe that their city is a safe place. However, I feel frightened, therefore I am focused on ensuring the safety of my sister and mine. For that reason, we walk little at night and we take as many taxis as necessary to avoid being in contact with some harasser.

In general, I don't like the vibe of the city; besides the hurried rhythm, I feel unsure at night. In Mexico I'm not accustomed to walking at night or being in contact with the whole society, thanks to my car. But here, being outside connects you directly with people.

However, here it is very frequent that random guys approach to ask for cigarettes as a way to flirt and sometimes only to annoy. For this reason, I don't want to be in this city right now. I want to be in a place where I can walk quietly, breathe peace, and get the best of vibes. I don't want to deal with nocturnal gargoyles.

My stay hasn't been negative throughout; overall we had a good time. We were fortunate to be at Victoria's house, the metro is 30 meters from the front door and her street Oberkampf in the 11ème arrondissement is full of shops, restaurants, and bars. If we want to go out, we don't need to go far, so we can be safe without spending money on taxis. That way, avoiding being alone at night and being very careful, I will be able to ensure a good holiday in Paris; enjoy delicious food, beautiful places, fine architecture, and cultural and historical wealth.

26 June 2013

I realize that I have been focused on myself. I have been learning and enjoying this trip, especially in the last few days. The relationship with my sister, a girl 3 and a half years younger than me, with a fun and extroverted personality, has been very pleasant. We have got along perfectly well, we have flowed together, and I have felt her as a real support in these moments where I need it the most. We are together all day; we even sleep on the same bed. Today we are very excited to move on to the next stage; to leave Victoria's house, and move to our own space.

Today I bought a new suitcase. I wanted something small and easy to handle in different places, especially to be able to carry it in all public transport. In the metro many times, there are no escalators and you have to carry your suitcase and climb as fast as possible so as not to block the path of rushing city residents. So with my new suitcase, I am ready for the next step. Tomorrow I go to the laundry, then packing in order to leave Victoria's house.

My sister and I are going on Saturday to a room of 15 square meters quite far from the center of Paris, next to *La Défense*, in *Neuilly sur Seine* to be exact. Something good is to have the metro line 1 that leaves us four blocks from the place, being to my taste the best line of the city passing through several tourist attractions: *Bastille, Louvre, Jardins des Tuilleries, Place de la Concorde, Champs Elysées*, among others. The neighborhood is very elegant and therefore makes it very safe. We can walk at night without being so afraid. It is the service room of a very old building with typical Parisian architecture. It's on the eighth floor without an elevator, with that we will exercise really well. We have a very nice balcony overlooking the *Seine* and *La Défense*, the modern part of Paris. Just by the sight, I fell in love with the tiny room, it calms me to watch the water flow. We got the studio through my friend Manuela, her friend Marie is going on vacation and we are going to rent it for a few weeks. Shortly after we saw the place and walked back down the street, she asked if 400 euros per month was good, but I had contemplated paying 200 only. I was puzzled and I said that because of the Mexican peso we could not pay that amount. I offered 250 and she accepted. So now my sister and I have a place for us, surely we won't spend that much time there because my friend from San Francisco, Andrina, is alone in a very comfortable apartment in the center of Paris. Chelsea who rented it at first decided to go to Barcelona. There is an available bed and we will probably spend some nights when we go out to party.

I am quite motivated to leave my belongings in one place and to be able to undo my suitcase; it will make me very happy. These days I want to keep buying some things and continue to create my style. Colors and prints do not attract me anymore. I have changed a lot of my tones. I like greyish blues, black, beige, coffee, wine, dark green, mint green, and others.

My goal is to fill my suitcase with garments that can be combined so I chose zero prints, just plain colors. For me, it was quite difficult. I went shopping with my friends, while they want to enlarge their wardrobe, I bought things to be able to diminish my suitcase.

This is how my days have been, in constant search to be more practical and to be as light as possible.

29 June 2013

    These days have been getting better and better. I feel different and that starts to be noticeable on the outside. This weekend my sister and I had a lot of fun with Andrina. On Saturday, it was the Gay Pride Parade and turned out to be taking place next to my friend's house. Neither Mariel nor I knew, so we just focused on taking our bags to our new studio and then head to Andrina's house. To our surprise, leaving the subway, we saw a tumult of people and music at maximum volume, in the Place de la Bastille where the Gay Pride party was being held. It was very entertaining to see people in disguise and joy on the streets. After a bit of partying, we decided to go to Andrina's place, and suddenly without planning a meeting spot, we found each other on the street and jumped on the excitement in the middle of the crowd and noisy surroundings. The three of us went to Andrina's house to have wine and prepare to go out again.

    Our friend told us about the intensity of the day, the crazy people in Bastille, and the surrounding streets. Andrina met some French people outside her house with whom she spent the day. Before they left, they shared the address where they would be that night, and we decided to go. I had just expressed to Andrina a few days ago my desire to talk to men. I love being among girls but I needed a change of energy. Although we had the address and the entry code, we didn't know the apartment number, so we walked through each door to hear where they could be. We were in the wrong apartment where an old lady came out with her dog to scold us, but we kept searching and going upstairs. At last, we arrived at the place where we heard the music playing and we rang the bell. I was feeling really awkward. Surely those guys gave the address to my friend and never thought we would come, but there we were, meeting with eight strangers. They had been partying for several hours, the music was strong, and they continued to drink. One of them filled a bottle of sangria and made us drink from it. In a short time, we reached their level of drunkenness and were having a great time. We danced, sang, talked in English, French, and Spanish, and enjoyed their good vibes and their party. They left to go to a concert so we left as well. A couple of them had no tickets for the event so we invited them with us and decided to walk to Andrina's house, and we were quite drunk. On the way, Romain, one of the French guys and I found an abandoned supermarket cart and without thinking, I climbed on it and he pushed me. I was laughing out loud in a cart in the streets of Paris. Then it was the turn of Mariel and Andrina, we took it up to two blocks before Bastille. After that, the girls and I said goodbye to the guys and went to a party on a boat on the Seine. The music was electronic with cumbia, afro, Balkan, and others. We danced and had a lot of fun. We didn't stay long and went back to Andrina's house to sleep. We were tired after the party with the French guys, the hour of walking with the cart, and several drinks on top. What a night.

30 June 2013

It was Sunday and we woke up hungover and very hungry. As we knew about the scarcity of open supermarkets that day, we decided to go somewhere more crowded and find something to eat. We went to *Rue de Rivoli* for a crepe made with egg, cheese, and mushrooms, accompanied by a litter of orange juice for five euros. The day was sunny and warm; we were very happy to remember our fun night as we contemplated the beautiful architecture of Paris. The three of us laughed and thanked the wonderful life, our beautiful summer together in this city. For them, it would end soon and for me, a long journey ahead; the beauty of having no date to return to the supposed reality. We arrived at Andrina's house, brushed our teeth, took our bags, and went for a walk. We decided to go along the *Seine* to see the magnificent *Notre Dame*. We spent some time sunbathing and watching the boats go by the river. We lay down in some gardens in front of the Ile St Louis, and we enjoyed the sun, played some music on the iPad, an afternoon of laughs and good times. Andrina is one of the happiest and most cheerful girls I know. She's always in a good mood and she spreads the best energy. Mariel and I love to be with her and have a great time, enjoying and laughing about anything. Besides, she is very generous; she made dinner twice to my friends and me. She invites us for drinks and food, she lets us be at her house when we want. I'm very inspired by her constant happiness, that's why life has rewarded her with a generous boyfriend who sponsored her two-month trip to Europe, something that so many would like. That day was very good, the weather was delicious, and we sunbathed beside the Seine. Also, I saw a friend from childhood and then we went back to Andrina's house. I cooked fried rice with vegetables for the girls.

1 July 2013

It's Monday and it's quite hot, so we decided to have a picnic near our studio. We left Andrina's house and took line 1 from *Bastille* to *Pont de Neuilly*. We went for groceries to the supermarket, fresh baguettes from the *boulangerie*, and then we came to our house to leave things and change our clothes. We then prepared our picnic bag and went to the *Bois de Boulogne*, a fairly large park/forest two blocks from the house. So we walked in order to find a place to settle and spend the afternoon. We walked for more than half an hour along the edge of the park because we couldn't find the entrance. We finally went a little farther and found the perfect place. The day was hot but a little cloudy, so we looked for the greenest pastures of the countryside to put our towels and scarves and settle comfortably. We took out the food, a very typical French picnic: red wine, Camembert cheese, baguette, grapes, and some delicious cookies for 90 cents. In France, the food is delicious; simply the section of cupcakes, biscuits, and chocolates in the supermarket you can't delight yourself enough with the exquisite flavors. Our vegetarian picnic, made with less than 10 euros was enough to give us one of the biggest delicacies in the world and a pleasant time in the forest with our friends. Once again we were happy with the beauty of life and how incredible our time together was.

On the way back, I found a small ring. Many times I look at the ground to know where I'm going. Also in Paris, unfortunately, people pee in many corners and you can see the liquid running down the sidewalk. Then taking care of my footsteps looking at the ground, something caught my attention—a small white object flashed and attracted my curiosity. I decided to lift it. It was a ring with white beads studded and a plastic shell with blue-sky tone, the quality was not exactly good, but I was surprised about the fact that it was a shell, of all things in the world was something marine. My mental resolution: some beach is calling me. For me, these surprises are not mere coincidences. I always pay close attention wanting to find clues to know what the Universe wants to tell me. Hence, in the spiritual world, we change the name and call them 'causalities'. They come from a greater cause and it is fundamental to listen to them. I immediately knew when I found the ring that a cosmic clue was being sent in order to make me direct energies and reach a beach. Just a few days before I was talking to Valentina, I said I would visit her with my sister, it would be around July 18. That's because Valentina's parents go on vacation on the twentieth and Mariel returns to Mexico on the twenty-fourth, so we could have a few days to enjoy together that amazing city. Valentina had contemplated returning to Mexico in September, but a few days ago she announced her return to Sayulita on August 4 or 5, which gave me a month of uncertainty without knowing exactly where to stay. I didn't want to go back to France, but in Italy, I had no one besides Valentina, so I thought about going to a secluded beach and looking for work there. It was just an idea and I decided not to think about it. I'll solve it when I get there. When I found the ring for me it was a sign; my way was then headed to the beach.

I put it on and told the girls I would use it as a reminder to go to the beach in Italy. I smiled, thanking the newly acquired cosmic gift. We came to the house and cooked pasta with mushroom sauce and tomato. We ate on our terrace appreciating the view from the eighth floor admiring the *Seine*, the *Défense*, and the typical Parisian roofs. Andrina returned home and my sister and I prepared to unpack. I was happy to finally settle in a place. Again, today was a perfectly fluid and happy day.

3 July 2013

Today in the morning, I got up and had the instinct to fix the house, being in my own property I become obsessive of order, so I began to clean and reorganize the studio. I decided to move some things from Marie to give us more space for my sister and me with our belongings. I put a lot of school papers in an empty plastic box under the bed. I also opened more room in the closet. I fixed some things in the kitchen, besides my sister and I had to buy basic things like salt, pepper, and oil; apparently, Marie doesn't even cook an egg.

After my order and cleaning session, I felt fulfilled. I went out onto the terrace and breathed the air of well-being; our holidays were being incredible and I was beginning to love our little Parisian nest. I was settled, just what I wanted since Victoria's house—order, cleanliness, and my own space. And now I had it, but there was one small inconvenience: a single bed. My sister and I would be forced to make an extra-human effort not to kill each other at night. I finally decided to sleep on the floor, there was a rug and I tried to stay positive. We put together a bed with a towel and a chair cushion, that to minimize the impact of the hard floor on the bones of my hip, then the bedspread of Mariel's bed and a sheet. Finally, it wasn't so bad. I was used to sleeping on the floor after my experience in Sayulita. To my surprise, I slept quite well.

After cleaning and tidying the house, I proposed to Mariel to explore the *16ème arrondissement*, a very elegant quarter of Paris, on the map was the closest to *Neuilly sur Seine*. We put on our most comfortable shoes and went for a walk. It was quite a distance but I motivated my sister by telling her of the incredible exercise we were doing walking around the city. We started almost by *La Défense*, and we went all the way to the *Arc de Triomphe*; on the way we enjoyed an icy popsicle. Then we went through *16ème* streets with very elegant boutiques; we headed towards *Trocadero* to see the *Tour Eiffel*. On the way, we stopped at the Sephora cosmetics store and to my surprise, I found exactly what I wanted, a soft brush to wash my face, and also was discounted. In the morning, I had put a liquid of Marie's on my face and I loved the feeling of having it fresh. I realized that clothes are constantly changed, but the skin is always there. I have always preferred not to wear any make-up. I like to look naturally pretty, but I had to ensure the best skin possible. At Sephora, I bought the brush, a nail polish, and a special soap for deep facial cleansing. I was very happy with my purchases. Finally, we arrived at *Trocadero*, we saw a concentration of people at the exit of an event, we knew of the Fashion Week in Paris but we didn't know the agenda or the locations, then we got close to see. It was the Armani Runway and we stayed like an hour watching models and designers come out. We didn't know anyone, but it was entertaining to see eccentric reporters and photographers going crazy to get the best photo possible. Among several models that came out, I kept looking at a blonde one; it was a mutual look, quite fixed and inevitable. The normal thing would be to look away when stared at by a stranger; it's an uncomfortable feeling that makes us look away. But for some reason I didn't stop looking at him, then he looked at me too, like two or three seconds later he took his eyes to the floor and smiled timidly. I felt ticklish and bragged to my sister the smile of that model. It gave me security and made me feel beautiful.

    Another externalization of my world, today I felt good about myself. I had my hair partially collected with a white flower, fresh face, and a sense of well-being and order after unpacking in our new place. The exchange of looks with the model asserted my inner state. I felt beautiful and apparently outside was noticeable too. In the end, the world we see is a reflection of how we are within, positive thoughts and love towards ourselves are going to manifest on the outside with harmony. Negative people have negative thoughts and therefore negative lives. It is important to change our interior to give a twist to our existence.

My sister and I decided to go back to the house. We were tired from so much walking, and we still had to go to the supermarket to buy some missing items. We took the subway and went for groceries. We ended up with a lot of things, especially because my sister bought almond milks, which made the bags quite heavy. One block ahead, we found a mattress. It was in perfect condition and was just recently taken out. It looked very new and came from one of Neuilly's bourgeois houses. It seemed to be waiting for us and we decided to take it. In Paris this is a habit, people take their things to the street and other people grab them; it's a very interesting exchange. The mattress even had two handles on the edge, perfect to be carried by two people. Then we put our bags in one hand and decided to take the mattress to the house. It would be a great challenge but totally worth it. We carried it for four blocks in total, paused several times to rest, and changed the arm that held the mattress. Finally, we arrived at the building but the worst was yet to come—climbing up the stairs all the way to the eight floors. So we decided to drop it down and deal with the shopping bags first. Arriving at our apartment was every time a physical challenge. So when we got there we had a glass of water. I ate a peach and my sister a chocolate then with our remaining forces, we went down to get the mattress. It wasn't very complicated but it took a lot of effort from both us, so we ended up exhausted. I was happy, I couldn't believe the new gift from the Universe, we had an extra bed and I wouldn't sleep on the floor again. Then my positive affirmation, which I repeat constantly as a mantra, regained, even more, meaning: 'I love the Universe and the Universe loves me.'

So far I had not narrated my trip with so many details, but lately I feel my days flow incredibly without any effort. I begin to notice details from the Universe, clues, and cosmic gifts, affirming that better energy is flowing within me and that I am on the right track. For the moment I will continue to enjoy my days in Paris.

5 July 2013

After a few wonderful days, I thought there would be a very positive continuation in Paris; however, there was an energy twist. The night I wrote the last day, I took several cups of vanilla tea without knowing its contents of black tea. In fact, over time I became very sensitive to substances, therefore I don't drink coffee, I don't smoke cigarettes and I don't use drugs, everything makes me feel bad except alcohol because it's a depressant of the nervous system. The rest gives me anxiety, my heart starts racing and I feel bad. That night I couldn't sleep until five o'clock in the morning, then my stomach ached, and in the morning I had a cold sore in my mouth. Suddenly that state of maximum pleasure was over, and I had a very annoying crack on the lip. In the morning I returned to take the vanilla tea and prepared to move from my small apartment. I would go one night with Victoria and others with Andrina. My sister received a friend so I decided to leave my place. When I arrived at Victoria's house, my friends noticed my level of anxiety and stress. I was very accelerated and exalted, and I explained the reason. Realizing that my vanilla tea had the same substance as black tea, I decided I wouldn't take it anymore.

I felt bad—I had a cold sore in my mouth. Besides being uncomfortable, it is demoralizing and I had trembling in the body, a direct effect of the tea in my bloodstream. I was extremely tired. I slept until late, got up early. It took an hour to get to Victoria's house, and another place of anxiety for me is the subway and suddenly several elements accumulated. I was exhausted. However, after reading a lot about plants and teas, I prepared myself a mint drink at Vic's house, which helped me calm down. I also had a few glasses of wine to relax in the company of my friends. After that, we went to take the appetizer at Justine's house, had a great time, and ate rich French snacks. Not too late, with the last train at twelve-thirty we returned. I slept at Vic's house.

In the morning I woke up with a terrible laziness, I simply didn't want to get out of bed. The bad weather and a general discontent for no apparent reason made me to lie down in bed. I got up, saw my sore, my morning face swollen, and my hair brings a total mess; I got depressed and went back to bed. Victoria went for a picnic with her French friends quite far from the house. She invited me but I couldn't find the courage to get up and go with her not very fun friends. I decided to stay alone. I had planned to go to Andrina's house, yet at two in the afternoon there were no signs of her, and so I just stood there, inert, watching the time go by. Finally, Andrina appeared in the social networks and invited me to her house. So I tried to take a better attitude, to bathe, to be presentable, and to move with Andrina, so I left at around three-thirty in the afternoon.

When I arrived with Andrina, I was exhausted, told her my situation, and complained of a semi-depressive state for no apparent reason. She told me that she felt exactly the same. The weather was also a disgrace, cloudy, and cold. Between talks, Andrina announced the news from Chelsea, who would arrive on July 8 with her boyfriend. So my friend needed to leave the apartment that day, and that's very soon. That change made us talk about some possibilities; we didn't know what to do. In my house were my sister and her friend, and in Victoria's house, we couldn't stay for the arrival of her mother and sister on July 10. Andrina, therefore, was thinking of renting a place in Paris. The terrible climate, the need for movement, and a strong desire to leave created a brainstorm of possible destinations. She had to find a place. I was tired of Paris, I wanted something more. I wanted to go to the beach, so did she and then we started the search.

My original plan was to go to Rome around July 18, and until then, stay in Paris; but now that Andrina became part of our trip, we decided to adopt something with her. A plan would be to leave Paris on July 10 and go a few days to a beach before arriving in Rome. One idea was to go to Croatia and from there take a ferry to Italy, then a plane to Rome. Seeing the prices of the flights, the time of transfer, and the expenses, in general, was a little viable plan. Then we started looking for options in the south of France; however, the flights were expensive as well. Another idea was to go to Montpellier. I have very good friends there and one of them with a car, who offered to take me to the beach. Overall the biggest trauma of Andrina and I was the lack of sun and water. We wanted good weather, being in swimsuit during the day, swimming and being happy by the sea. In Paris, the closest to that is the Seine, but you can't swim there. We were just fed up and wanted to leave. Andrina has an incredible application on her cell phone to look for houses and apartments for rent. We saw many options and places; however, calculating the final costs of renting became impossible.

Among the different options and plans, something especially called my attention. We could go to Nice, with the cheapest flight found for the moment at $120, and then take a ferry to Corsica, a dreamy French island. We started to find out more about that, saw photos and traveller reviews. Apparently, it's a paradise with crystal blue sea and white sand. This place caught my attention for several reasons: it's France and I have the nationality, they speak French; it has nature and beach, something essential for me at the moment.

Reflecting on my future, I remembered that Valentina would return to Mexico on August 4 or 5, giving me a month and a week of waiting to go to Australia. My idea was to stay in Rome or look for an Italian beach to live and work for a month. However, I feel a great need to go to the sea, it is where I most wanted to be. I do not want a city again. In my case, apart from seeing Valentina, I would be wasting time in Rome. I have been there twice, it fascinates me but I need to settle down and live somewhere.

Andrina didn't have enough money to stay in Paris for the rest of her trip. She had $700, her boyfriend was paying for her trip, and she was ashamed to ask for more, but there were no alternatives. She had to find a way to tell him about her situation and wait for a new deposit. After a day of frustration, my head was spinning in a state of confusion. We then decided to change the attitude, think positive, and go out and have a few drinks to take away the stress and leave the house a couple of hours. That we did. We also chose to stop talking about travel for at least an hour. We finally had a good time and we returned calmer.

10 July 2013

Today we decided to start different, we got up, meditated, did yoga, I bathed, and I felt much better. I am calm within my heart and trust in the natural organization of things. I trust the Universe, I know the way it functions, and it will take me wherever I need to be. For the moment I will not stress a bit. I will take advantage of the beautiful sunny day. I will see an old friend and I will seek tranquility. These days we were having a crisis, but these are always positive if we want to see it that way. A crisis indicates change; it breaks into our world and so many times our mind thinks it's something catastrophic. However, it's necessary and indicates the end of a cycle to open another. We know what we want: to go to the beach, to go south. It's a form of a petition to the Universe. Now we leave it in its hands to see events accommodate themselves in order to fulfill our desire.

Later . . .

I'm lying on the *Champ de Mars*, sunbathing and watching the magnificence of the *Tour Eiffel*. I am wearing shorts, barefoot, listening to music, feeling the sun on my skin; the wind comes at the right time to brush my body and refresh me. I lie down and watch the birds fly with the clouds behind them. Beside me, Andrina reads. I do not think about anything. I just listen to my music. I smile subtly and enjoy my inner peace. Everything is perfect in my world; I am where I must be and where I want to be, always.

11 July 2013

Finally, we have a destination. Andrina, Mariel, and I are going to a house that Andrina found on AirBnB. The house is 2 kilometers from Biarritz, a surfer beach in the south of France, in the Basque Country. Our next home is 200 meters away from the sea, with a beautiful view, for six nights. The girls will return to Paris, and I will stay there for a couple of months. I will look for a job, a place to live, and a surfboard. We finally chose Biarritz because it's close from here. It is a recognized place for surfing, and in the photos, it looks very beautiful. On the other hand, I am very excited because I have a French side of me, and I am interested in learning more about this country outside of Paris. I'm now pretty excited to stay in France and solve a part of my identity. Only a few foreign people are fortunate to speak fluent French. So now my visions are solid; living on the beach, surfing, and hopefully finding a job.

These days have been a bit the same as before. I bought a new suitcase (the third one), now smaller to take as little as possible, and I continued to buy things to finish feeling perfect. When we leave Paris it will be a new me, with a suitcase full of cute clothes, renewed and ready for my adventure; alone around the world.

12 July 2013

Today Andrina and Mariel went to the Louvre, I decided to stay. I wanted to buy some books and have some time alone. After their departure, I got up, meditated for thirty-five minutes, and ate two peaches with oats. Then I cleaned the house, vacuumed, took out the trash, and organized my things. Once I finished my domestic duties, I waxed my body, took a long shower to wash my hair, and put on treatment, then I filled myself with cream and put a refreshing product on my face. Feeling incredible, I lay naked in bed; and during that state of bliss, I affirmed the need to live alone. I wanted to enjoy the silence, the perfect order, and the time to be with myself.

Today I went looking for a book, in the end, I bought two. One short book about adventure and the reasons to experience it, and another with 450 pages titled *Sur les épaules de Darwin* or *On Darwin's Shoulders*. I will translate the first few lines of the reverse: 'This book is a journey, a journey to the discovery of a Universe that is even richer and more mysterious, a Universe that gives birth to us, and which we will never end up exploring a journey to the discovery of our cousins, birds, and flowers, and our distant relatives, the stars.' Of course, this caught my attention and I read some pages. It's a book to daydream about, mixing poetry and philosophy to contemplate nature with other eyes, also to see inward with the help of our exterior. It's a large book and it will take some time to finish it, perfect to be on the beach, to immerse myself, and devote myself to reading beautiful French literature.

15 July 2013

At the moment I'm on the train with my sister Mariel and Andrina, direction to Bayonne. We have left Paris. It was a nostalgic farewell together with the birthday of Mariel and the anniversary of the *Prize de la Bastille*, but I'm glad to leave the city. It was an incredible way to end it. On July 14, we had a surprise dinner in the house to celebrate my sister's birthday, even though her birthday was on the next day. Andrina came with a beautiful French cake and champagne. I also bought some cheeses and other provisions to do our small dinner. The weather was perfect and we were on the terrace appreciating the beautiful view. After that, we took the metro and headed to *Trocadero* to see the fireworks show in celebration of the end of the monarchy and the establishment of the Republic. We took line 1 at 10:00 p.m., the event started at 11:00 p.m.; however we couldn't take our connecting line to the destination because the subway was very full, so we walked. We didn't get to *Trocadero* but found a place where the Eiffel Tower was seen more distant, and we sat on a little garden where other young people were. From that spot, we could see for forty minutes of the fireworks and pyrotechnics in honor of the French nation. We had a great night. Yesterday, we had lunch at a pretty elegant place in St. Michel. After that we strolled a bit; we were by the *Seine* ecstatic with the beauty of the city and saying goodbye. It was the end of a cycle, after a month of living here. From there we returned to pack and prepare for the trip.

We got up at five-thirty in the morning to leave at six. We fell asleep at 3:30 a.m. because of insomnia—some bad sleep habits acquired during the holidays, and because we watched a movie. We did a little nap and I was quite stressed because on my trip two years ago in Europe we always arrived at the last moment. In Barcelona, in fact, we missed the train for four minutes. In the morning, I was a little stressed. I bit my nails and I was constantly watching the clock. The tickets were too expensive to loose, we had to be on time. In the end, we ended up getting into the train three minutes before its departure. I never considered its length and our car was the last one. It was like seven minutes of walking along the train, but we finally made it; we were inside.

I've been nervous for a few days, thinking about my future. My vacation would be over in a short time and my serious journey would begin. It would be me, my money, my decisions, and I should look for a job and a house. All these changes make me think about how I would go to ask for a job. If I would find something quick, where I would work, what the Universe was organizing for me. I had ideas of an ideal house with a beautiful ocean view. I wondered if I should be alone or maybe I would meet people, my mind was full. I wanted to go to Australia and I was excited, but at the same time, I was scared. One of the authors of the compilation of texts on adventure speaks of something particularly interesting. According to him the word *adventure* is linked directly with commitment. An example is with climbers, and he says the following, 'The mountain is a true commitment: we leave and there is no other than to reach the summit because, in the complicated parts, the descent by the same road is impossible.' This way the commitment for the adventure is established, once you get to a point of no return, you must go ahead at all costs until you reach the top and fulfill the mission.

I identified perfectly with this understanding of adventure. I have a commitment to my ideals and with my project, there is much ahead before enactment and completion of my trip. For a long time, one of my greatest fears is to repent halfway, to want to go back to Mexico sooner than planned, but this definition made me understand: I am a climber-traveller, I do not return until I reach the top. The road will be full of obstacles and adversity, this to test myself, to learn to deal with difficult situations, and handle stress; however, I must be strong and always think positively.

17 July 2013

I have been in Biarritz for two days and I don't need much more time to know something: I am exactly where I want to be. Yesterday we arrived in Bayonne, a small town about half an hour from the ocean, from there we took a bus towards the beach and walked following Morgan's directions in Airbnb. We waited outside the apartment, then she arrived at 2:10 p.m. and showed us the place. It was quite cute and with a view of the sea. In the end, she pulled out a deposit of 300 euros in case we broke something, which was not indicated on the website, and this annoyed Andrina. Finally, we paid, already concluded our stay she would return the money, less 60 euros required to pay the cleaning and 10 euros to the government. Andrina would write our experience in Airbnb, exposing the lack of information and warn future tourists about the surprise.

Morgan is half Australian and half French. We spoke the two languages with her, because Andrina doesn't speak French, but her English had a very strong accent sometimes incomprehensible. After seeing the apartment, we went to a cashier to get money and pay her, then she took us in her car to show us a little bit of Biarritz. She gave us several tips and told us about the best places to party. We could tell she loves to go out. I asked her if she knew someone renting an apartment. Currently, Biarritz is in its peak season, and she said it would be a bit difficult. She then took us to the supermarket and we did our shopping for the week—lots of vegetables, fruits, lentils, oatmeal, and others, quite healthy and economical in the end. The day was not exactly very hot or sunny. However, we decided to go to the beach. We stayed there a while and we went back to the house to watch TV, read, and sleep.

18 July 2013

Today Andrina and I got up early in order to finish my resume. We went looking for a cyber cafe; however, we didn't find one so we browsed in the library. It was complicated to understand the mobility with the buses. If you don't do a signal to the driver, he doesn't pick you up. We didn't understand this until we saw some buses passing by in front of us. Already in the library, we had to register and take out a card, but I didn't have an ID, and we could only get one for Andrina. When we started to work we were rushed. It was one o'clock and the workers were having a lunch break really soon. We decided then to return to the apartment with my sister and make the most of the day. Tomorrow we would get up earlier, and knowing how to use the buses and with my ID, we would arrive on time and start working straight away. I would do my resume in French while Andrina would finish my English one, which was tailored to fit social organizations.

After our somewhat unsuccessful mission, we arrived at the house, ate some lentils, and prepared to go for a walk around Biarritz. The day was a bit cloudy, perfect for visiting the center. Since yesterday I had noticed the beauty of the place, a very French style with a coastal touch, more colors, and more life in the buildings and houses. Today while walking with the girls, I was amazed by the beauty of Biarritz, in addition to the summer youth everywhere. There were a lot of handsome guys with surfboards and skateboards. I said to myself, 'You have arrived in paradise.' The ocean is perfect, lacking waves at the moment, but it has an extensive beach area, and the water is not very cold. Ninety percent of the tourists are French, and the rest are foreigners looking for some good waves.

    My sister wanted to see her friend from high school Margaux in the center. We ate some homemade ice cream while we waited for her. When she came through, we went to the beachfront where there was a large spread of stones and corals. The ocean passed over them and you could walk around and see the colors, touch the water slightly, and find some holes to swim. The water was crystal clear. Then Margaux arrived and warmly welcomed the three of us to her beloved summer town. She kept talking about Biarritz and how wonderful place this was; according to her experience, it was the best beach in France. She comes every year in summer because her parents have a house here. I was already thinking about how I was going to ask for temporary asylum while finding a place to rent, but the issue came naturally between talks. She opened the doors of her home as long as necessary. After that, I went alone to a few rocks and sat down to see the corals through the water. At that moment I felt the beginning of a life with more sense. I found a place to stay and that took away many worries. I felt a huge relief, an honest smile, one that comes from a personal victory. Things were in perfect order and the Universe was supporting me. I could not believe the beauty of the place I just landed. I would stay for two months and according to Margaux time would go very fast, unlike in Paris where it became quite eternal. Compared to the gargoyles in the underworld of the Parisian subway, here people vibrate happiness, everyone comes to enjoy life at the fullest.

    Since my arrival, I have decreased my consumption of chocolates, breads, and desserts. I spoke with my sister today on this subject. Depression and anxiety create a compulsive way of eating—you seek pleasure on the outside coming from an internal emptiness. However, being on the beach makes me feel incredible, and suddenly that need for external pleasures is less necessary. I feel complete and happy by the sea. Now that a greater concern for the body has arisen, I would like to lose that extra kilo I gained in Paris with so many chocolates and cheeses. Eating healthy becomes a cycle of wellness. I feel good so it makes me choose a healthy meal, then I still feel wonderful and light, and I want to continue feeling that way. I believe that being on the beach gives us different cravings. We feel more attracted to fresh produce such as fruits, vegetables, and salads, less cooked food, and more raw vegetables, and that's healthier.

At the moment I'm a bit burned. It seems to me that the sun here is stronger than in Mexico; despite this, I feel calm and excited. My life begins to take shape and I am delighted to have landed in such a magical place. Tomorrow I will do my resume and start searching for a summer job. Here the employees are largely students on vacation, many are quite young. They hire even without experience. I'm calm and I trust the way I'm acting. I will sleep in peace, thanking my fortune in life.

19 July 2013

Yesterday I got up very early and went to the library to write my resume and my motivation letter in French. I browsed on the web for some CVs to give me an idea. In the end, it was pretty good. I started with my three languages, adding the Italian with 'solid notions', then my experience in Machetes, Sayulita, adding two more months. Second, I put my summer job in the Mexican shop *Liverpool* selling toys. Finally, I looked at my resume, and I was pretty satisfied. It showed me as a qualified person for any job around.

After spending the morning in the library, I organized seeing the girls in the center of Anglet, a small square with two restaurants and some other businesses. Mariel accompanied Andrina to the doctor; she had been sick for several days in the throat. I arrived early and was quite hungry. I decided then to spoil myself and go to the restaurant and order a dish. It was while I was eating fish fillet with mushrooms that the girls arrived to accompany me. I was very happy with my achievement, had with me 20 CVs printed with a letter of motivation each, had taken a big step on the subject of getting work. While I was eating, I was very calm and happy. I would find a job, I trusted completely on that.

After the appointment with the doctor, we went to the house to look for our swimsuits and then headed to the beach. We decided to rent a surfboard and venture to the sea. First, we got in my sister and me, I asked her to let me enter with the board first, we would see each other inside. I was nervous but very excited. I had not done it for months, and I was expecting a good reunion with the waves. With the board held by my right arm, I took a few steps in the water until I had it by the knees, then I put the board and I jumped on it. Quickly I began swimming passing over the waves and being splashed and shaken by them. Instantly I was filled with adrenaline and absolute happiness. I had not contemplated surfing in Europe, but in the blink of an eye, I was already on the board doing what I love.

My sister and I took turns, I pushed her in the waves, managed to stand on several occasions, and was very happy. In my case, it was a bit more difficult. I struggled to swim and grab the waves. I finally stood up in some white water just to feel the surf. Naturally, my few teachings from the skateboard, the movements of feet, and the changes of weight made me move from right to left. I didn't want to do it for a long time because after several times I already learned my lesson. I must always act calmly and with flow. Also, my foot is not perfect yet; the sprain I had is not fully healed. After my fruitful day, I went out with the girls for a while to some restaurants and bars on Anglet beach. They decided after a few drinks to go to Biarritz by bus and continue their party. I didn't go because I was exhausted, so I went home by myself.

Today I got up later. I had planned to go to the beach to surf in the morning and then look for work in the afternoon. However, at night, I felt quite sunburned and didn't want to abuse my skin. I decided to stay in Airbnb. I got up, I ate a pear, then a fried egg and oatmeal for dessert; cooked with water and a touch of rice milk, jam, sugar, and cinnamon—a very complete and nutritious breakfast to have the most energy in my job search. I took the bus at 3:30 p.m. with the intention to arrive at an hour where the restaurants were quieter and the bars were just beginning to open. I was a bit nervous but I knew how to proceed. I stopped in the middle and started my tour. My dialogue was always the same 'Hello, I have a question: do you know any place where they are looking for someone to work?' And so I continued until I spread sixteen resumes. I went to more places because sometimes I didn't leave a resume. I walked a long time underneath the rays of the sun. After three hours I was already exhausted, so my sister picked me up and we went to Margaux's house. The result of my tour: a place probably needs a kitchen assistant, another place is looking for someone but when I was talking to the manager about my learned skills, they called him to attend a problem with the waiters. He asked me to leave my resume and he would call me later. Margaux's boyfriend works in a restaurant where they could need someone. He told the owner about me and asked to go talk to him tomorrow.

My day was exhausting, but I am very happy with the result, currently, sixteen restaurants have my phone number, and the smallness of Biarritz makes people relate faster. If a place is in need of new staff, I will be ready and available to work. Tomorrow I'm seeing the boss of Margaux's boyfriend and the restaurant where they need someone. I hope to find something these next few days. So far nothing gets me out of my stress-free state. I just flow and resolve my affairs day by day. I'm happy and calm.

20 July 2013

Today I got up to arrive at twelve o'clock to see Olivier, the owner of the place. I arrived ten minutes earlier and I killed some time around. Then I went to the restaurant and looked out for a bald man that would be Olivier. I went in and I walked directly to where he was. I told him that Margaux sent me. He then asked me if I had a little experience preparing coffee. I told him about my work in the kitchen for a few months. Without understanding very well, everything happened too fast. He asked me to come back tomorrow for a test at 8:00 a.m. He told me without being very clear that later we would see about a social security number and so on, said goodbye, and left. At that moment I entered into a shock state, it was not even three minutes of talk. I didn't understand properly and the only thing in my head was the social security number. I didn't count on that! It would be better to go tomorrow, to take the test, to carry my French passport, and when he asks my social security number I would explain the situation. Anyway, I will go soon to the *Mairie* of Biarritz to process that paper. I hope this is not an inconvenience and I can get the job.

Today a person spoke to me about 'Couchsurfing'. It is a page where travellers and property owners with open houses and hearts meet. On one hand, we are many with restricted resources for travelling; on the other hand, there are many people with extra space in their houses—that's the idea of Couchsurfing. We only need to create an online profile, writing our interests, philosophies, and some photos, specifying if we are offering or seeking a sofa. After that, we look in the place where we want to travel someone to receive us, and we get in contact. Users usually make public comments among them. I comment on my stay with that person, and they write how it was to shelter me. This way we can see the reviews, and give us an idea of whom we want to be with. For security it is better to look for someone with more reviews, which shows a greater experience housing travellers.

I created my profile and I wrote to two men to see if they can receive me. One of them is 40 years old but with similar tastes to mine; ecology, sustainability, altruism, and so on. The other was the first on the list, when I looked in his photos, he looked handsome and I decided to talk to him just to try. Today I spoke on the phone for twenty minutes with Yann, the 40-year-old. He would receive some people this week, but from Monday I could stay with him. He recommended contacting some friends of his by Couchsurfing to see if they can receive me on July 22. Anyway, I could stay a few days in Margaux's house and then go with someone else. I told him about my search for an apartment but he was not very optimistic about it. It's the peak season and according to Yann, it would be very difficult. While talking to him I explained my situation with social security, asking for some advice. At the moment I cannot solve this, first I will go tomorrow to my test and see the reaction of the owner.

I returned with the girls to the apartment and we went at three in the afternoon to the beach. We were tanning topless and were very much at ease as the French do; more adults than the young girls. This would eliminate the marks of the swimsuit and get a better tan. For many years, from the beginning of my adolescence, I lived with a strong insecurity related to my breasts—it was always my greatest trauma. However I have been slowly working on it, and I feel I overcame it. I always considered it a great defect, but now I want to change it into positive and make it something distinctive, being different from others and feeling proud about it, a big step. For me to feel safe showing that part of my body today on the beach was a great event. I had never done that with so many people around me; however, I managed to enjoy it.

Being on the beach and seeing such a variety of breasts around me, I realized how different they are. Also here almost no woman's breasts are augmented or operated, unlike in the United States, especially in Miami. The bodies around me were very different from the standard of perfection displayed in advertising and media; however, each was beautiful in its own way. The horrible system where we live wants women and men hating their bodies for not matching with the beauty standard. This way consumerism is created. Through advertising lies such as 'the wonderful pills to lose weight', 'miracle device that you step into, shake half an hour and with that, you will have the abs of your dreams' are created. Clothes, cars, travels, creams and make-up, anything to make a person feel better. If wellbeing isn't achieved after the acquisition of all products on the market, then comes diseases, eating disorders, bad relationships, and many more. With this, unsatisfied people create work for the pharmaceuticals and other corporations living of human misery. An unhappy life begins with hate for our body, this being our temple, the physical home of our soul. To transcend and live in harmony with the Universe, we need to love ourselves, to see ourselves in the mirror, and respect our imperfections. I love being on the beach because it has made me recover the relationship with my body. When living by the sea, people spend a lot of time in swimsuits and underwear, the sun improves their color, sand contributes to exfoliation, and salted water helps the skin. On the other hand, spending a lot of time with little clothes brings an extra motivation to loose weight. That's why I love surfing. It's an extremely fun sport and because of the adrenaline effect, I do not feel a great effort. Swimming to move with the board is exhausting. However, when I manage to take a wave I get excited and want to go for more. After an hour or two in the water, I come out victorious, feeling incredible, and it's very entertaining. At the end of my stay in Sayulita, my body became quite different. It became more masculine with stronger muscles in the back and the arms, but the change was nothing dramatic.

    To resume this, I believe that being by the beach can help people to reconcile with their body. Because a self-approval of the naked body is a really important step in the spiritual path. For the moment I will continue recovering my condition in the waves, and sunbathing topless being proud of having nothing to show. Tomorrow I get up at 6:00 a.m. to go to my work test.

24 July 2013

These last days have been the most intense of my trip. I would've wanted to write before but I didn't have a spare moment. Right now I am quite tired; however, I want to do it before accumulating more days. On Sunday, I went to my test at Bar Jean. I got up early and I arrived with exact punctuality at eight in the morning. I was still in my rhythm, getting up a long time before leaving, waiting more than twenty minutes for the bus, going through life slowly and quietly. When I arrived at the place there were two female workers.

I explained to them about the owner's request to arrive at that hour, then they introduced themselves very kindly, and they began to explain some peculiarities of the bar of small French breakfasts. They asked me for help with the *pains au chocolat* and the croissants. They showed me the functioning of the coffee machine, and they put me to squeeze oranges for the juices. Quietly, in my Zen rhythm, I performed my tasks. Eventually, I got to clean three furniture pieces where the glasses and dishes were, after that, I filled the baskets with bread. At the moment it was good; however, at 11:00 a.m., the rest of the team started to arrive. Every time new people came to greet me, to ask questions; suddenly I was surrounded by boys, mostly young because they are doing seasonal summer jobs; they were handsome also, and the place became chaos. Clients arrived and orders began. Suddenly the staff of about thirty people was going crazy from one side to the other. I didn't know what to do, the girls from the morning were much more stressed and didn't have time to explain anything. Suddenly I became a nuisance. The owner asked me to go from eight to twelve, just before the place started with its accustomed madness. When I finished I approached Olivier and I made a sign to go talk to him. He asked me to wait, then I sat at a table in a less crowded area of the restaurant. I was calm but a little scared. I didn't quite understand what was happening around me. After a few minutes, Olivier left the main bar and approached me, sat down, and asked me how I had gone, and with an innocent smile I replied 'well'. Apparently, I didn't do anything right, was very slow, and was not the person they were looking for. So he took 50 euros from his bag, gave them to me, and wished me good luck. Suddenly it was like being a light bulb and getting turned off. I believe my blood pressure went down because I was livid, so simple like that he had said you are useless, 'too slow'. I left the place completely confused, tried to escape as soon as possible, and avoided contact with any of the cute guys of the staff; I felt very sorry for my situation. I went out as a zombie, walking away from the restaurant as fast as I could, moving quickly, not knowing where to go. My head was elsewhere trying to recapitulate facts and understand the event. The only thing that occurred to me at that moment was to go to the bus stop and return with the girls, surely they would be in bed. However, I decided to make a detour in restaurant number two and inquire about the work. They told me to come back at five to talk to the manager. On the way, I reflected. I understood the process of recruiting in France. The first day is an essay to see your reflexes and behavior, so they can see the experience, your skills, and speed. But I was in another rhythm, the opposite of the total stress of the place.

    I felt very demoralized but in spite of it I said to myself, 'That was not the place, the perfect work will come for me, things will fall into place.' But my emotions were different, so I tried to fill my mind with positive thoughts. Arriving at the apartment I ventured with the girls. I told them my lack of knowledge about the test. It was an essay to observe my abilities; they wanted to see me doing everything as fast as possible and in the same stress to go according to the place, and I didn't do it like that. Shortly after, confused and tired, I had a little nap, waiting to leave again to the restaurant number two and talk to the person in charge. I woke up an hour later with the girls still there, and they motivated me to get up and eat something. I should return to Biarritz soon.

    Still feeling confused and demotivated, I heard my cell phone ringing. I responded quickly to see who it was—

happens to be the owner of a new restaurant requesting me for a work test. I accepted and I was summoned at 11:00 a.m. on Monday morning. Suddenly the joy returned to me. I told the girls and they were very excited. I had the choice of place number two and tomorrow a new test. I trusted the arrival of a job for me. After lunch, I went to Biarritz again. I went to the restaurant to ask, but the manager told me about his recent lack of time. He had not seen my resume but he would talk to me soon. So I thanked him and left. Being in the center I went to see restaurant three *Le Corsaire*. I looked from afar to see the place, saw many tables and I was scared, could be worse than the *Bar Jean*. On my way back, I realized the change of pace—I was no longer on vacation in Paris but I was still a bit slow. It was time to speed up my mind and body. I had to adopt a faster and more efficient way in order to get a job in a restaurant. My experience at the *Jean Bar* was a wake-up call. Working in France is very different from my experience in Sayulita. Here it is very serious and I should be more professional. In my test tomorrow, I would give the best of me. I would always be active, as efficient as possible. I wanted that job, besides it was in front of a beautiful little port.

    I arrived with Mariel and Andrina feeling much more motivated and energized. I had adopted a new rhythm as an instinct for survival. My sister, on the other hand, was also restless and wanted to go out to see a French guy she had met the night before. It was our last night together, and I agreed to accompany her. We got ready and left. Andrina chose to stay. Leaving the apartment, I saw something moving on the sidewalk. I approached a few steps and I could quickly recognize the silhouette of a porcupine. My sister and I were amazed so we got closer to see it better; we were very excited. Neither of us had seen one in a state of freedom. That little thing, insignificant for many, gave me a hint of going in the right direction. It was time to exteriorize and move faster, and that motivated me to pursue my chosen path.

    After our meeting with the porcupine, we took the overnight bus to Biarritz, and then we went to a place where the French guy was supposed to be. We walked to the other side of the village, my sister apologized, she recognized her stubbornness in chasing the guy. When we finally arrived, we were ten minutes with him before he decided to leave us and go with his friends. He didn't even invite us. He textually said, 'Excuse me girls, but my friends are complaining and I must leave. I can explain to you how to get to the bar and we could meet in an hour.' My sister and I were outraged, the return to the center of Biarritz we were cursing the French and their strange behaviors. I proposed to my sister to go to a bar, it was our last night together and it would be a good idea to go for a few beers over there, that's what we did. Very strangely we ended up getting to know two charismatic Australian surfers, and after the bar, we went with them to their friend's house to have wine. We talked about very interesting subjects: politics, Australian economy, a lot about food, vegetarianism, veganism, I remembered the reason which I'm dying to go to Australia. Unlike the French, the Australians are open and friendly. My sister and I had a great time. We laughed a lot, and she had never talked to Australians. I ended up sleeping at four-thirty in the morning, and in a few hours I would have my second test and probably would not be in the best shape, but I would give the best of me.

With a few hours of sleep, I got up and prepared to leave. In addition that day I would move, Mariel and Andrina would return to Paris, and I would go to Margaux's house. I finished my suitcase and left it ready for my sister. She would see her friend in the morning and give her my belongings. I would concentrate on getting the job, and then I would go to Margaux's house at night. So I arrived at 11:15 a.m. to the restaurant. I spoke earlier to warn of my delay when I arrived there was a table of young people eating. I looked straight for the boss and he introduced me to everyone and offered me to eat. I greeted him kindly and I self-served a little couscous with guacamole. After that, we started to work. The employees explained my responsibilities little by little, unlike at *Bar Jean*, here I would be working as a waitress, not simply cleaning and squeezing oranges. In a short time, I felt good, I was working fast, following the instructions of my colleagues. I attended three tables. I was the most smiling and kind to the staff and the clients, frankly, I did well. Finishing the shift, at three in the afternoon I had a talk with the boss. He said I had a good attitude; however, he was looking for a waitress and I didn't have enough experience. He explained about the total saturation at night. As I expressed my great willingness to work with them, he offered me to return in the afternoon and try the role of carrying the dishes, I accepted. Leaving my job, my sister called me, my idea was to take the bus to Margaux's to know how to get there, rest, and return to work, but Mariel changed my plans. She had forgotten to take my hat to Margaux's house, and I had also left my vegetable pencil sharpener to make flowers and 100 euros from the deposit of the apartment. I decided to go with the girls and recover my money and what I forgot, Morgan was supposed to arrive at 4:00 p.m., we would return the keys, and she would see the state of the place in order to return our deposit.

I arrived at 3:50 p.m., shortly after Mariel and Andrina were nervous about Morgan's delay. The train was leaving at six and we were getting late. Morgan finally arrived and after arranging the affairs, she offered to take them by car to the station; as I had time, I decided to accompany them, then she would give me a ride to Biarritz and I would return to my work. On the way, I received a call—it was another place asking about my availability. I didn't want to limit my options so I arranged for a test for tomorrow, which was Tuesday. Suddenly a feeling of happiness and self-esteem enveloped me. I was receiving calls and the possibility of having a job became a reality. Shortly after we left Mariel and Andrina at the train station, I affectionately said goodbye to them and got into the car with Morgan, suddenly a new feeling appeared: freedom. I was enjoying being alone, not relying on anyone to do anything. I was excited about the new changes and the possibilities of work.

At 6:30 p.m. we, the employees of *Le Corsaire* and I, arrived; we had half an hour to eat before starting to work. We talked at ease and then we started to prepare the tables to receive the customers. In that interval of time, I tried to learn the number of tables and train with the plates to be able to carry three at the same time. Each of the servers had a different technique, and I tried to adopt the most convenient for me. In a short time, people began to arrive. Within half an hour, more than forty tables in the restaurant were full. My job was to go to the kitchen, wait for the output of the dishes, punch the paper of the order, and carry the most possible number of orders to the corresponding tables. At first, I managed to take twice three plates at the same time, then they began to weigh me and to burn my hands. At some point, I felt that the fingers would fall from me. My hands were red and trembling, with the heavy plates I could not even carry two. Besides the tables were very far. I had to cross a street to reach the terrace where majority of customers were. At one point I wanted to cry. I was about to go talk to the owner and ask for clemency,

instead, I tried to carry the light and cold dishes, so I ended up killing some time in order to finalize my day without dying. It was exhausting. I got confused on many tables and I took the wrong dishes, it made me feel really embarrassed. I couldn't load enough, and I recognized my lack of experience. I didn't think I would stay, I didn't want to, I mean if they offered something I couldn't refuse it either, but I hoped not to be part of *Le Corsaire*. It had been a painful and very difficult experience for me. In the end, the owner told me what I already knew. He finally offered to come in the afternoon to watch the movement of the place. I was not ready for a restaurant where they served between 220 and 250 covers per night. He paid me 60 euros. I called Margaux, and we went to find his cousin to make our way home.

I was totally exhausted, the day had been too long and heavy, then I decided to relax and watch a movie before going to sleep. For being so tired and sore I considered not going to my test number three, I would call in the morning and tell them the truth. However, in the end, Yann (Margaux's cousin) offered to take me early by car. It would only be fifteen minutes away, then I cheered myself up and decided to give it another push.

My appointment was at 9:00 a.m. at the *Ventilo Café*, at that time I arrived. While there, I greeted the owner, an elderly lady, a guy at the bar, who would be my future colleague on the test and other girls. The situation was as follows: the chef's mother had an accident and he was forced to leave to take over the family restaurant. So his only assistant would take the position of chef and me, if everything went well, would take the helper position. We started working early, my partner Fabio, of 26 years old, explained the position's tasks, where the ingredients were located, the refrigerator things, some dishes, the toaster, the dishwasher, the table work, among many more. Quickly I started to work, I felt good. I had done that in Sayulita and after my failed attempts as a waitress probably my place in restaurants was in the kitchen. Fabio, a French guy with Italian nationality, seemed friendly. I liked the idea of staying with him, a nice and noble guy, not a shouting French ogre with no patience. We would both be new to the position, and we would team up in the kitchen. A few hours later, I knew that I would get this job. The owner came to ask about my passport, without telling me much but the reason was to make my contract. I worked until 6:00 p.m. to know all the details of the kitchen. In the end, it came out wonderful. They even made a compliment to one of my salads that had a beautiful presentation. I left there happy. I already had a job.

When I finished I met Yann at the train station in Biarritz and went to Margaux's house. There was Pilu, the lady of the house that I introduced myself to. We took a delicious Jacuzzi—Yann, Matias his friend, and Margaux's brother. I celebrated my new job. After that we had dinner together and remained talking until late. Pilu doesn't seem to bother with people in her house and apparently I can stay here for now; I'm delighted. Today I got up and my life was different. After the storm came the calm. I had a house, a job, and I lived on the beach in France.

25 July 2013

Today at work was good, the chef left early then Fabio and I stayed, and we put some music to make the atmosphere more pleasant. Quite curiously, in addition to having arrived at the exact moment, the next person to take the position of chef arrives on September 15, just the last day where I can work before returning to Paris to leave for Australia on the eighteenth. Fabio leaves at the end of September; he will then have a week to train the new person and leave the responsibility of the kitchen in his or her hands. Mere coincidence? I don't think so, my situation managed to fit exactly with the *Ventilo Café*, opening a perfect space for me to fulfill my needs, flowing to the rhythm of the cosmos.

26 July 2013

Yesterday I had my first day off from work after the crazy week where I did my resumes, went to several restaurants, did two failed tests, and three days of continuous work. Now I had a day to relax. In the morning I got up, did a good meditation for thirty minutes, ate several fruits followed by oats, then washed my panties and I went with the guys to the terrace and swim in the pool. The day was beautiful; it was 30 degrees and the sky completely clear. So I put on my bathing suit and went to read on the long chair beside the pool. Matias and Yann soon forced me to join them. After being half an hour in the sunbeam, I was already sweating, a perfect moment to enter the water. Before that, I put my iPad to listen to ambient downtempo (perfect music for the moment). Once in the water, I felt completely on vacation; when you are so relaxed and you are doing perfectly well in the company of water, in addition, I didn't stop talking with Matias. In the pool, I visualized how fortunate and how beautiful my life was, suddenly who knows how I was in a pool in France, accompanied by two very fun French guys and listening to my favorite music at a generous volume.

That day we stayed most of the time on the terrace, except when Matias and I went to the kitchen to cook. I put my whole grain brown rice to boil, and he set to cook meat and a salad. Once ready, we ate—Pilu, Margaux's brother, Matias, Yann, and I. After lunch we did some digestion, and then we had a plan to go surfing. We got ready; we took the old convertible Jeep and decided to look for some waves. When we arrived at the beach, we noticed the lack of swell, which is when there are no waves. Besides the tide was very high and it was impossible to surf. It was a disappointment but nothing very serious. The truth is that I was having an incredible time with the guys. I was laughing so hard, plus the drive was the best. Matias drove the return, a madman at the wheel. I was scared to death but drowned in laughter. We returned to the house and Pilu told us that we were a band of losers. We finally decided to carry out some activity and we had failed, not so much for me but especially for Yann and Matias, dedicated only to drinking and partying. After the scolding of Pilu and a demoralizing sigh, some of us took a little nap, the *Fêtes de Bayonne* were next and we needed to rest a little.

The *Fêtes de Bayonne* are celebrated every year. It is half an hour from Biarritz, and the city closes its streets to make them a public nightclub. The tradition is to wear white and red clothing, with bandanas on the neck and a red belt. There are concerts during the night, and people drink alcohol until they lose consciousness, a magical place. Although I didn't want to party in an abusive way, I wanted to experience a city turned into a nightclub and people dressed the same. So I decided to go with the guys; besides I was having an incredible time with them and they could be a good night team. Later, we put on the bicolor uniform and went to the nearest bus stop from Margaux's house. On the bus, I could see the general madness: individuals in white and red shouted and beat the windows incessantly. They sang things like 'the driver is a homosexual', 'the roundabout, the roundabout', as we passed by and shook the bus from one side to the other. They also sang other rude French songs. I was laughing out loud. Yann and Matias talked with Dutch people who didn't understand the songs and the people's shouts. It was quite a journey.

Bayonne was exactly as I imagined it—the streets and squares were jammed, everyone had a high level of drunkenness, there was music in every corner, and I just couldn't understand the French way to party, doing childish nonsense all the time. I tried to have a good time. I drank a little, although I really felt out of place. I perceived, I analyzed, and I laughed at the people, but I couldn't get into that delirium. Yann and Matias quickly went with the girls, kissed more than ten each. Apparently, that's what people come to Bayonne for, it seems a competition to see who gets more kisses. Quentin and I got bored a bit together. I didn't have much talk about with him. We then decided to return at 3:00 a.m. It was perfect to see the collective madness, but it's not at all the kind of place I want to be.

27 July 2013

Today I got up at 10:00 a.m. to go to work. Supposedly Yann was going to take me by car to avoid wasting time on the bus stop and thus having more minutes with the pillow. I got up a little earlier to see if Yann was there, to wake him up, and have a quick breakfast, but he was not there. I was ready to leave when suddenly I received a call from him announcing his arrival to the house shortly. He would take me to the Ventilo, such a lovely guy. He arrived at the time he said, and we left.

In my work, there was a lot of movement, something normal for a Saturday. I have the cosmic fortune to have arrived in the little crowded days to learn how to move in the kitchen. Today we were incessant; in total, I spent less than ten minutes sitting in a seven-hour shift, exhausting, however, was fast. Leaving my job I went to find a waitress girl from *Le Corsaire*, when I worked there she told me that she was looking for an apartment and a roommate. Pilu leaves two weeks on August 4 and wants to close the house so I need to find a place soon. If I had the idea of staying here longer, the mobilizing alarm arose again to help me find something. The girl from *Le Corsaire* was not there, but I sent a message to her cell phone. Besides that, I was in the afternoon looking for places online. I made some calls. I registered on a French page to find roommates. I put some ads online and I asked Pilu to inquire some of her acquaintances. As I was very happy in this house, spacious, tasteful, and very comfortable, I hadn't put any batteries to seek for other options. However, I can't be here forever; they are doing such a big favor to me and I don't want to abuse their kindness. It's time for a new challenge; find my perfect place. It will not be easy because the owners rent out their apartments weekly for the high season, but it will not be impossible. These cosmic events are like putting your clothes to wash, requires the first step to want to do it, then the effort to gather what is necessary and put it in the machine. Once inside, we just have to flow and continue with our activities. Finally, the clothes will be clean and ready; in a state of tranquility what we need will appear. In the case of finding an apartment, I must start the necessary movements, talk to people, make phone calls, search on the Internet. Finally, this energy enters into the washing machine of the Virtual Plane, there all things move and adjust to their form. The result: my perfect place to live. At the moment I have to act and move many resources in order to get the results I want, and probably tomorrow I will go to the stores to ask the employees.

28 July 2013

Today I am alone for the first time. I didn't have time to be as I went from being with my sister and Andrina to being with Matias and Yann, but today they went to Bayonne and tomorrow their train leaves. Quentin goes to Martinique then Pilu and Pierre invited him to dinner tonight. I stayed alone in the house, very unaccustomed to this silence. It's in these moments of reflection when I start to see from another perspective my new reality. Today I felt that I was in a dream and that soon I would wake up in my bed in Mexico, with my dog, my parents, my boyfriend, and my family and social obligations. However, that is not the case. I am alone, on the other side of the world, on my own. I like it but it also scares me, to be honest. I feel a new crisis before the change, uncertainty, and restlessness, despite this I trust in the guidance of the Universe that knows exactly what and when to do things. For the moment I go to sleep and tomorrow I will mentally enter with strength on the subject of my apartment.

29 July 2013

Today I got up normal to go to work. According to the bus stop, the bus would arrive at 10:00 a.m. I waited for half an hour and when I had already decided to do an auto-stop, finally the bus appeared. As a miraculous act, I arrived on time. At work, it was quieter than yesterday and the dynamics were good and quite entertaining. Leaving work I began my search for a place to live. I went to several stores and restaurants where I saw people of my age working. I first asked them, then I left my name and my phone number in case they found out about something. I did that for about an hour, not for long but at least several people had my cell phone. All movements and adjustments are fast; if someone leaves their apartment these days I could be the backup. Tomorrow will be the same, after finishing my work I will continue my search.

Heading back to Margaux's house, on my walk between the bus and there, I stumbled across a huge rainbow landing on a distant hill, a typical French landscape. I was stunned; it gave me great joy to have the opportunity to see something as beautiful as a rainbow. Again I saw in it a cosmic sign. I was on the right path; my Higher Self spoke to me and encouraged me to move on. I stared at it for a while and then I kept going on my way. Before arriving at Margaux's house I found a cat.

I caressed him for a while and played with him. It was 8:30 p.m. but it was still daytime. And because there was no one in the house I decided to go to the pool, it was a total joy. I was frolicking like a little girl, jumping and doing turns. I was happy to be in the water. Several times I lay on my back to float, at that time the outside noises were inhibited by the water. I could only hear my yogic breathing with a deep inhalation and a strong exhalation. At the same time, I appreciated the beauty of the sky, feeling my insignificance compared to this great world. I saw carefully the colors, blue and white, colors of peace and tranquility. It was a beautiful moment in the pool. I connected with myself; inhibiting any outside sound and being able to hear only my breathing turned my attention within. I was finding moments to pamper myself and feel happy alone. After being in the pool, I went to take a bath. As in France, the traditional shower is not very common. I decided to take advantage of the tub, so I filled it with hot water and I immersed in it, another moment of relaxation and total pleasure.

After my special evening with Natalie, I talked to my parents for a while, told them in detail about my daily life in Biarritz, then I prepared my dinner. I ate orange lentils, broccoli, cucumber, and some flowers made with carrots, all from my organic supermarket, perfect food.

Nutrition is one of the most important aspects of my life right now. It's the gasoline of my body and I am very careful about it. For me the perfect diet is vegan; however, for the moment, it is ideal to achieve and I don't want to force myself when it comes time to convert I will know. For now, I try to eat the best possible: lentils, oats, fruits; however, I still eat dairy because in France as a vegan you starve. I am not very much against fish, and chicken from time to time. Of course, red meat is my enemy and I have not tried it for more than a year. It gives me a horror to think of the violence towards our brothers, the pigs, and the cows, so noble and beautiful mammals, able to love their own. It is an absolute barbarity and cruelty the way they raise them, and the way they kill them. I am very much against it.

There is nothing more important in life than health, and it must be achieved in every aspect. The body is our temple, without it, we can't do anything. To achieve integral health is necessary physical, mental, and spiritual health. Physical health is obtained with an excellent diet and exercise, mental health is obtained with positive thoughts, spiritual health is achieved by meditating and accepting the existence of the Universe and its unlimited power of pure love.

This is how I seek to have the best health for my trip and for my life. For the moment it has helped me a lot, I feel very good in my body and this allows me to focus on succeeding in my missions.

30 July 2013

A couple of days ago I registered on a web page to find roomies in apartments and houses. I sent several messages to different people. Yesterday at work I received a call from a house in Anglet, not very close to Biarritz: it's a room for 500 euros a month, for now, it seems far and expensive; however, it has something interesting, they could lend me a bicycle. When I arrived at Margaux's yesterday, I looked for some other options on the page and contacted more people. Today, I also received a call from an available room in Anglet, it was a man with a doubtful voice. I asked him if he knew of a direct bus line from his home to Biarritz, but he had no idea. At the moment I don't care if it's a little farther away, but taking a double bus doesn't seem the best. It's already complicated enough with one; it always comes late and it's quite annoying to be waiting to see when it decides to appear, especially during the weekend.

Today, I was calm to think of the house in Anglet. I was motivated by the bike idea, but today when I spoke to the owner, she doesn't know how the route is. Biarritz is an uneven town full of hills, but maybe from Anglet to my work, it wouldn't be that bad. However, it's a risky decision, to enter a place, pay 500 euros and in the end, you have a big problem with transportation. At the moment I'm a little bit stressed, to be honest. I want to trust in the work of the Universe, but the uncertainty is sometimes a bit frustrating. I have until Monday to see where I'm going, and it's several days to solve it. Tomorrow I'll probably go back to leave my phone with more contacts. This is the life of the adventurer, you can't know what awaits for you, therefore it's better to meditate, breathe and say, 'I am where I must be, always.

1 August 2013

Yesterday, I went to my work and it was quite good, as always, and finishing I decided to stay in the Ventilo to have a juice and then a couple of sangrias. My co-worker Georgina, originally from London, put a set of electronic music very much to my liking, I decided to stay listening and avoiding going out, it was 34 degrees and it was 6:30 p.m. For some reason, I didn't want to repeat my quest for rooms. My plan was to come to Margaux's house and talk to the neighbors. They were doing some repairs and in my opinion, they were moving; with that, they would probably be leaving some property or something interesting. I finally stayed for two hours at work, the atmosphere was fun, although the girls were working. So I just listened to the music and I got entertained with my iPad. Marine finished at seven and we stayed an hour talking. Afterwards, I returned, to be honest, the minimum alcohol I took kicked in. I also decided not to talk to the neighbors and went straight to the house. A few minutes later I received a call from Manuela, one of my best friends living in Paris. I kept talking to her for hours, then I kept looking for options online.

Today I made a home appointment with an osteopath masseuse. I found her card in a surf school and I took it. I had a small osteopathy treatment in Mexico and it caught my attention. Their work consists of placing ligaments and tendons in the right place. My foot kept bothering me in some movements, I felt a blockage and for that reason, I decided to call her.

Agathe arrived at Margaux's house promptly at nine-thirty in the morning. I had just woken up and it was evident in my swollen face and slow reflexes. So we placed the massage table on the terrace in order to keep silent and respect Pierre and Pilu's sleep. Quickly Agathe began to manipulate my foot, she moved it and used her hands to feel my ligaments. I didn't understand anything because I never had a treatment like that. I felt several thumps and things moving. Agathe not only focused on my foot, but she also manipulated the hip, according to her I had the sacrum displaced. I felt the adjustments, just the biggest thump and the most painful was where I had that annoying tension. I'm going to have an appointment with her again. We need to give the body some time to get used to the changes and then to manipulate again and make me feel better. In the end, I was very satisfied with her work. I don't know if that's enough to eliminate the annoyance in my foot forever, but I felt very good after the session. It gave me hope to be in a perfect state of health.

Finishing my therapy I went to rest before that Pilu put some pressure on me regarding the move; then quietly I started to see my options with people renting rooms in appartager.com. I had asked a vital question to one of them if there was a direct bus stop to Biarritz, that person replied that it was possible and gave me a telephone number. I dialed and I perceived a rather strange voice. Before that I got to see the bus lines and locate the house on the map, finally, there was a line from Biarritz to *Anglet La Barre*, about 800 meters from the place. Pierre encouraged me to go to see the room; he advised me never to wait when there is an interesting option. Then I prepared something to eat, I got into the pool a little, and I left to my appointment.

From Pilu's house, I took two buses, then followed my planned route according to Google Maps. Ten minutes later I was in the apartment. I rang Stephane and waiting for him to look out of the window, I felt a strange sensation in my body. With two seconds of looking at him from bellow I knew I didn't like him. I was hesitant to go up to the apartment but I decided to do it; and as I vibrated it from before, the guy was horrible and the place was filthy. I literally remained less than five minutes there looking at the space—it was messy and dirty. I wanted to leave immediately. The guy looked harmless but unpleasant, fat, and terribly dressed; he was a gardener. I quickly got out of there. It was a very strange reality hit. For a moment on the bus, I was excited to have found something, but I quickly woke up from the illusion. I would rather pay 100 euros a night than living with someone like him. I waited for the bus for half an hour. At that moment I felt pretty bad, completely alone in the world. If I lived with a gardener no one would find out and no one would care; I had no one at that time. From being a princess in Mexico to working as a cook living with a person as dirty as him, what a world!

After my terrible appointment, I was fortunate to see Victoria one afternoon in Biarritz. We went for an ice cream to the fishing port. I was very happy to be with her. I told her about my adventures in Biarritz and I shared my concern for finding a place to live, my only desire for the moment. Finally, I could calm down a bit, I was on the right track. I didn't have much to lose either, I lived on the beach and I had a stable job.

At the moment this is my situation, I don't have a place yet. However, I will try to visit the house in Anglet from where I would have to move by bicycle. At least there are five rooms. I hope one of the tenants is a traveller or a sexy surfer.

3 August 2013

We are in peak season in Biarritz and I haven't found anything yet. News: I leave Margaux's house tomorrow. Yesterday my attitude changed completely, I left a little aside from the option of finding an apartment or a room before leaving here because there was very little time. Then came the feeling of adventure. I had to look in 'Couchsurfing', sleep in some hostels, instead of crying I rather started to laugh. In the worst and last case scenario, I would sleep in the *Ventilo Café*. Then in my head, I designed a strategy. I would leave my suitcase in the kitchen cellar and take what was indispensable. I would move from night to night or for short periods. I should wait for a descent in the season in order to find something.

One would think about this situation and would start to cry, but I was happy. I would never miss a place, and I knew I have money for any inconvenience. But spending more than my salary per day seems illogical to me, that's why only a hostel of 20 or 30 euros would be viable. On the other hand, I stayed after work in the cafe with Marine, my colleague at Ventilo, and a gentleman that is a good customer. I told them about my situation and they both offered me a roof in case I had nowhere to go. It's precisely that point of the journey wherefrom the solidarity of the other depends on your survival. It's a beautiful feeling to have unknown people willing to help you, fraternity emerges. When someone helps you in situations like this, you feel very grateful for their generosity and you want to return it in some way. You probably can't do it with the same person but a greater solidarity has been born within you. This is how a circle of love is created among us. When I was younger I was not necessarily the friendliest of all, but now I give away my smiles. Finally, we are humans, we are equal, so let's be brothers and sisters.

6 August 2013

After the last writing, I went with Pierre, Pilu, and his friends to talk for a while. They made me try different alcohols from the Basque Country and a little wine. Then I learned that two of them were surfers in the '70s. They started to tell me about their stories and I was fascinated. At that time the sport was much frowned at, far from being fashionable. However, surfing was the only thing they had in mind—they were obsessed with the waves. As it was very rare, there were no more than twenty people practicing and they knew each other well. They had the ocean to themselves. The two lived in Bayonne, twenty minutes from the beach; they also had a kombi. That has been the biggest dream of my life, my computer had a kombi sticker and now my iPad has also. For some reason, it has always caught my attention. I love the idea: hippie trip and movement. Pilu's friends spent much of their time moving around with their kombi. They went to the beach, parked, and spent the day analyzing the waves and currents. Nowadays, the sport has changed enormously, surfers enter directly into the water, but these guys didn't know what being in a hurry meant. Time was spent on the beach, and they enjoyed looking for a greater connection with the ocean.

I ended up sleeping late, in addition, I had to finish my bags and leave Margaux's house. It would be Sunday and there would be fewer buses than usual. At 10:00 a.m., I would be at the stop to arrive at eleven at my job. For fear of losing it, I arrived ten minutes earlier. I sat in my suitcase and waited. Last Sunday, the bus had arrived at 10:30 a.m., although it was not marked as such; having enough time I was relaxed. Suddenly it was 10:30 a.m., and the bus didn't show up, then I started to worry, but I couldn't do much about it. I kept waiting. It was 10:45 a.m. and nothing, so I told Fabio the cook about my delay. I decided to wait for the next bus marked at 11:13 a.m., it was 11:30 and nothing! Then I spoke to Fabio to explain my situation. He suggested doing auto-stop, I tried a few minutes, but it didn't work either. Finally, Sabine, the daughter of Josie, the owner of the Ventilo, picked me up. As I waited for her the bus passed through, two hours late! The lady waiting with me went up to ask. Apparently, the driver had an accident in the morning.

I arrived at work quite tired for my ordeal, in addition to the waiting for two hours that was not exactly pleasant. Then I set to work, trying to take a positive attitude even when I didn't know where I was going to sleep that night, plus my belongings were in the filthy cellar of the kitchen. I started to chop vegetables and get ready with my materials and prepared to receive the orders of the customers. Then I heard my cell phone, a text message by the sound. It was Margaux: 'Nat, your sister just messaged me and asked that you get in contact with her as soon as possible. Your dad had a motorcycle accident and he is in the hospital'. In a matter of seconds, I fell 10 meters underground, very anxiously looked for my iPad. Surely on Facebook, I would have the news; it couldn't be true. With trembling hands and heart at full speed, I logged in at Facebook, then waited a few seconds to load the page. I opened the message of my sister. In several lines, she wrote that Dad had a very serious accident in the motorcycle, had broken the femur, destroyed the knee, a rib, and fractures in both hands. I began to cry immediately. I was drowning in my crying. I felt a huge helplessness—my father was hurt and I was in a kitchen on the other side of the world. I was at a level of maximum anxiety. I wrote to my sister on Facebook but she hadn't logged in in four hours. I didn't know how to communicate with them, my state of shock wouldn't let me concentrate. I walked from one side to the other not knowing what to do. I was tired of trying to speak through Facetime and decided to dial Mexico. Sabine lent me the Ventilo phone, and I quickly searched how to dial from France, and called my house. My mother answered and she began to tell me some details through a very curt voice. I stifled another choked sob with the gasping breath, and she asked me to calm down. My dad was fine, fortunately, it was only the bones. There was no spill or something cerebral. However, I was still very scared, crying non-stop. She asked me to call him in the afternoon through Facetime to see him, so I hung up and returned the phone to Sabine. For seeing me in such a devastating state they gave me the day off; however, I didn't know where to go. I had no one in Biarritz, no friends, and no house. I felt too bad.

    I left the kitchen to take a breath and continue to cry, although I had to do something, I wasn't going to work that day. I went to get my wallet. I wanted to contact Didier, Pierre's friend. I called him but it entered the mailbox, I left a voicemail telling him about my situation, I didn't know where to go. I needed someone's support deeply, then I dialed Manuela. I talked to her for forty-five minutes. She asked me to calm down and to find a decent room to sleep, leave my things, and go somewhere pleasant. She was right, I couldn't do anything else. It was time to pay for a hotel and pamper myself. I had to be prudent and not risk myself sleeping who knows where. Never in my family had anything like this happened. And when it happened, I'm on the other side of the world, doing my life, away from my family when they need me the most. I felt really bad about myself. The man who gave me life and took care of me so much, at the worst moment suffering terribly. I began to doubt my decision to have moved away from my family. Nevertheless, I didn't think of returning. This had to be another test, Manuela also told me. It is a difficult decision to leave your country and you have to accept the consequences.

Leaving my work, I went to a few hotels around the corner of the Ventilo. In front of my favorite place in Biarritz, a parking lot with beautiful houses and an incredible sea view. I like to go there before work to contemplate on the view. I like to sit on a bench and stay there for a few minutes. The first hotel I tried was closed at the entrance, so I went to the second and asked for a room. It was a simple one for 50 euros; I took it. Then I grabbed my suitcase from the Ventilo and returned to the hotel. They gave me the key and I went up to my room. I had a sea view, right to my favorite place. Immediately I put on my bathing suit, I took the sunscreen lotion, my bag, and went to the beach. From far away, I saw too many people in the *Grande Plage* and decided to leave Biarritz, then I took the bus to Anglet. I felt too bad but tried to stay calm. I couldn't do anything. I went to Anglet like a zombie, walking by instinct, with a long face and sunglasses to cover my swollen eyes. I didn't think too much. I couldn't do it or I would cry in the middle of the bus. Then I got to the beach, I put my towel on. I took off the top of my bathing suit and lay down. I was very sad but calm. I couldn't believe or accept my loneliness at that time. It was too hard for me. I could hardly deal with my own situation when the worst scenario imaginable occurs. Of course, it could always be more serious or fatal. I spent a lot of time on the beach thinking and talking to myself. I went to the ocean for a swim—always the water somehow cleans you.

Finally, I thought of the advice of Manuela—it was good and I could feel better.

When it began to cool, at around eight at night, I decided to return. I would dial at 9:00 p.m. from here to see my dad in Facetime. I took the last bus. I was hungry and I would look for something not very expensive to eat. I took my usual way to work and I stopped at a place for sandwiches, crepes, and Panini. I was annoyed to see that the only ingredients to assemble your meal were an animal. I asked for something without meat. They offered something with cheese and I accepted but was not very excited about it at all. In this country as a vegetarian you have problems. I cannot imagine with a vegan diet, they literally can't cook without butter, cheese, cream, and milk. Their stellar vegetables to accompany the dishes are oil-fried potato chips. I say this from my experience in the restaurant, and I find it disgusting how people eat. A greasy hamburger with bacon, cheese, and some delicious potatoes, fried five times, at eleven in the morning. In addition, the French eat raw meat; they are very attached to their carnivorous dishes. When I discuss my reasons for not eating animals, many people insist on the nature of human beings; we have done it forever. In that, they are absolutely right, since centuries human beings have always vibrated in dark and negative frequencies; wars, violence, destruction, disease, savagery, hatred, power struggles. But we are entering the New Age, the spiritual awakening. The world can't be conceived as before, the current system is obsolete. We need to start the transition to an environmentally friendly world. We must leave behind the wild domination of our Mother Earth. We must respect it and love it; otherwise, we will soon die from global warming or any other environmental issue.

I believe that in order to achieve this transition, human beings must seek to enter into a frequency of love, to eat with love to ourselves and to others, to eat healthy, to give our body foods from Mother Earth, to leave aside junk food, meat, and synthetics. I believe that when you eat animals you consume violence and abuse; you absorb the negative energy and toxins released by the animal at the time of murder. When you eat grains, vegetables, and fruits grown organically and naturally, you give your body the love and nutrients necessary for its proper functioning. I probably went a little far with this, but I bring the subject related to something that caused a deep conflict. Today at work I couldn't open the ice cream refrigerator because on top were four kilos of a piece of animal to prepare *entrecôte*, a corpse, and I couldn't touch it. Mathilde and Fabio began to laugh, but later I expressed my repulsion towards violence against animals. I can't deal with it, it's too painful for me. I stayed in a frequency of anger and impotence at the same time. I then talked about the book I was writing. Besides that, I would spend my life dedicated to build a better world.

Returning to the subject of my dinner, I ended up ordering the Panini with a thin slice of cheese, lettuce, a piece of tomato, mayonnaise, and mustard. Quite bad, dry, and devoid of flavor. Afterwards, I went to my hotel. On the way, I got a message. Someone had found me at *appartager.com* asking if I was still looking for a roommate, in French *coloque*. I replied that yes, in his second message he presents himself, his name is Maxime and he is 20 years old. That was good news for me, the fact of not being an old man was highly comforting, especially because of my experience with the gardener. He also asked me if I had any way to move or if I only searched in Biarritz; my situation to find something was desperate so I didn't care about the distance. Then we sent several messages to each other. He asked me to get together to talk and meet. I explained my need to move quickly. If I moved where he was it would be with my suitcases. With my work, I didn't have time to go to Bayonne, thirty-five minutes from Biarritz, see him, and return. The buses stop passing between 8:00 and 9:00 p.m. I didn't want to continue spending money on hotels and hostels, and more now with my family situation. I wanted to be somewhere where it is quiet and not be on an adventure every day. He called me on the phone and I explained my situation in more detail because he didn't know me, he didn't want to let me in. So we started joking about the risk of being murderers or something like that. I suggested adding each other on Facebook to meet us there, see if we were normal people, and prepare the move for tomorrow. Then he added me, and I saw his profile without rummaging too much.

Surely he did the same. I saw a normal guy with a normal life and it seemed more than enough.

I slept that night at the hotel, the next day I packed my bags and went to work promptly at 11 a.m. I told Fabio about my new place to live in. I would pay only two weeks while I found something in Biarritz. That day I focused on doing my job well, I didn't have time to be nervous to move away with a strange guy. Finishing my day, at 6:00 p.m., I had a drink with my colleagues and at seven I went for my bags. Maxime finished work at eight. To make my way to his place, according to the indications on Facebook, I had to take the A1 or A2 bus from B*iarritz Mairie* to Bayonne, from there I would take bus B to Tarnos and get off at the mall. It would be about an hour's journey that I did without difficulties. When I arrived at the mall, I texted Maxime; he told me that he was leaving his house. I sat at the bus stop and waited, somewhat nervous about our next meeting. A few minutes later he called to find out where I was. I explained and soon saw me, greeted me from afar, and hung up the phone.

We walked one in front of the other, we saluted and soon after we joked about our appearances, neither he nor I seemed murderers. Very attentive, he took my rolling suitcase, strange thing in the French men, first good impression. For some reason when I'm nervous with a guy I start to talk a lot, make jokes, and laugh at myself, something good because we quickly broke the ice and started talking. He also laughed at me or with me. Maxime in person looked more handsome than on Facebook, definitely a very appreciable extra. First, he showed me the apartment: it had a room of about 30 square meters, without much furniture, only two chairs, a table, and a large bookcase, a terrace with a view of the forest, and a small kitchen. Separated by a door, were the bedrooms and bathrooms, a space for the toilet, and another for the sink and shower. Maxime had prepared the bedroom, changed the sheets, and moved some belongings from his closet to leave space there. He would sleep on an inflatable mattress in the living room. Suddenly my life succumbed to a dream blow mixed with reality. Last night I was in a hotel and now I was with a cute guy and also had a room for myself. I could breathe now. I had a job and a place to live, exactly what I needed.

This previous segment, from Margaux's house, has taken me five days to write it. I have done it on my long bus routes to go to work and return. The truth is that when I arrive at my house I start talking to Maxime, then we have dinner, and we see the series 'Californication'. Now we see a chapter in English subtitled French and another in his language. He never sees anything in its original language and we had a culture shock towards that. However, we managed to solve it. My life has taken a routine turn. I was definitely looking for it; especially with my dad's accident I really need stability, security, and the Internet to talk daily with my family. Now I am well and I also have a lot of fun. The work is very entertaining, time passes quickly, and the employees are young so we laugh, talk, and play music. Then I go home and spend time with Maxime.

9 August 2013

Today I woke up much more tired than normal. I did a pretty good meditation and I dedicated it to my mom and dad, then during the day, I was like, missing energy. My life was going fine, however, I was lacking something in order to be well, I didn't know the reason, I asked myself out loud and I asked the Universe to send me that missing element.

After a few hours came some answers, I might need to party or have an adventure, something to entertain me and get out of the routine. Time is slow, it's also because I already want to go to Australia and because of my dad's accident; therefore

I need some new entertainment. In Biarritz I had been worried about two things: to find work and a place to live, I already have the two so I can think of something else. In addition today something strange happened to me, in the bathroom of the Ventilo I found a poster announcing a cultural event and the title was 'Coco and Pablo', something that caused me a shock. In my life, these are two guys who have turned me crazy: Coco my recent ex-boyfriend, and Pablo a motorcyclist with whom I was quite obsessed for a long time. Could that sign point me to men? Another important event also, one day before my father's accident, I moved to Maxime's house and I dropped Coco's gift bracelet. Several weeks ago, I had realized that the knot would soon be undone, but it would be at the right time when I was ready to let go of it. It's been more than two months. This week, I was already planning to upload photos of Fabio and Maxime to Facebook. Coco would not like to know that I work and live with handsome guys, so he would stop sending messages. I have not yet done so, but soon he will find out. Anyway in Australia, I will surely have a boyfriend and he will have to deal with it.

10 August 2013

Today was a better day, I didn't feel tired although at work I had some failures due to lack of concentration, I don't know why besides I was practically not thinking about anything. Today my meditation was very good, I was able to go blank for 20 percent of the session until I lost track of time, I usually never set an alarm but I know perfectly when it's 20 minutes or when I'm in the half-hour, today I couldn't distinguish it. On the way to my work came the answer to my question yesterday, I must return to surfing, in my stay in Sayulita the main reason for my balance and well-being was surfing, so I must go back to it. With this I would have a full day, I get up very early, I meditate, have fruits and oats for breakfast, I take the buses to go to Biarritz, go surfing, I work seven hours, I have a drink with my colleagues and I return to the house. There I would be with Maxime, talk to him, dine, bathe, and watch some series. At the moment I can't ask for anything more, if I want to surf again, I can't go late to bed, so the party would not be a priority. In the matter of guys, I don't have the control now, for not being able to get much party, only if the Universe wants to give it to me, otherwise it will be in Australia. At the moment I am very well, excited to go surfing tomorrow and that's what I think about. Maxime will not be in the house because he is partying in a neighboring city, I will be quiet and I will read.

11 August 2013

Today was definitely not the best day. I got up before seven in the morning to meditate for half an hour. It was a good session, then I ate a peach and oatmeal with organic oat milk, and I prepared to go surfing until there everything was going all right. It was Sunday and I knew of the shortage of buses. I would do a little more time but there was no hurry, I would arrive at nine at Biarritz and the surf school would open at ten o'clock. So I arrived at the *Grande Plage* and sat down to see the people surf and try to understand the waves a little. After some time of contemplation, I rented a board, 6 euros for an hour. I took a seven-foot one. I saw some waves breaking less loudly at a far point; so I went there, left my backpack, put on the leash, and went into the water. I quickly felt the force of the ocean—the waves shook me violently, I tried to take a couple but I was not doing well. I was between currents and almost onshore, so I decided to go where I was watching other people surf in the beginning. On the left side, there were more beginners, so I went in there. The same happened to me, I got smashed by a couple of waves so I decided to leave. I had to work at 11:00 a.m. and it was around 10:30 a.m. It was pretty bad, I lost time going to a remote area and then I didn't do it very well. I also noticed a bigger and faster wave.

I tried to forget my bad start with the surf and walked towards the Ventilo. I arrived punctually at 11:00 a.m., went up to the kitchen, ate two bananas before starting to work. After that, I was still hungry, so I made three scrambled eggs with tomato and onion, accompanied by salad and bread. I started my morning chores feeling very tired. Fabio looked the same; we thought that we wouldn't have a hectic day. However, the customers arrived and the movement began.

It was a horrible day at work because Fabio was really stressed. I tried not to take personally his attitude and his manners, and in addition, I was not very happy either. I tried in the quiet moments to have a talk and be nice, but it didn't work either. Soon his heavy attitude returned. We practically didn't talk, and we worked hard. Afterwards, I went to the beach to watch people surfing again. It was crowded and there was almost no room to sit. I felt tired of being alone for so long. I had enough of Biarritz. I wanted to go to Australia. However, I understand my process, for now, I must remain here. I need to strengthen myself physically and mentally, and that way I will arrive in Australia totally ready and open to involve more people in my life. Now it's time to train my surfing skills and focus on it.

Finally, my day didn't end so bad. I arrived at my house and Maxime was with a friend. I like to be with him and with a simple greeting I smiled, my first true smile of the day. I don't know what I would do without him these moments. It's incredible to return from work and spend the night accompanied, a very good surprise gift from the Universe.

16 August 2013

These days have been good, nothing very extraordinary. Yesterday was my day off and I went to the beach for hours of solitude. On the other hand, I had not been surfing. The surf school schedules leave me very little time to practice. The school opens at 9:30 a.m., sometimes later, with that I have little time to go to the ocean, return the board and get ready to go to work. In the afternoon, they close at 7:30 p.m. and I leave at 6:00 p.m. Going surfing seems at this moment somewhat stressful, running from one side to the other with the pressure to get to my work or the same in the afternoon before the closure of the school. On the other hand, having a board and transport it with me on the daily bus, leave it in the Ventilo and walk around with it sounds very impractical. Today on the beach I didn't have a book or my iPad so nothing to do, just sunbathing, watching people, and listening to conversations around me. Now I only think of Australia and my happiness in being there. I will find paradise in that part of the world. The date is getting closer and I look forward to it. Despite a certain discontent, this stage of loneliness is necessary. I must learn to be alone to know how to be with me, to find happiness, and rejoicing in myself. Once the plenitude is found inside, the feeling of loneliness disappears. For that, it is necessary to spend time alone, to find passions and entertainments, of course, meditation is fundamental to have inner peace. Loneliness and death are probably the greatest fears of the human being today, yet loneliness is something beautiful. It is a space where you can be with yourself, reflect, and question things. When peace is found, there comes a feeling of fullness because God is with you always. I will continue working on myself in order to feel this way, someday maybe I will.

I decided to write this day not for my life right now, but for something very interesting in my book. The Universe is currently expanding, expanding into infinity by an unknown force opposed to the law of gravity. That force created by energy is something that physicists and the most intelligent scientists have not been able to explain yet, and according to the book by Jean Claude Ameisen, matter represents five percent of the Universe, more than 70 percent is pure energy and nobody knows how it works. Why do we, if we are inhabitants of this infinite system, live only in the 5 percent relative to matter? We are 70 percent energy and somehow our world system turns around that. Being a relatively normal woman, coming from a conventional family, I can't fully explain how it works, but I have several ideas. That part of cosmic energy dwells within us through the soul; for that reason I practice meditation, to contact infinity and feel it through tickles on my body. That strange force lives in us and surrounds us in our material reality, creating a perfect connection between the interior and the exterior. The intermediate stage between the cosmic and the tangible world is our mind. With it, we can manipulate our life and obtain the desired results. If things have worked well for me until now, it's for a good harmony with the Universe. I listen to my Higher Self and I know exactly when to act. It's not about messages coming to me, there is no voice or anything like that. I simply follow my instinct and let things flow naturally. Many times the Universe knows your needs better. For example in my case, I landed in a job with an excellent atmosphere and I'm living with a cute roommate. As I vibrate in a frequency of positivism and try as much of love, I attract the same; it's not a casualty to have reached such places. In addition, the Universe compensates you and gives you more of what you are looking for. Arriving in Biarritz, I just wanted a job and a place to live. At the moment I only slept in the hotel once; it has been excellent.

That is the principle of the Law of Attraction it's all about setting our intention clearly, and the Universe will work its way for that dream or idea to manifest. Once we are moving through our natural path and flow, the Universe will communicate with us through clues, and what I call causalities. Connecting with our intuition is necessary, the internal compass that will make us take the right decisions, at the right time. Making that idea a tangible reality requires optimism, faith, and positive thinking. It's necessary to trust fully about the realization of our dream, and it might take some time to appear, though we need to keep pursuing it with passion and determination. Luck is created as we look for it, and it requires a lot of energy and effort.

At this stage of my journey, I feel like my dreams and my reality are in perfect harmony where I don't lack anything, achieving my objectives and my mission. That's magic, right? And I'm achieving it by listening to my heart and blindly following what it tells me, knowing that it's my Supreme Intelligence. When we live in our maximum potential, being the best version of ourselves, being honest, and being free of mind and spirit, we can just surrender to the forces of the Universe, that will show us the way little by little. And I believe that by doing so, we can truly achieve health and happiness. So if that's the end result we are looking for, we need to search within and find that dream of ours; the place which holds true happiness and our mission on planet Earth. Since the incorporation of meditation in my life, I have experienced so many changes, because when you wake up everything seems like a dream. It sounds ironic, doesn't it? Sometimes I really feel confused, living between a dream and reality, but I start to get used to having a life like that and it's highly rewarding. Many times I wonder how I got here. I think of Mexico as well and what it would be like to be there. Sometimes it just seems like an illusion, living on a beach in France alone. However, when those moments of fear and excessive reflection arrive, I wait for a little and a few minutes later I feel the certainty of being in the right place. If I were in Mexico, I would be in depression, with thousands of stomach problems and insomnia, dreaming every day what my life would be like outside the country. Now more and more I approach the date where I'm going to flow impressively. At the beginning of my trip, I was very much afraid of wanting to return before, but now I am about three months out of my house, surpassing my record with Sayulita. The most difficult thing has undoubtedly been to leave Mexico, to be in Paris, to start from scratch in Biarritz, my father's accident, and my moments of solitude. But when I go to Australia, I will have a huge fortress and a quiet spirit. Here I only think of being there, but in Australia, I will be living my dreams therefore my mind will stop thinking and I will be able to connect with the present. When my fear of going back sooner than expected, around three or four months over there is when the flow of energy will be better, and I will be able to experience unthinkable events for the moment.

For now, I try to enjoy as much as possible, saying to myself, 'Time is passing by quickly in Biarritz. Soon, I will leave Europe.'

20 August 2013

If I could put a title on my day yesterday it would be 'The Light at the End of the Tunnel'. I could see it this time. I have been locked in fears, uncertainties, and solitude for several months, but yesterday I could see the exit. It doesn't mean that I'll definitely leave the tunnel. I'm still in it, but I don't have much time until I get out and surrender to the light. Finally, my requests to the Universe and a manipulation of my mind about the speed of time are giving results.

Yesterday we had a very hectic day in the Ventilo. We worked too much. When the weather is rainy, people go to the restaurant instead of spending the day at the beach; for that reason, we were saturated. We quickly started to get tickets and orders, so we had three hours of madness. A time came when we no longer had space to hang the tickets. I was beginning to think blurry and we had the kitchen as a battlefield. However, we continued, trying to do our best. When we managed to get a large number of tables, we still had a lot of work, but I saw fewer tickets hanging, so finally, I could breathe. There I exclaimed, 'It's the light at the end of the tunnel!' my colleagues laughed. That didn't mean that the job was over, we still had a lot to do, but it's that minimal hope saying 'The worst is over.'

I paid Maxime two weeks for the apartment, which expired on Sunday. A small inconvenience though: he has guests today, tomorrow, and Thursday. He had told me last week but it was not a fact yet, so I tried not to think about it. Now I'm forced to sleep a few nights out. I don't really care, it's only a few days and then I could go back. He's going to Spain on Friday and he can leave me the apartment for a week. The most complicated situation is the accommodation for the two weeks of September. I have been asking some people about that, but I didn't have many options yet. Talking a few days ago with my colleagues in the Ventilo, Mickel one of them, announced his next move. He would leave his apartment and give it to Sonia, a waitress among us. Knowing that information,

I decided to speak with Sonia yesterday afternoon and ask for accommodation for two weeks in September. I was nervous about her answer if she told me no I needed to continue the search.

Finishing my hectic day yesterday, I took my phone and noticed a new message. It was Thierry from Couchsurfing accepting to give me accommodation for three nights. I was happy. Then I asked for a beer and I sat down with my colleagues to talk; very nervous I decided to ask Sonia about the apartment, without thinking much she said yes. Now I was even happier. In one day I had resolved where I was going to sleep in my future stay in Biarritz. Leaving the Ventilo, walking to the bus to go to Maxime's house, nobody could take my smile off. I felt light and in perfect harmony, as in an advertisement of soda drinks. On the bus, I put on my headphones and I listened to the recent album of the band Kashmir 'EAR'. I transported myself somewhere else, I closed my eyes and let go with slow movements to the rhythm of the music, surely the French saw me with their typical long faces of criticism. I didn't care. At last, I could breathe; it was the light at the end of the tunnel.

This week I'll be at Maxime's. I'll be back early so I can take the last bus at 8:30 p.m. from Bayonne to Tarnos. I'll take advantage of my last days of solitude before living with Sonia and going out to party. These days I will write about my three nights with Thierry.

Coming out Tuesday from the Ventilo, I was pretty tired from so much work. I couldn't even think about my future nights with an unknown couchsurfer. I left the Ventilo carrying bags and a sleeping bag because of the day before he asked me to bring one. Then I walked to my destination where I would find him, in the *Bleu Café* on *La Grande Plage*, the main beach of Biarritz. I felt a little stunned, my mind was suspicious but my instinct told me to move on, then I got to the place. I put my backpack, my bag with a cushion and clothes inside, and the sleeping bag on the floor. I sat on the stairs and I sent him a message. I didn't wait very long and suddenly Thierry came to get me, a hairless man, with a red shirt, muscular, but a bit overweight; he was 42 years old. He then took me with his friend Stephane and we sat down to drink some beers, talk, and get to know each other. Soon we started to talk about surfing and travel. Thierry is a man who has travelled around the world, knows many countries in Latin America, Asia, Australia, and some others in Africa. Later I learned about the death of his father when he was 19 years old, with the inheritance he bought apartments and lives off from his rents; with that, he travels the world. We had an excellent talk. Thierry and I found many topics of common interest. His friend didn't have the slightest culture, was just an extra, making the situation less uncomfortable with the fact of sleeping at his house. Thierry seemed reliable and good, but I could see a flirtation with me, at least with the presence of his friend, it diminished the tension a little. Thierry being a traveller, he could understand my complicated situation. He gave me some security. I never thought of an act of evil from his part, but there was obviously a strong attraction for me.

My instinct for some reason made me accept his accommodation, then we paid the bill and went to leave my belongings at his house. He lived in an apartment of 30 square meters in a building in front of *La Grande Plage*, a perfect location. The place was on the eleventh floor, we headed all three, and we went to his studio. Opening the door there was a short hallway, the first door was the bathroom, only with the toilet, in the second door the sink and shower, to the left was a kitchenette, and separated by a large bookcase was the room. There was also a small terrace overlooking Biarritz houses. It had two single beds and an extra mattress. I would sleep on the bed and Stephane on the mattress. Then I left my things, the men took a shower and I got ready to go out. We decided to have dinner at the Steak House, I ate a very good cactus burger, and then we went to the *Palacito* to have a drink, to finish in the *Carre Coast* for clubbing. I had a good time that night, the music on the *Carre Coast* was electronic of the best quality, with an excellent sound system and I was happy dancing. They invited me for a few mojitos and with that, I was quite in the mood. At four in the morning, they decided to go to sleep; however, I didn't want to. After paying 10 euros cover, I wanted to make the most of the music and my party, so I accompanied them to the room, I grabbed the keys and I got off. The club was just below his house, perfect. I was happy alone, I started to dance and soon after I met a very nice guy, originally from La Reunion, an island near South Africa. He had lived in Australia for two years and one in Mexico; so we talked and danced as well. It was a bit late and we left the club to talk better, then his friends left and I decided to go back to sleep, the day after I had to work at eleven. I came back very satisfied. I had a great night.

On Wednesday I went to work with a bit of a hangover, but very happy and much to talk about with my colleagues. After all, my night with Thierry had gone well. At first, it was difficult for me to take the pace of work but then it flowed well. At six o'clock in the afternoon, when I finished my shift, I sat down with the girls at the tables outside to chat and enjoy the afternoon, after that, I reached Thierry and Stephane at the Steak House, around eight o'clock at night. Later we all returned to the apartment; we were too tired to go out again, so I prepared quinoa for dinner. When Stephane was asleep, Thierry and I immersed ourselves in an intense talk about multiple issues. He told me about his mother's recent death and the endless legal and family problems. I told him about my history and my life in Mexico. We talked about the evil in the world. We saw pages on the Internet about very interesting subjects at the present time. One of his fascinating themes is about the death of bees, so many chemicals and pesticides in crops are killing them, and without them, humanity is lost. A third of what we take to the mouth depends on its pollination, the flowers would die, also fruits and vegetables, except transgenic crops clearly. Even the great genius Einstein said that with the extinction of bees, mankind would have four years to live. It's a very critical situation; millions of colonies have died, and continue to do so. They are becoming an endangered species. Unless we drastically change the way we treat the planet, our future doesn't look very positive. There would be a need to ban pesticides in plants and fight against transgenic seed companies. That is why I expect a great change of consciousness on our part. If bees disappear, we are in serious trouble.

That night Thierry and I talked for hours on other topics such as nuclear power plants and radioactive waste, garbage in the ocean, animal abuse, and destruction of the environment, among many others. It had been too long since I had had such a long and intense conversation with someone. We were both very excited about our meeting in Biarritz. It was late in the evening, but I proposed to walk to the beach, he accepted and we went. We sat on a big rock at the edge of the ocean, we kept chatting. That's when he asked me if there was anything between us, and I answered 'a simple friendship'. It was a bit uncomfortable but after that moment I felt more confident. I clarified that I was not looking for anything else with him. It was good to find someone interesting to talk to but that was it, no more. Already tired we decided to go to sleep. I had my rest day on Thursday so I wasn't very worried. However, I wanted to go to San Sebastian. I desperately needed to leave the village and change my atmosphere.

I got up later than eleven o'clock in the morning. I ate some fruits and had oatmeal for breakfast. I was pretty calm. Once fed and ready, I decided, at one o'clock in the afternoon, to go to San Sebastian. I arranged with Stephane and Thierry to go alone in order to write for a while, and then they could reach me later in their car. Then I left the house, took the bus, and went to the train station. Being there I realized that the last ticket back was at 6:00 p.m. and it was already 2:00, so I decided not to go. I didn't want to depend on Thierry with the risk of getting stuck in Spain. Then I took the bus back. When I reached the apartment I noticed Stephane's absence, apparently, they had an argument. I suggested to Thierry to take the car and go outside Biarritz. That afternoon we went to Hossegor to stroll quickly, then passed by Cap Bretons, and then we went to St Jean de Luz; a place that I loved, a mixture between Bayonne and Biarritz, with typical architecture of the Basque region of France. There we drank beer in the main square. After that, we took the car and drove to the end of the bay. We climbed a hill where we could better appreciate the view on St. Jean de Luz and there we stayed for a while. The weather was cloudy and there was a lot of wind, but being at the top made me feel incredible, stretching my arms and allowing myself being pushed by the wind. I cleansed from top to bottom and didn't stop smiling and inhaling fresh air. At that moment I could only feel one thing: freedom. Suddenly I could put my life in front of me, how I could reach the top of a hill, in the ocean, on the other side of the world. I felt deeply happy, with nature, the wind, doing exactly what I wanted, besides just that day I wanted to flee Biarritz. Thierry and I returned home very happy. We had an excellent day and talked about many subjects. We continued our conversation about our family situations and later we went back to the studio and fell asleep early.

Finally, my three days with Thierry were very good. I got away from the routine and sleeping in Tarnos. I had the opportunity to meet him, the most interesting character of my trip for the moment. I was very happy. It was a great experience, however, I doubt I would do Couchsurfing in that way—as a woman I can't allow myself to enter a man's house so easily. It doesn't matter if you are a traveller in complicated situations, men see you as a woman, sleeping in their house, for their minds it can be associated with something else. I would go back to doing Couchsurfing but with women. Age is also very important; the older the more perverse they can be, that's why when Maxime told me that he was 20 years old it was excellent news. At that age, they don't have such twisted minds. They are more likely to enter into relationships and therefore are less desperate. I don't know if I heard that from somewhere or I invented it, but it says, 'Don't go to the wolf's cave if you don't want to be eaten.'

In addition to my Couchsurfing experience, I have not had anything extraordinary these days. I had Maxime's apartment for me alone for ten days, and tomorrow I move in with Sonia. Lately, I've been pretty nervous about going to Australia. I have a strong vertigo; the immensity of the world makes me feel so small, a sensation of being a fish in the middle of the sea. Today I'm better, despite feeling many changes at work, now I remain calm.

I don't know if it is because of meditation, but I have become more sensitive, for example, today at work. I felt even dizzy and couldn't concentrate very well, but later I began to order my mind understanding future changes. Marine, my favorite colleague had her last day today; Fabio is going to have different schedules. Lea another afternoon girl ended today, Diane had her last night yesterday. In the kitchen, we will have fewer dishes to prepare, this as a result of the upcoming end of the season. However, this doesn't mean a decrease in the pace of work, now I'm forced to clean like Cinderella. Every day I clean the refrigerator, taking out the food and putting it back in, simply because the owner wants to put us to work even if it is removing the last stain in the kitchen. Sometimes I'm tired, but the end is coming soon. I'm going to get paid with a lot of euros, and I'll go to Australia with more money than I initially planned. For now, I am very happy to move with Sonia; my house will be walking distance from the Ventilo. I can go out in the evenings and enjoy my last days in Biarritz. It will go very fast.

5 September 2013

Sunday I arrived at Sonia's. Four nights have passed and my life has had a radical change. I knew that I would enjoy my last days but not in this way, it has been incredible. My colleague Mathilde had been trying to take me out for a few days, but because I lived so far I never could. On Sunday, as my first night in Biarritz, my colleagues decided to take me to a party at the Blue Cargo, about ten minutes by car, a restaurant by the beach. At Sonia's house when I was preparing to leave, I bought a bottle of wine that I would carry it in my bag to reduce expenses and have a good time. Fabio told me that it was the party night of their roommates and they would reach us later, with that I was already clear with my new goal. Fabio's best friend, Gabriel, would be there, that motivated me to go. Of all my stay in Biarritz, the only guy of my interest is him. We met at Bar Jean when I did my first failed essay. We had a little talk, I told him about my Australian plans, he would also go in December with Fabio and other friends. While doing the smallest jobs in the Bar Jean, I watched him pass and stared; something in him caught my attention. Working with Fabio these times I would occasionally ask about him and his roommates, trying to get useful information. I quickly knew his schedules, his rest day was on Tuesday, but he worked in the evenings, until two or three in the morning. Already with my clear objectives, I decided to go out with Fabio and Marine, we went to Blue Cargo, the music was electronic at very high volume. From the beginning, I was liking it, quickly Marine and I started dancing, there were many handsome guys but no one who really attracted me. In my head, I thought of Gabriel. At two in the morning, we decided to leave. I found out in the car about the arrival of the roommates to the apartment. I was nervous and a bit deaf from dancing by the side of the speakers. Then we parked the car, we went into the apartment, entered the TV room, and there he was; sitting at the edge of the window. I noticed his new hair cut, he looked very good.

Being that time in their apartment I knew, I was very attracted to him, totally my physical style, obviously way better than what I was used to in Mexico. He had something very special that caught my attention from Bar Jean; young but with grey hair, as they call it 'salt pepper'. His hair shined and made it look silver, that with light blue eyes like the ocean of the Mayan Riviera. I always liked men with fine features on his face, and that was him; nice nose, thick lips, perfect smile with very white teeth, in addition to his 1.85 meters tall, thin and marked in all his muscles, also well dressed. I saw him and I felt ticklish. I had to plan how to get his attention. I would use my usual strategies. Then the plan was to go clubbing, for some reason they had free entrance to the Duplex with a gift bottle, then we went there. The music was commercial not my style, but I would be in a good mood anyway, acting cool and fun. Soon Gab gave me a glass of vodka with juice without asking. We communicated a little without saying much. I was struck by his insanity, from the beginning he didn't stop dancing, and not long after we were dancing together. I had him . . .

That night I had a lot of drinks and I was pretty wasted. I spent almost all my time with Gab and I had a lot of fun with him. Those euphoric nights where you lose any sense of time, where you dance, laugh, and the flow of energy is impressive. Our attraction was something completely chemical, not even because we got along good or because we had an interesting talk, it was simply energy and irrational connection. There were some kisses accompanied by dances, but I didn't want to go with him. I don't know if it was a personal decision or the Mexican conservatism, but he accompanied me to Sonia's house, I went in and went to bed directly.

Monday morning and I received a call from Sonia at 11:10 a.m. to know about my whereabouts. I was supposed to be there at eleven, but when she spoke to me I was deeply asleep. I didn't know anything about my life at that time, so I got up and I prepared to leave as quickly as possible. The wonder of living there: I would arrive in ten minutes walking from Sonia's to the Ventilo. Finally, I arrived at 11:30 and it wasn't that bad. I went directly to the kitchen to start working. My level of concentration at that time was critical. I had to read the ticket several times to know which dish to prepare. I was slow and inefficient. We had a busy day in the kitchen, and Fabio as always was unnerved and rude. Some time from now he had taken a very negative attitude, didn't know how to handle the pressure and exercised his authority to oppress me. I was having a hard time working with him. We had probably reached a point of mutual saturation. I tried to apply different strategies to calm him but nothing worked. That day after overcoming the saturation of meals, I was happy, enjoying myself, singing, talking about the beauty of life. I had moved to Sonia's house, it was ten minutes from my work and five from the beach. I had an incredible night with the only guy of my interest in Biarritz. In a short time, I was going to Australia. And a few days back I got paid 1,400 euros. I was in total ecstasy, I loved my life. Fabio ended up hating my attitude of maximum happiness, behaved worse with me, Josie the owner asked him to leave early for lack of customers and left the kitchen like a real battlefield. Fortunately, I had arrived half an hour late and so I could have time to finish cleaning, then I would leave at six-thirty.

I spent three hours without stopping for a second between cooking and cleaning up the mess. Being happy and trying to uplift him with my good vibes didn't work either; instead, he punished me by being mean and leaving mess everywhere. That day I felt tired of France, here, there is no one with the same way of thinking. Everyone around me is negative and bitter. I was finally opening up but I couldn't find the right people with the same energy to relate to. However thanks to my mental strength, I didn't absorb any of Fabio's crap. I was still happy, with many good things ahead and a few more days to finish my work. That day in the afternoon I was with Sonia, we bought some food and then went to the beach to watch the sunset. We talked about many things and it was lovely.

Tuesday was the same with Fabio, he just didn't know how to handle a position of authority. Every time he did less and demanded more from me, never with a please or thank you; I was tired of him. This time I tried to carry the strategy 'I don't talk to you' because the day before I was very chatty and he said, 'You talk a lot' in a very contemptuous tone as if it was something bad. The situation became strange because of my new love affair with his roommate friend. I tried to be as diplomatic as possible, and of course the peace and love always present, hatred does not kill hatred, only love can do it. I tried that sometime before but it was impossible with him.

Something was no longer working in his head and I couldn't do much about it, just being patient. That day I finished very tired, had worked a lot again, cleaned like Cinderella, and was tired of the French bitterness. After work I had a drink and then I went to my house.

    On the way, I saw two men, one young and one older, with big backpacks indicating their street situation. They asked for money but in a nice way and smiling at the tourists in the street. I had the instinct to give them a euro, it was nice to see their smiles and that's why I approached. I quickly started a conversation with them, shared my despair with the French people, and how they attracted me by their smiles on their faces. I decided to stay with them. They were about to finish their show in that corner, the young man juggled and the other played the guitar and sang, so we decided to go to another place to continue with their activity. When they started in the new spot, there were not many people, so we decided to go to the beach instead; they would go to their old vehicle, I would go to Sonia's house to find other supplies and we would meet at *Place Clémenceau* to go to the beach. We went together to watch the sunset. I was having a great time, talking about different topics, their lifestyle, philosophies, among other interesting things. Max, the youngest had been six years in the street, sleeping wherever he went, but I couldn't tell if he is happy or rather thinks he has no other choice. The other said to me, 'I live like this because it's a life decision. You give me a house and I don't want it.' At the beach we ate, Max of 24 years didn't want to, he sometimes didn't eat apparently by decision; Christophe ate a lot and I just had a peach. After eating Christophe took out the guitar and began to sing political and social issues in a form of criticism. I don't know how they achieved it but they made me sing as well. I had never done it that way and I felt very good; singing is a meditative state. I had an excellent evening with my friends from the street, humble people with a noble heart, more valuable than many others in Biarritz. I was happy with our gathering. I finally got back at midnight, bought Christophe a five songs album, exchanged phones, and everyone headed to their destination. I was very satisfied.

Yesterday Fabio left at 2:30, we were left, only Mathilde and I, dividing her time as a waitress and in the kitchen. Josie put us to clean new places very disgusting, again I worked a lot. In the afternoon, I stopped to meet Thierry and go see the sunset, we gathered at the *Bleu Café*. I told him my many problems with Fabio. The night before, after being with my friends on the street, I went to bed at twelve and decided to turn off my cell phone. Fabio had written to me while I was on the beach to invite me to a bar, surely because Gab told him. However at twelve, I didn't know anything about his whereabouts, and I preferred to turn off the cell phone. Wednesday morning I had messages from Fabio and Gab, inviting me to take a walk, but it was too late. I answered in the morning telling him that I was sleeping. As I watched the sunset, Gab texted me again. We spent the afternoon writing to each other, but not continuously. Sometimes, it took me half an hour to respond and him the same.

I understood where everything was going; he would invite me with him, but not so directly. I was with Thierry, then he went to eat at his house and I was alone on the beach, I had arranged to talk through Facetime with my mom at ten. Then I returned, I chatted with my mom, I made dinner and I had a shower in order to get ready to see Gab. We still hadn't defined anything by our games of not responding quickly; finally he invited me to the Ventilo. I took my time and I left quite late from my house. When I arrived at the Ventilo, I went directly to him; within minutes he had a shot in his hand and a drink in the other. He was very energetic and didn't stop dancing, as always. At first it was difficult for me to understand him, we were not in the same frequency, besides being someone with whom I can't have a normal conversation. We took some time to adapt and then we managed to tune in our vibes, without ceasing to be weird either. Finally I had a very good night with him. After the Ventilo, we were wandering the streets, playing, dancing, laughing, pushing each other, he was telling me stories but we didn't talk about anything serious, he told me very little about him. Something I could notice, is that he spoke Brazilian Portuguese very well, he put songs and sang them, that made it even sexier, of course I didn't know why he spoke the language. At the end I could tell him about my life, I talked a little about Mexiro and my spiritual philosophies, without being very specific because I didn't want to frighten him. I don't know if he was interested, but apparently he listened to me. We walked together and a block from my house we said goodbye. We didn't organize another date or something similar. I came back seeing stars and with a smile from ear to ear. I had spent an amazing time with this emblematic and exotic guy.

7 September 2013

Today on my rest day, a phone call from Christophe, my friend from the street, awakened me. I wanted to go to San Sebastian and the day before we talked about the possibility of going together. However, after my evening I was quite tired, therefore I decided not to go with them. I got up, ate breakfast, and stayed in the house for a while, lying down, thinking and smiling, remembering my strange and fun night with Gab. I suddenly received a message from my Australian friend John. I met him with my sister on her last night in Biarritz. Tim and John had returned from Corsica and stayed another two months in Biarritz. They had also been in Ventilo yesterday, where we talked for a while. We decided to meet soon to go surfing and cooking vegetarian food. John invited me for dinner today and I accepted. My plan was to go to Ventilo to write, then we would meet there at 7:30 p.m. to go shopping together. While writing I received a message from Samuel, another guy from Tarnos. I met him one night when I returned to Maxime's house and he approached me to ask about an ATM. We were chatting and then he asked for my phone, later I specified that the only thing I was interested in was friendship. Today I forgot about him. Yesterday I was supposed to see him to have a beer and talk, so I told him I was a bit busy and it was better to see each other at another moment. At the same time, I was texting with Gab. That's when I realized that I had been in the center of Biarritz for six days and already had a busy social life. I was happy.

My chrysalis is over; this concept refers to the stage of transition between the caterpillar and the butterfly when it becomes a cocoon and remains inert enclosed in itself. When this process ends it becomes a wonderful being, leaves the earthly world to fly freely through the heavens. I felt exactly like this, being a caterpillar in Mexico, a cocoon in Biarritz, and now I felt that butterfly in me. A Natalie that had been found; renewed, and strong, ready for the following step. In life there are many chrysalis, some stronger than others; we have all experienced similar processes. I felt that in my future, there would be no moments of absolute solitude like this last month. I felt ready to socialize and meet different people, make the most of my new days in Biarritz.

Later that day I met with the Australians. I cooked a ratatouille (a vegetarian dish from the south of France), accompanied by quinoa, it was very good and they loved it. We were talking very happily about Australia and how incredible their country is. According to John, I will love that place and I will not want to return. We were also listening to good music and eating chocolates. Their apartment is next to the Ventilo. It's so amazing to be in a place as safe as here, where I walk back alone, a distance of ten minutes to my house, going through various bars and places with atmosphere. I felt very lucky and grateful to life.

I'm starting that stage where I'm going to feel great, where I'm really going to have fun. It really surprises me to see the level of synchronicity of my interior in relation to the outside. Tarnos meant my last days of solitude but I didn't think to open myself so quickly. However, it happened without much effort on my part. When you are in harmony with the Universe there is a perfect synchronicity between your desires and your reality, and incredibly always better than expected;

the Universe knows the needs of your soul and gives it to you, or vice versa. I am entering a state of openness, where I'm ready to let more people into my life. And is great to see that I have a response back, like with my friends from the street or the Australians. Tomorrow is Friday and I'm going out with the Aussie guys. It will be a lot of fun.

9 September 2013

This weekend was very entertaining. On Friday, I went with the Australians to the Ventilo to have a drink, then we went to the only good night club (to my taste) of Biarritz, the Carre Coast. In the end, they decided not to enter and they went to another bar. So I went in by myself and had an amazing time. I became friends with some Swedes and enjoyed the excellent music, dancing until five-thirty in the morning. After that, I came back walking to my house, ten minutes away with total security in the streets. On Saturday I was with Gab, who is definitely a key element for my last week in Biarritz. It's a distraction to stop thinking about Australia, and besides, it's one of my requests to the Universe being in Tarnos. I am impressed by how fast things arrive, since my first night at Sonia's house our little romance/game had begun. Gab is absolutely incredible, it's not a traditional relationship with normal talks, but for that, it becomes something more special. He is spontaneous; very funny, probably the man who has made me laugh the most. He has no worries or complains about anything; we have a crazy chemistry. I still don't know anything about his life; he hasn't told me why he speaks Portuguese, or if he has any brothers and sisters. Information is not important between us, I love our conversations in French and how much fun we have. That Saturday to be with him was a spiritual experience; perfect harmony, happiness, total delight, laughter, an absolute forgetfulness, and an escape from reality. I was able to share my spiritual beliefs with him. I read a paragraph of my book and with his minimal notions of Spanish noticed the high spiritual content. He told me that he has a yoga teacher friend, so a lot of mines was not something completely new. He seemed to receive the information with a lot of interest. I also played my music and appreciated it. I never imagined having such a special encounter with a guy. I asked the Universe for a distraction and brought me something much better, as always. In a moment of maximum saturation of France, where Fabio and Josie the owner are driving me crazy, where they don't let me go up and pull me down to avoid my well-being, Gab arrives and transports me away from here—magical. I hope that tomorrow I can be with him. I have too much desire to see him, that way I can escape from Biarritz and give each other a journey of good vibes and happiness.

    For the moment I'm resting from my busy weekend. I went out yesterday with Mathilde and his Portuguese friends. I got along perfectly with them, but in the end, I only thought about Gab; he didn't come out that night, because he fell asleep after eating two whole pizzas. Because of communication games practiced in this relationship, I have not been able to make any plans with him. When I want to see him he's not there and when I think I would not see him he appears, well, for a week playing is fun. Thanks to Gab and my friends my days have been good, but the work has been more complicated. Today, Josie was scolding me all morning. I even burned my food and ruined my breakfast. She can always find something to annoy me. If I'm not fast enough, not organized enough, she came to the kitchen and almost threw her fish and chips because she had found a piece of onion, and because the chips were cold, when it was the fault of Fabio for putting them ahead of time. Another thing she hates is my next departure to Australia. If she hears me talking about trips, she comes to scold me and asks me to focus on work. This kind of bitter and dark people detest happiness in others, for that reason they try to crush me, yet my strength keeps me standing. I am fortunate not to depend on a miserable job for my existence. I am creating my own path because I have several problems with authority. So I don't have the need to start crying or anything like that. It just slips away from me fast. These are my last days having to deal with them. I will never work with bosses with such low energy frequency. I can't stand it.

Today after my work the osteopath came to carry out my second session. I postponed our appointment for financial reasons; I wanted to have my salary from August to do the payment. We had a very intense session; she moved many joints in the foot and she almost put everything together. I felt much relief however there was still a ligament to put in place. She told me, 'This is not the time to do it.' I was stunned as I thought 'I'm still not ready to be completely healthy.' The advancement of my foot was huge, however, we have not finished yet. I will see her next Friday to conclude the last details. I always felt my foot problem as a probable representation of a fear of walking, or something related to walking, with flowing. I am impressed with how my life is getting together, I am a week away and my foot is almost ready. Now I'm going to be able to go to Australia liberated, cured, aligned, and with 80 percent of the fears overcome. In addition, she came to the most appropriate day. I'm exhausted by so much social life and wanted to rest quietly in my house. And that's exactly what she asked me to do; to remain at home and avoid much activity.

14 September 2013

This week I had a good time, Monday and Tuesday I rested, on Wednesday we went out to take the *aperitif* with Fabio, Marine, Mathilde, Rita, and other friends of theirs. After that, we went out for dinner and then to a bar. At first, it was weird with Gab. I had not seen him since a few days back and didn't know what to expect. A short time later and a few drinks on me, I learned the reasons. Gab told me that there was a lack of respect on my part towards him. I obviously didn't understand why he told me that, later I made him talk. He took his cell phone and opened Facebook; there he showed me a photo where I was tagged. It was the night when he fell asleep with the pizzas, and I went out with the Portuguese. In the photo, I was hugged and taken from the hand of Francisco, and that was enough to drive him crazy. I could not believe in which moment he was making a fit of jealousy. I tried to calm him and fortunately, after a few drinks, his anger passed away. Halfway through the night, he tried to convince me not to go to Australia so fast. He would go in January too and we could leave together. I tried to be the most kind not to hurt his feelings, although something was very clear; nothing could stop my departure. No man has succeeded to date, and in Europe, I would do nothing but freeze in the winter. I finally managed to explain more about my life and my reasons for leaving. He understood and tried not to continue doing dramas.

Thursday I spent it at Gab's house, the weather was terrible so I took the opportunity to lock myself in their apartment. He had gone to work but I stayed with Marine, Fabio, and other roomies. We watched TV, played cards, made crepes, and waffles. I had a good time. On Friday I went to work and I was alone with Mathilde. Josie basically spent the whole time yelling at us, taking advantage of her last opportunities. The situation at work was boring, there were less workload and time was slower. However, Fabio had regained his best moods at the beginning; in that I was lucky. I only have tomorrow left, my last day. I cannot wait to finish this and get out of here.

15 September 2013

Today in my country they celebrate Independence Day—the day we got rid of the Spanish, although in my case I celebrate getting rid of the French. Today is my last night in Biarritz. I have finished my work and tomorrow I return to Paris. Now I'm at Sonia's house, alone, with the suitcases ready and with a lot of desire to leave. Today I was supposed to have a farewell party with my colleagues but Mathilde was very tired and nothing was done. Probably I will see Gab later at night when he finishes his work. To conclude a night like this assures my mission in France: getting money to go to

Australia more at ease, besides being alone and suffer a little, but nothing more.

Finally, the only people with whom I made a minimum bond was for work, based on spending hours with them, except Gab and a few others. Biarritz and France, in general, could not give me anything else. It was more of an internal work of strengthening, of being with myself, of overcoming my own fears; but once I was ready to open myself to the world, I realized that I was not in the right place. Here I didn't meet anyone with the same mentality. In fact, my colleagues and supposed friends have a rather limited head, so I'm very happy to get away from here. I need to be with wise people, intelligent. I want to know that I am not the only one in the world living an applied spirituality, using it to be happy and to be in harmony.

I felt absolute happiness when I finished work today, leaving forever the hellish cuisine full of fats, meats, and low energy frequencies. Never in my life would I do something like this again, not because of the work itself, but for some colleagues. When I had a few goodbye drinks with Mathilde I felt very strange to have finished, it was the end of a phase. Suddenly I looked back at the experience, remembering my beginnings in Marguaux's house, my month of loneliness in Tarnos, my father's accident, so many memories, and now three and a half months out of my house. If I could choose a word to describe my time here would be nostalgia, a stage of missing my past and not really knowing where I was standing, trying to see ahead without any certainty or guarantee. A period of limbo between past and future, with a pressure on myself, trapped without many options but to move forward. Now I've finished the hardest, I knew it from the beginning, here it would be the worst, but I've passed that stage and I'm ready for the next. I am going to Australia with experience, much more mature, and strengthened.

16 September 2013

Now I'm on the train to Paris. I have been talking to a Parisian about travels and some writers, I told him practically my life and he did the same—a man of about 40 years, very French but charming, pretty handsome. Today was my last day in Biarritz. My plan was to get my salary and say goodbye to my colleagues in the Ventilo. Josie asked me to arrive around 10 a.m. However, as a good Mexican, when they don't say an exact hour I may take my time, so I arrived at 10:40 a.m. There were a lot of people and Josie asked me to wait for her, she even made me clean the tables outside, taking advantage of the last second to boss me around. I did it laughing. At eleven, she took out the papers for us to sign them together. I didn't care or wanted to read anything, I just wanted to get my money and go fast. After about ten minutes of signing, she gave me 952 euros in cash, about 200 euros more than expected, I was so happy. Sabine would arrive at noon, so I decided to take a final tour and return to say goodbye to her and my colleagues. I wanted to see Biarritz for the last time.

Leaving the Ventilo, I walked slowly, trying to appreciate every last detail, marveling at this city with such beauty. I had 900 euros in my pocket, my happiness elevated me as I walked to the rhythm of the wind. I felt light, smiled, and wore my head high. That last hour I could live the word of my time here: nostalgia. Being a Monday, many shops were closed, weekend outsiders had left, the empty streets made me hear the sound of the icy wind announcing the arrival of autumn, young people back to their school life, I could only see couples of old people walking as if everyone agreed to leave the same day. Biarritz had changed its air completely, as I never felt it before. An ambivalent city with much to offer in summer and very little in winter. I was struck by the change of buses in their schedules and routes; there is the summer plan and the winter plan, from September 1 is winter, autumn and spring do not exist in Biarritz. It's winter or summer, young or old, life or death. That day I could live the city in its winter, boring, dull, rainy, grey, and cold. I said to myself, 'It is the perfect time to leave, you have completed a cycle.'

It was beautiful my last hour in Biarritz. I was able to recapitulate my travel story so far, how the events had developed, and the excellent results. I thanked the Universe for so many blessings. After my nostalgic farewell to the city, feeling cold I got to say goodbye to my colleagues, first I started with Mathilde, she was eating outside and I sat for a moment, we talked. Then Fabio, although we had some arguments, I care about him, then Sonia, I thanked her for letting me stay in her apartment, finally Josie and Sabine. Even though I had been hallucinating this place in some moments, only love could come from me, even Josie I love for having taught me so much and paid me many euros. I left there with joy and total satisfaction, something that comes with finishing something and doing it well. I returned for the last time from the Ventilo, taking the most important and beautiful pedestrian avenue. It would be my last time in this place, at least for many years I would not return. I then went to Sonia's house to finish my suitcase and meet Gab at Colonne for coffee. I had not seen him since Friday and I noticed his new haircut. I was happy to see him. My last moments with him were incredible; he made me laugh out loud, there was a point where I could not breathe anymore. I had teary eyes and wet nose. I really don't remember another guy with that ability to make me laugh. I adore him and I will carry him in my heart forever. He stayed with me until the arrival of my bus. We didn't have much time to say goodbye and regret the separation. He behaved like always making jokes every second. On the bus, I received a text message from him. I will write it in French because I never want to forget it. I will also put the translation. 'Je te souhaite un excellent voyage, et qu'il ne t'arrive que de bonne choses dans ta vie! Tu es vraiment une bonne personne et je t'aime beaucoup! J'espère que l'avenir nous permettra de nous recroiser et partager plus de temps et de moments ensemble . . . Dommage de t'avoir quitter :(je t'embrasse fort, tu va me manquer tu sais . . . Allez sors du bus et reviens!' (I wish you an excellent trip, and that only good things happen to you in your life! You really are a good person and I love you very much! I hope the future allows us to cross paths again and share more time and moments together. I'm sorry to have let you go :(I send you a big kiss, I'm going to miss you, you know? Get off the bus and come back!)

My encounter with Gab was the best of Biarritz, the most special and magical. He is an incredible guy that I will never forget. In spite of his attempts to avoid my departure, I know my duty; my destiny is not in France, it's in Australia and that's where I need to be. I would hardly stay. In Mexico, I had a much harder separation with Coco. Let's say I'm already trained. I'm an Artemis; my projects go first. However in Australia, it will be completely different; my only objective is to reach that country, and for that reason nothing and nobody can stand in my way. However, being there I will have an open heart. From now on, only God knows my future. And because of that opening, it's very probable an intense infatuation being there. I know myself and there are always guys in my life. Nevertheless, I have had in mind the barrier 'freedom' that prevents from making a long-term commitment. In this case, I will be completely free because that's how you free the soul, standing in the way of the Universe and living your true destiny. I am willing to embrace the cosmic will. If my mission in life is to raise children on the beach with an Australian, so be it. I doubt it widely but until I don't have a clear exit, I will not go back to Mexico. A free soul is where it needs to be and lives the greatest happiness through the connection with its Higher Self.

I mentioned this concept earlier, and I would like to put more emphasis on my beliefs about it. In my world, there are two selves, the Lower Self and the Higher Self. Most people live in the first; it is the Self-related to the Ego and the physical plane, the thoughts are also part of the Lower Self. When there is fear, doubt, anger, and a series of negative feelings this comes from the Lower Self because they come directly from the Ego. Life here is in the lower plane of consciousness. In contrast, in the Higher Self is where the soul lives, the highest part of our being. This Self is connected with the Universe, with God, and infinite energy. People living in Higher Self love rather than hate; they don't care about the future because they trust fully in God's work; they know that things (whether good or bad) happen for a reason and everything is for a greater good. People connected with their Higher Self live in a spiritual way in their daily lives, obtaining a total connection with the force of love and the Divine.

Most of our thoughts belong to the Lower Self because the Ego is involved, but the intuition is completely attributed to the Higher Self. Intuition expresses with messages from our elevated plane of consciousness. It's our Higher Self trying to speak to us, seeking to do so in several ways, and if we ignore intuition it manifests itself in our dreams, in causalities, in diseases, among others. Intuition cannot communicate with us in an easy way to understand our reason. Nevertheless, it's our most perfect intelligence. It's necessary to listen to this Self and seek a connection with it; it will always lead us in the best way.

One of the objectives of my journey was to establish a connection with my Higher Self because I know that living in harmony with it, I will accomplish the mission of my spiritual life, connected with the human of course. My Higher Self communicated through my heart in order to send me to Australia. I decided to trust and that's why I'm on my way.

I am ready this time, not like my departure from Mexico. I left my past behind. After three and a half months out, my life is my trip. Sometimes it's a bit difficult because it's a dream where you never wake up from. People when they travel always have a return to reality; to routine, to everyday life, but I don't have that. In Mexico I don't have a life built, I don't have a job, nor school, only Mexiro, but I would be practically starting from the beginning. Constantly, I feel in a dream; the things that happen to me, the places I'm at, the feeling of well-being. Sometimes I wake up in the morning and tell myself, 'What are you doing here? Where do you live?' I still believe that one day I'll wake up in my bed with my dog, and my parents next door somehow bossing me around. Part of this process is adapting to this peculiar life, full of unforeseen events and magical situations, such as sitting next to a Frenchman identical to Hugh Jackman and talking to him. The more I practice meditation, the more I live in the present, and the more I eliminate negative thoughts, the more magic happens. I now believe that if we work hard in ourselves and decide to pursue the spiritual path, our lives can become a virtuous cycle of joy. Love frequency creates and attracts happiness, and the higher we vibrate, the more we attract wellness.

20 September 2013

I'm four hours away from Sydney. I cannot believe how little time is left to arrive. The trip was very heavy. I feel a strong jet lag. I wanted to write in China but it was impossible. I was exhausted and couldn't even read. I left at 8:20 p.m. in France and arrived at 6:00 a.m., 12:00 p.m. in Beijing; on the flight, I couldn't sleep at all and saw three films. For a long time, I've been thinking about this day, but I was more nervous in the past. In France I was calm, breathing softly. I was very excited to think of Australia. In China I didn't understand anything about my life, the jet lag didn't let me see clearly however I tried to make the most of it and look around in the stores to see some Chinese products. Many things I know well, the typical Chinese textiles in purses, bags, and shirts, but I noticed an obsession with panda bears. There were thousands in the form of stuffed animals, cookies, chocolates, an impressive variety of articles with pandas, so I decided to buy a gift to Neto as a thank you for receiving me in Sydney. My ex-student of French language, cousin of my friend Alejandra, turned out to be studying a semester in Sydney. So I had a conversation with him through Facebook and he agreed to receive me at his house. I was happy to have someone with whom to reach on the other side of the world.

One of my fears was not to take the plane, to have some inconvenience, to lose the passport or something. Of course, being a product of the mind, as always it puts unnecessary worries creating stress to get us out of the present. Finally, I had no choice. I would not be able to skip the plane and return to Mexico. I just had to focus on doing each step at a time, that I did and it seemed to go well.

Leticia and I in Sayulita said that with the Universe you have to get 'loose and cooperative'. It would be equivalent to 'go with the flow', and John Lennon's famous 'Let it be'. Now, thanks to that, I almost circled the globe; left Paris, passed Eastern Europe, and crossed Russia and China to reach Beijing. I passed over South Korea, Japan, Indonesia, and now I'm flying through Northern Australia, quite surprising. I thought I would be much more scared or astonished, but let's just say I'm getting used to a dream life, where you wake up in China surrounded by pandas and strange people. At the moment I don't manifest too much happiness. I am uncomfortable, tired, I urge to take a shower, and get to Neto's house, but soon I will be very ecstatic jumping and behaving like a little girl at a Sunday fair.

At the moment I have a bag with 1,950 euros in cash in addition to my Mexican card with about 2,000 euros. Here is the secret of how I managed to have so much money. Actually, the only expenses on my card were the top of a bikini for 37 euros and the train ticket to the airport for 10 euros, other than that I spent almost nothing being in Biarritz.

This is how I did it: when I was with my sister and Andrina in the Anglet apartment we gave a deposit of 100 euros each, that came back to me when the girls left, by that time I had received my payment for 50 euros at Bar Jean and at night I would be paid 60 euros in Le Corsaire, on July 23 I started working on the Ventilo and on August 1, I received 450 euros. The first two weeks with Margaux I didn't pay anything, then with Maxime was 150 for two weeks in the beginning and at the end, I paid him 80 euros for the rest of the month (counting my nights out with Thierry). With about 500 euros I survived the month of August, paying rents and other expenses. Clearly, I never went out, every time I left from work straight to Maxime's house, which allowed me to save a lot. The only expenses were my daily transport of 2 euros, my routine *pain au chocolat* for 1 euro, some fruits in the morning and some simple and cheap dinner of vegetables or grains, eating in the Ventilo allowed me not to spend on food. In the last week of August, I had about 50 euros, but it didn't matter, they would soon pay me. On September 1 they gave me 1,400 euros, with that I paid 150 euros to Sonia for accommodation, my train ticket to Paris for 100 euros, my therapies with Agathe for 100 euros, and some food expenses. Even though I went out a lot these two weeks, I planned how to not spend money. For example, taking my own wine inside the bag, and Gab always invited me drinks, so I managed to have a good time and spent very little. On September 16 I got my last pay, in France, in the end, they pay you one day a week of vacation, the *congés payés*, then for my almost two months of work they gave me about 200 euros more, so I left with 950 euros.

In my belief system, money is energy. For example, wanting to be a millionaire is not a valid end; desiring large sums of money is associated with the Ego, with the Lower Self. Noble purposes, linked to the Universe or to God, are not banal, could be purposed such as: climbing a very high mountain, travelling the world, having a partner, being happy, among others. Opening a restaurant just to make money has not a very strong purpose. Instead to do it by passion for food activates the magic of the Universe. It's important to distinguish whims from desires, the first one serves to feed the Ego on the material and physical plane, the second comes from the soul and therefore is connected to a higher purpose. Money will come as a means to an end; it's all about aligning ourselves to our cosmic path, and trust that we will always be taken care of.

In Mexico, my plan was to get a job in Europe for a month to pay for the stay. My idea was to spend my Mexican money but to replace it to go with 2,000 euros to Australia. I never imagined an economic abundance like now, I'm taking double! My plans now are to open an Australian account and put the 2,000 euros that should be enough to pay the initial hostel in Byron Bay, the rent of the apartment, buy a surfboard, and survive a month without work. For now, I don't know the reason for this amount of money, but the Universe knows it better than me, everything is linked to the future. My Mexican money will be a reserve, trying to use it as little as possible. Now I have a new cosmic clue, the fact of not having the pressure to find a job since the beginning gives me the freedom to see several options and choose something good. These times I will dedicate myself to public relations. I want to meet society in Byron Bay and then get something; however, I have a new project in mind: get a job in a social organization. My friend Andrina recently sent me my CV for organizations in English, with a very professional appearance. That is the only cosmic clue to know where to move the energies. I have a month to look for something in that, I will search the internet, I will send CVs by mail, I will ask the people in Byron Bay, I will move the 'cosmic washing machine' to see if the Universe wants to send me a job in some social organization. I have enough time so I won't worry. However, I must be aware of my expenses—apparently Australia is not a cheap country. At the moment I'm a few hours to reach Sydney. I urge to arrive I'm quite tired. I will go with Neto and spend the weekend with him.

21 September 2013

Yesterday I arrived in Sydney at 7:00 a.m., between migration, security checks, and the recovery of my suitcase, I left the airport at 8:30 a.m. I took the train to Wynyard Station, the closest to Neto's house. My first impressions of Australia made me feel a bit like in the United States but with friendlier people. When I entered the subway, I found it very slow, with a reference point of the Parisian metro. Later walking through the city, in the center, I felt like I was in Manhattan. I had a very strong jet lag, I understood absolutely nothing. I only tried to get to Neto's house as soon as possible. At 9:15 a.m., I rang the doorbell of the Rex building on Kent Street. A very sleepy English voice answered me, for a moment I doubted if I was in the right place. I spoke to him in Spanish and my friend was able to react and answer me in Spanish, he asked me to wait for him in the lobby, he would come down for me. A few minutes later Neto arrived in his pajamas and with one eye closed, he had gone partying with his friends and they were very hangover. We were both in deplorable conditions. I felt disgusted with the urgency of a bath; however, before proceeding to the shower we were talking for a while. At last, I felt safe, I had crossed the world but I arrived home with a Mexican friend in a very comfortable apartment. A couple of hours later, the roomies Rodrigo and Jorge arrived, we talked for a little bit and then they decided to take me for a walk.

At one o'clock we left the apartment, we walked to Darling Harbor. The weather was delicious, sunny but with a cold wind, ideal for strolling around the city. I easily found trust with the boys. I couldn't believe my luck to be with Mexican friends in such a distant place. I walked with them and I felt like I was with a clan. I laughed and I talked without stopping. After Darling Harbor, we went to the famous Opera House. The weather changed quickly and grey clouds with high possibility of rainfall made us return. Here it gets dark at six o'clock, at about that time we arrived at the apartment. We spent some time resting and in the evening we went to a market in Chinatown. We ate some crepes with Malaysian curry specialty, walked around for a while, and then we came back home in the evening, watched a movie, and slept at two o'clock. I had an excellent day, a great welcome to Australia.

It's a gift from the Universe to have arrived with the guys, they keep me company and that way I can avoid doubting and returning to my usual fears. I'm in Australia but I feel like I'm in Mexico. It's an excellent transition, that way I can see the city a little and know more about the country before starting the adventure. I'm also fortunate to go with them and their seventeen friends to Byron Bay because they organized with other Mexican students of the building a trip along the East Coast. Speaking on Facebook with Neto, he told me about his flight to Byron on September 24, which I had defined as my final destination. Of course, I would go with them, it just couldn't be more perfect.

22 September 2013

Yesterday I went with the guys to the Saturday market in The Rocks, the oldest part of Sydney, which was founded around 1800. The market was very pretty, and as an accompaniment, there was a red-haired guy with his guitar playing beautiful folk. I was quickly hypnotized and I gave him 2 dollars. Then we went for a walk and when we came back I decided to buy his album, the title was 'All about to Change'. I saw that and like a magnet I approached, I asked him if it was his first album, he said yes, an EP of five songs. I congratulated him and I said, 'Never give up.' Now I'm looking to buy meaningful items, not only for aesthetics, there must be something in its background. If it is to support an organization, ecology, an emerging artist, the organic field, is a way to keep money circulating in a good energetic channel, of positivism and love. In this way instead of giving our money to large corporations, we are supporting small projects, where dreams and aspirations reside, led by people with a great courage to start something on their own.

I was very satisfied with my purchase of the record. It reminded me of my ex-boyfriend Coco. Thanks to him I had become more sensitive to music and unknown artists. To my surprise, the album had a lot more to offer. I felt a big shock when I read the title of the songs: 'Brighter Lights', 'All about to Change', 'Golden Sun', 'Burn Away', 'Stay'. The album showed different stages of my life last year. 'Brighter Lights' for me means the initial illumination, when I began to meditate, and therefore my life changed, the beginning of my awakening and the path where I am now. 'All about to Change' is when I finished University. I was not aware but radical changes were coming in a few months. 'Golden Sun' is Sayulita; that's when the Universe taught me how it worked, where I fell in love with the beach and the heat. 'Burn Away' is that moment where I decided to leave Mexico, in a somewhat violent way trying to leave my past behind. Now I'm in 'Stay'. I've arrived in Australia and I plan to stay here until further notice.

I was really surprised to have something like that with me, how the synchronicity manifested itself so accurately. Somehow that small object reassured me that I was in the right place. Again it was like dreaming, I felt in the clouds thanks to that connection so magical. I kept smiling, I tried to explain to one of the guys without sounding too strange, obviously, they don't understand these unconventional ideas, fortunately, I have my book that allows me to express these incredible events.

I learned the concept of synchronicity through Deepak Chopra. As I understand it, is when you find 'casualty' situations that show how you were in the perfect place at the perfect time. If you had arrived two minutes later you wouldn't have found that person, or that object. The more we are connected with the energy of the cosmos, flowing in peace and harmony, the more we perceive these magical synchronicities, making life a place of surprises.

When we finished walking in the market we went to Surry Hills, from there we walked for about three hours to Bondi Beach. We never imagined the distance, and nevertheless, we followed our intuition mixed with a little ignorance from one of the guys, although we ended up exhausted from so much walking. I was pleased to see several organic stores, massage centers, yoga, and surf. In Bondi, I felt much more in a place of my style; there I had a feeling of gradually approaching where I really wanted to be. Australia was definitely the country for me; the vegetation, wildlife, people, language, beaches. I hope Byron Bay is everything I have been looking for.

Today I also had a magical day. This time I went alone to stroll through Sydney. I knew about a museum showing the history of the convicts and I decided to visit it. I looked for the address in Google Maps and I left at one in the afternoon. Without much trouble, I arrived at Hyde Park Barracks, a red brick Victorian building, in the middle of a piece of land surrounded by a wall with barred doors. Without much understanding of the place, I went straight in to find out more about the dark Australian past. I was surprised by the history of this nation; in the nineteenth century, England sent 50,000 convicts to colonize the territory. The industrialization period created more crime in the cities, therefore, the government made a policy to humanize criminal sentences; and those people were expelled from England to work in Australia. That is how this country was founded; forced labor built Sydney, a very sad past. The museum was empty although in the list of UNESCO World Heritage Sites there are eleven places of Australia and Tasmania, in the subject of convicts. People here have blocked their past, and many families erased their ancestors from their family trees. I was fascinated by the museum and to know the origins of this country. At some point I will try to touch this subject with some Australians to know how they feel about this, I am a sociologist wanna be and I find it very interesting.

After the Hyde Park Barracks, I went to the Australian Museum. I was recommended to visit a wildlife photography exhibition in this museum; the winning photos of a Nat Geo contest were exposed to the public. I would also take the opportunity to see the rest. Before arriving a man asked me if I was lost, with that, we started a talk and walked together to the museum. He had a guitar with him; he was a writer of songs for artists like Bonnie Tyler. The strangest thing was when he heard my name, he told me that he had returned to music after leaving it for 20 years, now he was writing a song for a French friend named Nathalie, recently deceased. It struck me very much that coincidence. He also in three weeks, would go to Byron Bay and look for me there. Then he said goodbye to me and said, 'stay beautiful'. I entered the museum with my head over in the clouds, feeling very grateful for all those strange beautiful moments that I've been living recently.

The Australian Museum showed me the richness of minerals and fauna of its territory. I loved learning about the species and the particularity of marsupials, a place completely different from the rest of the world. Leaving the museum I saw a few white cockatoos with a yellow crest, making a scandal above the traffic lights. My first reaction was to look for their owners, then I decide to get closer to the scene. Soon I realized that those animals that I had only seen in captivity were flying around the city like any other pigeon. I was fascinated. Sometimes being in a city makes me forget 'It's Australia!' The exotic fauna was also in Sydney. After that I decided to visit St. Mary's Cathedral, one block away from the Australian Museum. First I saw it from the outside and I noticed that the front door was closed. So I decided to surround it to see if I could find a way in. There was a small door and through there I got in. I decided to sit for a moment to appreciate the architecture. A few minutes later, I turned around and saw children dressed as acolytes and priests from behind. I then realized they were a chorus group, so I stayed. The organ began and so did the voices of the children. I enjoyed a concert in the form of a sung mass, very special. Leaving the cathedral, I found an ice cream cart next to Hyde Park, I bought one covered with chocolate and nuts. I ate it walking through the park in the middle of the night. The park seemed really special; the huge trees echoed the chants of exotic little birds. I felt like I was inside a jungle in the middle of the city. In the park, I saw a photography exhibition showing the everyday culture of Sydney.

I had a very special day, an introduction to Australia, its history and its megadiversity. It was perfect to have started in Sydney and not in Melbourne or Perth. I was in the core, where the English began to populate the territory. I'm leaving tomorrow, so I'll do banking procedures, I'll walk around a little and then I'll get ready to leave at four-thirty in the morning to the airport. And soon I'm going to Byron Bay, the Promised Land.

23 September 2013

There is a famous saying of Bertolt Brecht 'The crisis occurs when the old hasn't died and when the new hasn't born', and that's how I felt this morning after talking to my sister through Facetime. In the chat she told me that she would soon sell her computer, she had taken mine and was very happy with a Mac. A few minutes later I asked her about my car, to my surprise I found out that my parents sold it in August. Besides my dad has been staying in my room for several days with his rehabilitation equipment. At that moment I understood that my place in that house was slowly fading; it was a strong shock and with that, I felt completely lost. I don't belong there nor here—crisis. Feeling quite disoriented and dizzy, I decided to leave the apartment to do my chores. It was good to be outside to clarify my ideas. Finally, I had a very productive day. I found the cheapest exchange house on George Street and bought dollars. Then I decided to cut my hair as a spontaneous act to represent a new beginning. After that I bought a cell phone and grabbed my passport to open an account at the Commonwealth Bank, from there I decided to go for a walk in Darling Harbor to think and to be alone. Now I'm with the guys making travel arrangements.

Today I realized something important. I have had enough expenses and Australia is very expensive. I will probably be forced to get a job faster than contemplated. I'm thinking of looking for something part-time, no more than five hours a day to be able to remain neutral and avoid spending my funds. I prefer to save my money to go travelling at the end; for now, I want to be more chilled. This is a way to integrate quickly into local society; work in an organization could be somewhere other than Byron Bay. For now, I need to create a home and start my life, especially after talking to my sister today. My plan is to focus on getting a house, then my surfboard, and a job.

It's 10:00 p.m. and I'm going to sleep. We get up at four in the morning.

27 September 2013

I have been in Byron Bay for three full days and too many events have happened, a difficult part, and the rest incredible. We left Sydney—around seventeen Mexicans together. Neto and the roomies became friends of all the Mexicans in their building; the Rex apartments have been among exchange students for some time, so they quickly became friends and decided to travel as a group along the East Coast of Australia. I joined their plan and I went with them to Byron Bay, they would only stay for one night, I would start my life there. It was a very fun day, at first it took me a bit of work to get involved and at one point I didn't want to hang much with Mexicans from rich families, but I remained grateful to be with people and not completely alone. The flight was at 7:00 a.m. so we arrived at Byron Bay quite early. We went for a little walk around the town without going too far and headed back to the hostel, the Backpackers Inn.

My first impression of Byron Bay was not what was expected. I was in a 1970s American town, like going back in time. I saw many hippies but I didn't understand the concept very well. At some point, I thought, 'Shit, this is the place you chose and here you are going to stay.' I was annoyed to hear people say Byron was incredible but not have experiences to affirm it. I tried not to think and enjoy my day with the Mexicans. In the afternoon, we went to the beach and we were playing Mafia. It was fun, that way I learned the names of the girls and I integrated better with them. At night, we went partying to a typical bar here, had a good time. I was surprised by the great quality of men, super handsome and amazing bodies, just like Vikings. I was very excited.

Finally my impression improved at the end of the day, people seemed much more friendly and smiling. I saw some places of organic food from outside, the village or rather the two main streets I found to be nice. The problem was coming from a place as beautiful as Biarritz, so it made me compare and I found this place not as nice. Although the valuable thing here is the people, and that takes more time to appreciate it.

Yesterday was horrible. I got up at eight in the morning because I couldn't sleep anymore. Neto and the Mexicans were leaving at ten and I wanted to say goodbye to them. On my second day in Sydney, I got a cold sore on the lower lip for having low defenses; flights, lack of sleep, and schedule changes that were lethal to me. I got two sores; they were pretty small but really visible to me. Yesterday I got up and they were much worse, had a disgusting layer of pus, it looked yellow and terrible. With that, I couldn't talk to anyone or do anything. So I decided to apply a remedy used on other occasions. I went to get salt in the kitchen and I was putting it for a long time, the pain was unbearable. I walked from one side of the room to the other waving my hands as a distraction; fortunately, there were no other travellers with me, so I could be alone and squirm in my pain. The salt acted with the pus and removed it little by little, then I rinsed and I put the salt back, as well as ten times. It was horrible, I felt terrible with that thing in my mouth. I didn't want to talk to anyone but if I mentioned it, I would give it importance, and people would too, so it was better to act normal. Finally, at ten o'clock in the morning, I said goodbye to the boys and girls. After a couple of hours of suffering, I could remove the disgusting yellow, the wound looked red and fresh but at least it didn't look that bad. When they left I had a realization, I was alone and I had to start from nowhere again; find a place to live, work, etcetera. But with that thing in my mouth, I didn't want to talk to anyone! I locked myself in the room and got into the blankets to whine in silence. After a while, I decided to take the reins of my life and try to look for an apartment. So I went to the reception and bought some Wi-Fi time to browse through a website recommended by an Australian the previous night.

I was researching and found some options. I sent several messages from my cell phone, I knew that the online search wasn't enough but I didn't feel like going to talk to people and ask. I wasn't comfortable. Shortly after I started to text with a woman named Mia, and she offered me a visit to her house. She could pick me up in the hostel; I couldn't lose anything so I accepted. She said, 'I arrive in ten minutes', then I went back to my room for my bag and I went outside to wait for Mia. She arrived in her car, a woman around her forties with a hippie style. In a short time, she told me that she has practiced yoga for years but now she was hurt. A few minutes later we arrived at the house. I never imagined it to be like this, a beautiful house, neat and clean, with good taste in decoration and Buddha's in painting and statues. I felt in peace and harmony since I entered. Mia lives with Lucy, a vegetarian yoga master girl, I would share the bathroom with her. I loved the house, however, it would be available by the end of October, and I needed something sooner.

Mia gave me a ride back to town and I walked to the hostel. I had only eaten a banana in the morning but I wasn't hungry. I got into bed again to rest and felt a little depressed. I needed to go search for a place but I didn't want to, the sore wasn't much better. At 3:00 p.m., I decided to go out again, the shops would close at 5:00 p.m., and I didn't have much time. Arriving at the village I saw a woman outside a shop and I approached her. She recommended I look for a blackboard where people put ads and so I went there to have a look, I found something and sent a message. After that, I went with another girl and suggested to see ads in the local newspaper *Ecko*. I took it and decided to return to the hostel to see it calmly.

As I hadn't eaten anything I went to the kitchen to prepare some organic beans. They took years to cook so I stayed a good time there. Meanwhile, I sent messages to the advertisers of the *Ecko* newspaper. One of them had only a local phone so I decided to dial. A lady with a more British than Australian accent answered me, a very sweet and formal voice at the same time. I told her about my situation and told me that she had a rental room for a month from October 6, she would send me an email with photos and she would wait for my response. After talking to her on the phone I was very happy; in one day I had two great options for accommodation. Right after that, I went back to the kitchen and a girl started to talk to me. She was German and was travelling with her Greek friend. It was instantaneous, when I felt better with myself a girl started talking to me, after that I was chatting with Canadian travellers. I left the kitchen and went to the room to go to bed again, this time I felt a little better. A few minutes later, my new roomies, a couple of Brazilians, came in. Then we began to talk and they invited me to have some drinks with them, so I changed and joined the table where they were sitting. The atmosphere of the hostel was very nice, young people chatting; many knew each other from there. I loved seeing the people opening up and how fast you could socialize, the opposite of France. After spending some time having a good time with people from the hostel, we went with a British girl to the same bar the night before. We stayed for a while and we returned.

Today in the morning my cold sore dawned better, but a couple of hours later it was bad again. I had to leave the room and change to another, then I went to the reception and paid another two nights. Again I spent the morning pouring myself salt and suffering alone in a six-bedroom. Shortly after I went to buy Internet to chat with my friends, and see Sheryn's mail about the room for a month. When I saw the photos I loved it and I called her immediately. She said that we could meet today at two o'clock in the afternoon, it was 1:15 p.m., so I rushed out because the place was a bit far from the hostel. It was something good because otherwise I would've stayed depressed and see every five minutes the progress of my cold sore. My flip-flops got me a blister from walking in Sydney, so a good stretch I was barefoot, as many people in Byron. I was feeling happy, every time I found the town more charming; the people around gave me good vibes, just what I wanted after my experience in France. While walking I wrote to a guy named Christophe to ask about a bicycle for sale, I wanted one to move faster, so I would see him tomorrow near the hostel. I walked for half an hour, and when I was near the place the concentrated vegetation amazed me. It reminded me of Mexico, not like in France where practically everything is touched by humans. The intense wind shook the trees strongly; at the same time songs of exotic birds accompanied that orchestra. I loved instead of listening to cars and the highway, to be surrounded by sounds of nature. When I got to the intersection of streets that we defined as the meeting point, I called Sheryn and she came out to get me. The house was very nice, neat and clean, she showed me the room and I thought it was perfect. I would share the bathroom with a German girl; they also had a Japanese student living in the studio.

Sheryn and her partner lived in the upper part of the house; basically, we would only share the kitchen with them. If I went out partying I wouldn't bother them because I was at the bottom. Soon I started talking to Sheryn about various topics, including about my book and spirituality. She had gone through the same thing and had left Sydney to go in search of a place in nature. She wrote a book about her story and I decided to buy it. She told me that Byron Bay was a center of spirituality in Australia; there were not many other places like this. I told her of my astonishment at the rapid movement of energies in Byron, I had been here for three days and so much had already happened. Sheryn assured me that this place is like that, has a very particular magnetism, and can absorb and impel you to adapt in a very fast way. Sheryn listens to guides, is clairvoyant, and I asked for consultation later. Finally, we had a very pleasant meeting. At three she had another appointment with a man to see the room too. She would call me tomorrow to confirm about it; hopefully, it's a yes.

On the way back I was really surprised, about the rapidity in the development of so many events, at the same time I was sending messages with another man to rent a place for a week, before moving with Sheryn. It's as if Byron Bay had a life of its own and was absorbing me in. Yesterday Mia took me out of the Backpackers, and today Sheryn also did it with her sudden appointment at 2:00 p.m. Back in town, I stopped by an organic shop to see the products. I was happy to just walk around. I couldn't believe the variety of seeds, dehydrated fruits, species, vegetarian, and vegan cakes. There was also a good supply of organic fruits and vegetables. I bought a shampoo and broccoli. After that I kept walking back to the hostel, feeling happier every time. Suddenly I see a job advertisement announcing the following: 'Are you fun and outgoing? Can talk to anyone? And have fun while working? Then become part of the Peterpants team'. Without understanding much I decided to walk in. I went to the reception to ask about the job. A young woman gave me a short explanation, but asked me to wait for the person in charge of it, he would arrive in an hour, so I waited. The job was to talk to people and invite them to the travel agency. At first, I didn't find it very attractive to be doing that, but while I waited, I started to see the possible benefits. I would be outside, having fun, talking to people, could be a perfect candidate for the position. Later the people in charge arrived and another girl was interested in the work too. They asked us questions obviously to see how we developed; they loved to know about my three languages. After a fairly quick talk, I left my name and my cell phone. In the blink of an eye, I had my first job interview. Leaving the place I understood something: that which had punished me in France, to be extroverted, chatty and happy, here is something precious. The ads specifically ask for cheerful people with good vibes, just what I want is to be happy and not in a place where people put me down. Now, all I have to do is move with the energy of Byron and see which job will come to me. Another thing, the payment in Peterpants is with travel money. It's amazing because I could travel to Australia and some islands; however, I need to have real money to sustain my living here.

My crazy day doesn't end there; I returned to the hostel and started writing this segment. During that time, I talked with an English girl and some guys from Denmark while cooking my beans. Before the closure of the kitchen, I was in front of a couple of very unfriendly French girl duo. I was curious to analyze their attitude by pretending not to understand French. They had the typical long face, complaining and were glued to their cell phone. There I said to myself, 'I am so grateful to be no longer in your country.' At 10:30 p.m., we were asked to leave because they were going to close the common area. On the way to my room, an American guy asked me, 'Are you Mexican?' he was sitting with the girls from Greece and Germany that I met yesterday. The guy was making jokes without stopping; he kept on talking and saying nonsense. It was pretty late, so we were forced to leave the tables and go to another place. I was tired and wanted to go to sleep, but this half Jamaican and half American guy proposed to go with him to the beach. I had shorts so I asked them to wait while I would put some pants in my room. At first, I doubted it, but I said to myself, 'These are not moments to close doors. It's necessary to accept this type of invitations'.

That way the group was created, one German, one Greek, one Canadian, one Jamaican, and one Mexican. So we made our way to the beach and looked for a place to sit. The Jamaican, honoring his origin, lit a marihuana cigarette, and I smoked a little without feeling the effects too much. We were talking, watching the stars, when suddenly one said, 'Everyone look at that light, it's coming here.' So I turned around and I saw a light approaching. At first, I was afraid, then I perceived a human figure and I was afraid too; a girl came up with the light of her cell phone and started looking for her tiger balm, and she was like crazy pointing in the sand. Everyone was really surprised, we thought that the girl was delirious; looking for a small thing in an ocean of sand in the middle of the night. She literally made us move to see if it was below us. However, we took it with humor and laughed. After a few minutes of searching, the German pointed in one place and the girl found her tiger balm. We were attacked by laughter at the absurdity of the situation. We asked her about her origin, and she didn't tell us. She didn't even want to show her face, it was hilarious.

From that moment on, we had an incredible time and too many crazy things happened, one after another. At one point, another individual with a light was walking along the beach. We invited him to join us, it was a local guy from Byron and he had a guitar. Then the tiger balm girl began to sing, with an angelic voice; the rest we hugged and moved to the rhythm of the music. Then it was the turn of the other guy. He sang a Bob Marley song and after finishing, he quickly disappeared. The Greek told the tiger balm girl, 'I love you and I want to marry you.' The Jamaican said it too, then we organized a wedding, and we couldn't stop laughing while doing it. In addition to our internal games, we watched a giant bat pass by, very common here apparently. We witnessed the appearance of the red moon on the horizon of the ocean, and a pink cloud flying too close from us. In the end, we were playing with the plankton and seeing the reflection of the red moon over the water. And that way, without any type of expectation, I had one of the most special nights of my life. A complete spiritual experience; where the union of good vibes and open spirits made a magical combination. Byron Bay is a very unique place; the portals here are wide open. I begin to be afraid because the movements are happening very fast.

1 October 2013

It's been several days and I haven't really found time to write. I'm at the hostel and all the time I have some incredible distraction or plan. Today I was chatting for hours with an English girl, then I was in the pool reading and sunbathing, then some Brazilians came and invited me to go with them to the beach, it's next to the hostel so it only needs a short walk through the bush to get there. At the beach, I found Matt, a friend from here, and he accompanied us. I returned to the pool and stayed there for a while with Matt, a cute brown-haired Australian guy. Then he invited me to buy vintage clothes in the afternoon and then we would go with more backpacker friends to a talent show in a very famous hostel here called The Art's Factory. My days here have been like this, all the time. I get to know more guys and girls and I have a better time. Many live in the hostel because they work a few hours cleaning and doing other tasks for free lodging. The atmosphere is amazing. We get along very well, everyone is happy, I get to know people of multiple nationalities—it's the most fun.

In the few moments where I was able to get away from the social gatherings at the hostel, I finished my resume, and yesterday I took it to three different places. The third wasn't necessary because I already have work! And it's in Byron Organic Kitchen; vegetarian, vegan, and organic cuisine. I arrived like everywhere else, presenting my CV and saying 'I'm looking for work for the summer' with the typical speech; however, I only went to vegetarian cooking places and organic produce stores. I knew I didn't want to work in anything different than that. I wanted something incredible, and I got it. I'm going tomorrow at 8:00 a.m. for the training.

The events since my arrival in Australia have accelerated too much. I have a very strong cosmic connection-level because I get what I want extremely fast. The energy flows perfectly. I feel incredible and I'm eating very healthy. Except for a slice of margarita pizza, I have eaten vegan every day, trying different dishes in organic stores, which I will learn how to make at my work. Every time I'm vibrating in higher frequencies, every day I'm more and more happy, I feel lighter and with great well-being. This is just the beginning. In the kitchen, the owner asked me for at least three months of commitment. Then it's official, I'm going to live in Byron Bay! I cannot even imagine how I'm going to be when I'm surfing, taking yoga classes, meditating daily, and eating organic vegan food. I think the day I'm going to free my soul completely and find myself in a state of total love and harmony is about to arrive. This place is my dream come true; the energy, the nature, people, and beautiful guys, the amount of things linked to spirituality—couldn't ask for anything more in life.

These days I already paid my room for a month with Sheryn. I bought a beautiful bicycle for 200 dollars, besides finding the job of my dreams. In a week I solved my life, Byron Bay wanted me in, swallowed me right away, and I'm part of this incredible micro-cosmos. Australians, travellers, locals, most say Byron Bay is the best, if not the best in Australia, and here I arrived. Pure magic.

4 October 2013

I have news regarding my work in the kitchen, at the moment it is one or two days a week, after finishing my 6 hours of work the owner told me that, I didn't know whether to be happy or not, with that I must find something else to survive. My job that day was wonderful. We did about twenty vegetarian pies, mostly vegan. I had to chop vegetables, I made some salads and put the preparations in the oven. I learned a lot, it was a paid cooking class. I was surrounded by pure beauty; vegetables, a wide variety of grains and seeds, many spices, fruits, and most organic. I had to cook; I almost didn't do the dishes. I couldn't believe the dream coming true.

My days have been absolutely incredible; however, soon I will leave the hostel and there will be several changes. On the one hand, I really want to have my room, unpack my suitcase, and create a private space to be able to finally rest. On the other hand, the hostel has been such a great source of happiness, that I'm having a hard time letting it go. Yesterday was a beautiful day; several in our group went to the beach and we sat in a circle on the sand. We were chatting, laughing, and enjoying the perfect weather. Sometime later, Matt and I ended up lying on the sand and got covered by it from head to toe, but as never before in my life, it didn't cause any discomfort. I felt free and I rolled over and over. Matt pulled out his iPod and we shared his headphone listening to music. That moment, I really felt far away, completely free and happy from within, integrated with nature, my body melted on the sand—I became the beach itself. If only I could freeze that moment and stay there forever.

Yesterday at the beach with the guys from the hostel we stretched our body a bit and did some yoga exercises and breathing. After that, I was talking to Matt and I came to a new conclusion, I want a free job. I'm very happy and flowing perfect with the magic of this place, I don't want to enter into a routine of excessive and tedious work. I also thanked my few hours of work in the kitchen. However, I must look for other alternatives. Yesterday I spoke with my dad and I learned that I have about 2,700 Australian dollars in my Mexican bank account and a thousand dollars in the Australian, with that I can last for about three months without problems, clearly spending as little as possible. Today I spent a lot of time with my wonderful Jamaican friend Steven; that crazy night on the beach necessarily created a bond of friendship. He just arrived because he was sent to Byron to open and manage a travel agency. He is a charismatic person full of love and positive energy. Unlike other travel agencies, he invites people to greet him, meet in the office, and stay as long as they want, opening a very pleasant space for social gatherings. Being there we can use free Internet, computers, watch movies, and we will organize a barbecue. I had a good time with Steven at his place, that after going to talk to the manager of an organic store. I went there to ask for work and talk a little about my experience in organizations and social movements. He told me that he has nine other resumes along with mine; in addition, they only accepted Australians by policy of the store. It was the only work option in my head. I really don't feel like doing anything else. So with Steven, I came up with a new idea: I'm going to give free yoga classes. The issue of getting a quick job is not precisely because of lack of money. It's because I get bored easily and I need to be doing something. Free yoga classes are a great project. I want to open a space to talk, do some stretching, and give an introduction to the philosophy and the magic behind it. That way I will be able to create a circle of love, attracting people to my classes, and sharing my knowledge. When you start a project like this, it's an investment at first: you need to meet people, make contacts, create some noise, and later it starts to work. With this, I can open many doors. I could even get some private yoga classes and get money from there. I need to do my own project, work freely, and be myself, show my happiness and love becoming the teacher. It's time to utilize what I learned; to share, to give away, I want to be heard, and I can't think of a better place in the world to do this.

Tomorrow I have a yoga festival entitled 'Are you ready to evolve?', which will include meditations, songs, food, yoga, workshops, talks—I'm too excited. It will be a concentration of interesting people, and I will be filled with the best and most positive vibrations of love. With that, I will take the necessary forces to start this crazy transformative project.

8 October 2013

It has been several days since my last writing and I have gone through some crises and decision-makings. Saturday was my yoga festival, it was amazing. First I took a class of an hour quite normal and simple. The teacher's partner sang live mantras with an oriental instrument. After that, I had a yin yoga class, in this, we kept the postures a lot longer on the floor, an approximate five to seven minutes by posture, quite exhausting. Later I went to an Ayurvedic food talk, also to talk about the revolution of the now. Then a session of breathings to get active and others to create calm. After that, I went to a school gym where we danced as a form of meditative yoga with movement. And lastly, Chocolate Yoga.

This last one was the most interesting, they gave us a shamanic cocoa drink from Guatemala and we did a ceremony. We called the spirits of the north, south, east, and west with a series of blessings, and then with a few breaths we sent that energy to the glass, then we drank the potion. It was a kundalini yoga, where we focused mainly on opening the heart and letting ourselves be guided by it. In a few moments, I entered into a trance with the music and the general energy; it was a shocking class. Finally, a group came to sing divine mantras. The festival was absolutely perfect.

That day I was very confused with my life. I had two options: either I look for a normal job or I become a yoga teacher, starting from nothing and not earning a dollar. My financial situation at the moment allows me to survive for two or three months; on the other hand, I don't want to indulge in another exhausting job simply for money. In France, I decided to avoid unwanted work unless it's very necessary. For the moment I'm calm and for that reason, I have decided to take the difficult path. The path indicated by my heart and my intuition; a new challenge in my life, to be a yoga teacher. Now I think that it really combines with my internal situation. Lately, I only talk about health with my friends and according to the person I talk about spirituality, and above all, I feel a great inner love and I have to take it out somehow. I have an enormous need to share and make people as happy as I am. This is good for Mexiro, I will learn to lead a group, to use my communication skills to create social and environmental awareness. Eventually, I could become an excellent teacher and be hired to give paid classes. I will meet many interesting people. I will have free time to flow with the energy of Byron Bay; my visualizations are good.

Now is a time where I'm going to fully focus on myself. In fact, I moved to Sheryn's on Sunday. It's about fifteen minutes on bike from the center, in a very quiet area full of greenery; huge trees, and multiple exotic birds. It felt extremely good unpacking and creating a space for myself; I also bought several kitchen items to start forming my pantry of organic and healthy products. Today I printed the posters and tomorrow I'm going to stick them on the community board.

My yoga classes will be on Thursdays and Fridays. On top of that, when my friend Jakob took me from the hostel to Sheryn's house, I immediately started to miss it. So when I returned to the hostel to look for my bike, I spoke with Dave the manager. I wanted to give free yoga classes for them and use the facilities. My friends are there, it's next to the beach, there is a pool, and the vibe is the best. I want to be in Backpackers without feeling intrusive. I thought the plan was good, so Thursday will be the test to see how the yoga class works. If the results are good I will do it a couple of days a week, and I will be able to walk freely so I can leave my surfboard there and not be moving from one side to the other.

Now it starts a very strong physical challenge, I'm going to give free yoga classes Monday to Friday at the main street park, a class on Fridays at my friend Steven's travel agency, and maybe at Backpackers. I'm going to buy a surfboard and I will return to the sport. At the same time I must get used to the bicycle; today I could hardly do the return. In a short time, I will be exactly where I want to be—eating healthy, doing yoga, and surfing all day and with free time to be with my friends and have a perfect time.

Every day I'm a little better, more calm, and content focused on my activities. However, I expect a lot of work and I'm a little nervous about directing groups. Of course, as a good citizen of a capitalist world, I had my doubts about money. However, I fully trust the Universe and the way it operates. For the moment I will not think about it, and I will follow my heart. Eventually, if I don't have money, I will learn how to proceed.

12 October 2013

There have been many events since Tuesday when I wrote for the last time. I have some important news: I already bought a surfboard and I'm back in the water. I went with a professional surfer I met one day in a store of second-hand items. I liked him and decided to go with him to buy a board according to the recommendations. He suggested a 6-foot shortboard to float better. I bought it and I took it the same day. A few hours later, I went to the beach in front of the Backpackers for a surf; the board was perfect; it floated well, it was very easy for me to stand on it. I'm going to go very far in my surfing. On that side I'm ready. I only need to recover my physical condition to last longer in the water, and of course, learn the duck-dive to pass under the waves with the board.

Thursday was my first yoga class at Backpackers Inn. I tried not to think much about it, I didn't even prepare for the class. I would let myself be carried away by the creativity of the moment. At around 10:30 a.m., I took out my new mat, acquired at the yoga festival, and I started to do some stretches by myself, a little before eleven, my students started to arrive. It was a group of nine girls and a guy. I started with a lot of emphasis on breathing, then we did a very pleasant meditation listening to the ocean, the leaves of the trees moving with the wind, and the songs of the birds. With our eyes closed, we moved the neck slowly and did some exercises to warm arms and shoulders, then we made the posture of the four points and did other stretches there. The class was a fluid yoga—free—and we made several poses. We finished in schavasana, and I accommodated the body of my students moving their legs, arms, neck, and head. They ended up happy, relaxed and exercised. My friends congratulated me on my first class, a success. That day I didn't speak with Dave the manager. I hoped he liked the idea and would let me be in the hostel and use the facilities.

The night before, on Wednesday, there was a barbecue in the hostel that became a farewell to Sarah, a girl from Sweden. Matt my friend, with whom I spent most of my time, had gone some nights to Noosa, a small town four hours from Byron. He returned and for some reason, we didn't hang out as long as before. That night I was chatting with my other friends feeling extremely happy. I even massaged them on the back. I felt that Matt was acting very strangely to me. I sensed his attraction to me for a long time; nevertheless, I felt certain jealousy from him when I was with other guys.

That weekend my Dutch friend Tihjs asked me about our relationship. I had put up a great resistance because I didn't want to deal so quickly with a guy in love. I had to concentrate on my affairs; it seemed a punishment. I tried not to think about it and go with the flow. However, that night I never imagined such behavior. We went to the club, and really quick Matt got drunk. He was flirting and taking many girls to the dance floor, a shy guy with any skills for dancing was suddenly out of control. That's when I felt some feelings for him; otherwise, I would not have minded. Suddenly I began to feel quite annoyed and decided to leave the club. Arriving at my house, I lay for a while thinking, probably this must happen to realize his importance in my life. I decided to go find him the next day to have a talk. For now, I would focus on giving my yoga class, go surfing, and then solve that situation.

On Thursday, I stayed at the hostel all day. After the class I was with my friends in the garden sunbathing, we practiced some headstands, we got into the pool and enjoyed a delicious climate. In the afternoon I decided to go get some food and be alone to think things through with Matt and me. My resolutions were as follows: definitely not the man of my dreams knows nothing about health and spirituality and doesn't do much with his life. However, being with him I could integrate even more in the hostel and not feel strange. Even with yoga classes, I don't live there anymore, unlike my friends. That somehow excludes me and makes me feel like an outsider. My decisions seemed rather selfish. I was thinking of going out with a guy from the hostel in order to be there, and have a different reason to simply not get over the place. However, I had to follow my intuition and go talk to him. I went back to the hostel to look for him. Minutes later I saw him from afar but I didn't dare to approach; shortly after, I armed myself with courage and went.

The talk was a total disaster. I never imagined that answer on his part. Basically, he told me that he felt a very close relationship between us and that's why he had gone to Noosa; he was forced to create a distance from me. He also thought that I was chasing him the night of the barbecue and didn't let him talk to other people. There I realized that life is full of surprises. I never imagined he would be such an asshole, and he basically didn't want to know anything about me. Finishing the talk, I felt quite hurt. Usually, I have to deal with friends in love with me; however, now was the opposite. In his head, I wanted to be his girlfriend and was harassing him. So I decided to leave the hostel. I wanted to be alone in my house to have a moment of reflection. On one side it made me well to be rejected by a guy, a novelty in my life. I was also glad to think it was not him. I was not sure about it, and the man of my Australian dreams must be more evolved and smart. That situation helped me figure out something else. I had to move on from the hostel and start looking for friends elsewhere. There was so much more in Byron than the Backpackers Inn. So two important things happened that night, I opened up to meet new people, and above all, I opened my heart to a partner.

Yesterday was Friday and I gave a yoga class in the shop of my friend Steven. Rose, Julika, and Emma, some girls from the hostel came, besides Steven practically forced to do the class. It was very good; we stretched doing a fairly dynamic class and the group created a special vibe. We laughed but also felt the energy connection through *pranayama*, the four were happy, even Steven loved it. Later I talked to my friend Simon, a surfing teacher at Backpackers Inn. He invited me with his friends to The Jonction and I decided to open up and meet new people. One is from the United States, about 40 years old, and has spent many years as a Pilates teacher and physiotherapist. He has been in Byron for a short time and was looking for a yoga teacher to do some classes on the beach, fusing other types of exercises; again the Universe was acting faster than me. I had been a couple of days with this mindset, and I already had a plan to instruct and earn money. In Australia, a yoga class costs between 15 and 20 dollars. Shortly after, we started to plan the classes brainstorming a little, and this is how I found a partner. After The Jonction, we went to Simon's house, Shaun, and his other friend, then we went surfing and Simon gave me some very valuable tips for surfing. The waves were big and very continuous. However, he pushed me to go pretty far. I was smashed several times but Simon's goal was to take away the fear, and he did very well. Now I feel stronger and prepared to look for better waves. After surfing we went to the hostel, rinsed my board, I went into the pool and enjoyed the best vibes. Simon worked at five and his friends also came with us. I spent a lot of time talking with Shaun while I was in the pool. Walking around the hostel I found Lauren, Rose's best friend, and she said, 'Hi, I heard your class was amazing. I would've liked to go but I had work.' At the same time Dave the manager came by, after talking with Lauren approached me and asked me about the next class. He said, 'They seem to enjoy them.' Those minutes I felt completely fulfilled and could continue with the classes in the hostel. Dave was happy, had met Shaun, and we decided to associate to create a very special and different classes on the beach.

Now I have a lot of work ahead of me. I would see Shaun today to do some routines on the beach. He's going to bring me some anatomy books, and he's going to teach me a lot about it. Now I will not be able to give free classes in the park. I have printed the publicity papers, but I didn't want to put them around. I will only be able to give free classes in the hostel and with my friend Steven. I will begin to work in my classes with Shaun. Now I am entering the phase of building an incredible life, the one in my dreams. I'm on the beach, I live ten minutes on the bike from downtown, I'm surrounded by nature, I'm back to surfing, I have paid cooking classes, and I'm going to work creating awareness and exercising. Instead of going to look for a job, I searched my passion internally and for love, I decided to become a yoga teacher. After that, Shaun arrived and now I will make it a job and live on this. I believe this is the way we can change our lives, instead of working to live, living to work. Finding something that creates passion from within, something that doesn't feel like work, that way we'll be fully happy and satisfied with our lives. To create happier societies, we need more people working in their passions, and I'm sure that the spiritual path will take us in that direction.

18 October 2013

My last writing was almost a week ago. Some events have happened but not too many. Mainly it has been a week of adapting and realizing some aspects of my life. I have spent a lot of time in the hostel enjoying my friends. I have not been able to surf so much because we have very strong winds and the temperatures have dropped. The waves are bad and the water is cold, I don't feel like getting in the ocean. On the other hand, I could only see Shaun one day to do a Pilates class on the beach, he has been very busy and we haven't been able to catch up very often. The winds and the weather don't help either. It was Tuesday I think when I had a big crisis. The work in the kitchen had been very slow, only two days; Shaun was missing; a guy I met had not answered my message, and so I was beginning to doubt the way to take. I was wasting a lot of time and I was still on vacation at the hostel. It was time to start seeing my options to make money. This small crisis happened in the shop of my friend Steven. There I had a talk with a girl and I was able to clarify my ideas, I finally decided to wait this week to see how my life gets together. If the work with Shaun is fruitful, if I return to the kitchen and for how long, if I see this guy on Sunday.

A couple of days at the end of this week I worked in the kitchen, on Thursday four hours and today eight exhaustive hours. I am happy because with that money I can pay my lodging for a week, 190 dollars. My work with Shaun didn't advance at all. I only saw him one day; the guy in question called me on the phone and invited me to a waterfall on Sunday, and overall I feel pretty satisfied with the results. I'm seeing how my life makes sense. This time I feel quite settled, I made many expenses to buy my bicycle, my board, my yoga mat, and my pantry, but now I'm only going to spend on food and lodging, not a dollar in alcohol. My goal for the moment is to maintain myself, not necessarily save as I did in France. If later I want to travel, I will seek a job that allows me to. At the moment this is what I want to do: I want to be able to stay here, live in Byron Bay, surf, eat healthy, meet interesting people, and be very happy. The goal is not to control things, from now on I'm going to let go, maybe one day I get up and I want to go back to Mexico or I want to leave Byron Bay. My intuition will tell me at the right time. It's a matter of living day-to-day and putting aside unnecessary worries.

Now the interesting part, a new guy is hanging around in my head. Last Sunday I went with my friend Steven to the Beach Hotel. He was half asleep however he got up and came, there was very good electronic music, but Steven didn't want to dance, so he decided to leave and I stayed by myself. I went in front of the DJ to enjoy the music. Then some guys came to talk to me and to dance, but I didn't pay much attention to them; however, beside me was a guy with a vintage shirt, dancing, and smiling. I liked his energy and I decided to talk to him. I said, 'cool shirt.' And from there we began a conversation. Later I could perceive an attractive physique, hiding the face behind its brown hair with discolored tips, quite disheveled, a very Australian style. We didn't have much light but I could see clear eyes, smile, and nice lips, a lot of beards too. His name is Jared, he is Australian from farmer families. He is 25 years old, studied photojournalism, lived in different places, and is currently working in construction to save a lot of money and travel around the world. He wanted to take me to some places around; he invited me to his uncle's farm. At that moment we were talking about plans in the air, but on Monday he texted to invite me to a waterfall this Sunday. After being on the dance floor, we decided to go out and talk. It was very nice and I thought he was someone smart, but his friends had to leave and he would sleep in a tent quite far. However, he was quite interested in doing something with me this weekend, then he said goodbye cordially adding, 'You are a sweetheart.'

The music stopped being good and I decided to leave. I felt pretty satisfied after having met Jared. For the first time since my arrival in Australia, I had met a guy who caught my attention right from the beginning. My interest in Matt, for example, started two weeks after meeting him. In fact, after my painful talk with him was when I realized that I was ready to have a boyfriend, and I asked the Universe, now in my head I haven't stopped fantasizing about the possibility of Jared, maybe he is my new lover, but I will not know that until Sunday. There are several clues on the matter: he works from Monday to Friday. In the kitchen, I can only work weekdays because Saturday and Sunday it's closed. Also, he wants to show me the area and go exploring, something incredible for me right now, to get out of Byron for a little bit. Again, I trust fully in the Universe. I asked for a boyfriend and let's see what will be sent. It's like writing letters to Santa Claus.

21 October 2013

Saturday and Sunday were the most intense days of my life, probably associated with the full moon. On Saturday, I was at the hostel about to go surfing on the beach in front, when my friend Simon, surf teacher, texted to invite me to another nearby beach, he would come to get me in thirty minutes. I was happy to go with him and his friends and get out of the routine in Byron. We went to Watergoes in his van with Marky and Travis. It was great to get in the ocean with them because they pushed me in some waves and gave me tips to paddle better. I upgraded my surfing level, thanks to that. I came out exhausted; I had swum a lot. After that, we went with the others to the beach. Shortly after I began talking to Marky about yoga, I started doing some exercises with him. While doing that Simon came with a marijuana joint and I smoked from it. At that moment, I didn't realize how strong the weed was, but I would be on another planet for at least three hours. It was the most fun and difficult at the same time to do yoga with Marky. Because he was on his board shorts I could see various problems in his posture. Men are afraid of yoga but they most need it. We can't live in inflexible bodies, that's where muscular tensions arise and bad postures are formed, besides the facility to acquire an injury. A free soul needs a free body. A healthy, flexible, strong body; only then the cosmic energy can flow and naturally align the chakras. If only people were fully focused on correcting their posture, they would probably change their lives. Many insecure people, for example, are humpbacked. If they would work on opening the chest, showing the heart, they could probably solve those problems of self-esteem and show themselves to the world with confidence. Also, body language is more than 70 percent of the communication.

It was exhaustive to work with Marky. I tried several exercises to release the tension in his shoulders. He must work on bringing the tension to the abdomen; it's the only place in the body that we are going to keep firm at all times. Many people don't know it, but that's the key, from there we will hold our torso, our back, and finally the head. The force must come from the abdomen and the rest should be relaxed. There I decided that I want to have a group of pure men in yoga, the most inflexible, those must come. It's a catastrophe to see people's bodies, terrible postures. I loved doing this for free; I just couldn't charge Marky for that.

Shortly after Shaun came. I don't know if it was the effect of the weed but I felt very 'repulsive' towards him in many ways. I had a perception of him as the typical American with a capitalist mentality; those people who invite you to do a class with them but you immediately feel a will to scam. I was in a very sensitive moment. I was too happy and I had connected deeply with Marky, but Shaun was quite disgusting. I knew since that moment that I didn't want to work with him anymore.

The rest of the day was extremely fun. We went to a park to sit on the grass and enjoy the sun, then went surfing in front of the hostel, then went with an Australian surfer friend of Simon, then to another friend's house. Night came, Simon and the others were starting to party, but I decided to leave early and prepare for my day at the waterfall with Jared.

The night before, we decided to meet at some point around ten o'clock on Sunday morning. I woke up very early to meditate, to paint my nails, and to do girl things to look pretty. At ten o'clock in the morning, I received a message from him to tell me he was running late, the first good sign of education. When he was in Byron he called me and offered to come to get me at my house, a second good sign. When he arrived, he was waiting for me in his old grey car; I noticed his hippy look with long hair and a careless beard, the little night light had not allowed me to see him clearly. I didn't know what to think. On the way, we were chatting, as always I mastered the microphone, something that happens to me when I'm nervous with a guy. I enjoyed so much the Australian virgin landscape, leaving Byron and knowing something else. Again, I couldn't believe how wonderful my life was, I was very grateful. First, we arrived at a very large terrain. There were cows and some hills forming small mountains. He decided to make a marihuana joint to enjoy the walk; of course, I smoked. A few meters after we parked, we found some people arriving from the waterfall. They offered us some sticks to defend from some supposedly aggressive birds. Jared took one and I decided not to do it, deep down I laughed about it. We started to walk where the cows were when a big bird flew very close to our heads. There I realized the seriousness of the situation, and I took a stick myself. It was a moment of considerable stress and paranoia because eight birds did the same. At the same time I laughed at the absurdity of the situation: I was in Australia, on the other side of the world, defending myself with a stick from assassin birds, just like in the Stone Age, and was also extremely blown up after smoking weed. Passing the land of the crazy birds, we found some other people that recommended leaving the sticks; later, they would no longer attack us.

    On the way I began to feel fulfilled, somehow it was like a return to Mexico and my trips through waterfalls and rivers, passing between rocks and weeds to reach the target. Jared was bringing me to one of my favorite activities. I enjoyed the most complicated passages, going on unstable rocks in the river, climbing a little. A good part of the way we were silent—he went in front guiding me, and I was connecting with nature being very happy. After about twenty minutes we arrived at the place: a small waterfall of about 2 meters with a relatively large hole. I had the impulse to want to get in as soon as possible. He offered to climb the top and jump down, I accepted. I followed him through the small sidewalk to jump into the water. The day was quite cloudy but it wasn't cold. I behaved like a little girl swimming and playing in the water.

It was an incredible moment in the waterfall. We climbed up again to jump, but this time I sat on the edge, just enjoying the contact with the stone and the sound of the water falling behind me. I stayed there for a while wandering. Suddenly I saw a few rays of sun where Jared was sitting, and I decided to jump into the water and go towards them. Shortly after, I started to cover myself with mud all over the body, that way I was exfoliating and absorbing organic earth minerals. That's exactly what yoga is all about, it goes way beyond a classroom with a mat; it's about connecting with nature, finding peace through it. Human beings have lost that connection while living in cities completely removed from the natural, but that is where we come from. We are one organism; spirituality requires a return to nature, where cosmic energy flows perfectly, a world governed by eternal and unbreakable laws.

That is how I was experiencing yoga in its splendor; thinking of nothing, enjoying every second, breathing, connecting with my surroundings, being myself, thinner after some time with a vegan diet, tanned, and feeling naturally beautiful. My body perfectly aligned, flexible, strong, healthy, complete confidence in myself, no shame to be criticized for my words or actions—that was the magic that Jared created in me. He made me feel absolutely free.

In the waterfall we ate fruits, then with a lot of inspiration, I started to take pictures of nature. We walked barefoot on the way back, very important to have a greater connection and activate the root chakra. We stopped at another small waterhole to have some food. I had some vegetables cooked in red sauce and the bottom had black rice with tomatoes and spices; the dressing I put it aside, he liked it. That's my savings technique lately. I have not eaten out in more than a week, or I prepare a little quinoa at the hostel or I carry my homemade salads with me. Now I entered a stage where I will decrease my expenses as much as possible. That way I will avoid buying unnecessary items, and I will eat very healthy, staying away from desserts and chocolates.

    It took us a long time to get back to the car, we were still rambling with nature. I stopped to take photos, and he took pictures of me with his film camera, enjoying the way, how life should be like, without a hurry to reach the destination. I stayed a good time with the cows. I told them how much I love them, then they started to follow me; it was very strange. I really enjoyed at some point when we started talking about philosophy, he asked me about my favorite authors and I ended up talking about the New Age philosophy of my interest, with that we approached the subject of yoga and postures; he wanted to try it. So I made the posture of the mountain activating *pranayama*. I loved seeing that he was open to the subject and wanted to practice with me, excellent signal again.

    After the waterfall, we had a picnic on a beautiful beach called Dream-time Beach, and I couldn't believe the food inside his blue cooler: organic bananas, organic honey, a kind of cream made with sesame seeds, pistachios, fresh bread, and a Roquefort cheese. The guy loves vegetables, fruits, and natural food, but he acted normal about it, I was impressed. Later some seagulls harassed us, we saw a rainbow and its end on the horizon, a pair of eagles flew over our heads, some border collies came to give me love. I ate delicious sandwiches by mixing the ingredients. After being on the sand, we went to some rocks on the seashore. On the way I was dancing, singing, and doing some pirouettes and ballet steps; Jared was happy watching me. I felt very good and I wanted to express it through my dancing moves, releasing my body in a meditative state. I missed my dancing a lot.

    I finally had one of the best, if not the best day of my life. I had never felt so good before, like if I was in another dimension. Jared and I have too much in common, but he does not brag or talk too much about those issues that I've been obsessed with for some time now, rather I need to get information out of him. He has always lived by the sea, started to meditate ten months ago, lived a year in Berlin, and has just returned from overseas. He is saving because he wants to travel more, likes vegetables and organic food, plays several instruments, and I can be the best version of myself with him, reaching a level of happiness and cosmic connection as I had never felt it before. I am very interested in his way of being—he is very different, mysterious even. I was fascinated to be with him and I want to see him very soon. Today during the day I haven't stopped thinking about him, how incredible our encounter and the magical moments, the beauty created between the two. Nothing physical happened between us, only, in the end, we said goodbye with a very strong hug.

Today I have been with inner tranquility. I don't want to go very far but I feel my soul wanting to be with his. My attraction towards him manifests in that plane. Jared yesterday transported me really high—it was a deeply spiritual experience. Many people say that regarding love, you can know it from the beginning, and now in my head, in my heart, they are telling me: *it's him.*

28 October 2013

It's been a week since my last writing and several cosmic adjustments. I left Sheryn's house on Thursday. Here's the reason: I ruined her blender by putting very thick beans, she told me to use some water, and I did; however, I broke it. The next day I wake up and find a letter from her, not only had she taken $135 from my security deposit, but she exposed to the smallest detail my behavior in a very disrespectful way, making me feel like the worst possible guest. That day I went to the hostel and I showed my friends her letter, many laughed at the exaggeration. I wanted to leave. I didn't feel comfortable with it. That night I returned to my room and being there I thought of staying, finally, it would be another week. In the morning, I received another letter from her, asking me to put the $135 of the blender to leave the security deposit at $250. She made me really mad and I wrote asking for my money back, I would leave tomorrow. I left the house without knowing her answer, had been absent for several days, and we had not been able to see each other. A few hours later, she left me a voice message telling me that she agreed with my departure, and she would return the money. That day I took care of packing my bags and organizing. I spoke with Mia, the lady from the second house where I would move on November 4. I explained the situation and asked her permission to leave some belongings with her, that way I would go lighter to the hostel. I was very happy to return to the Backpackers. My friends live there, and I always went anyway.

On Thursday while I was at work, I received a message from Mia. She had decided to give the room to someone else because she was not comfortable with my recent experience at Sheryn's house. In a way, I felt bad, but on the other hand, I felt free. That house is full of rules too. There I thought I needed something more relaxed, without being chaotic either. The cosmos is making some adjustments; I didn't belong to Sheryn's house or Mia's. Now I had to look for something else. Deep down I know, I'll find something perfect for me; something better will come.

Now I am in the hostel, a few days are fine but I'm already focused on finding something. I finally think I'm managing to overcome this place. My new friend from work Andrea is very right. She hates hostels because most backpackers lack brain, young people of many nationalities but to date, I haven't found anyone like me. The other day, I decided to go on my own to the surf festival, I met Andrea there. We stayed together the afternoon and night. We are exactly in the same frequency, we are both vegetarian, we meditate, surf, love spiritual themes, and we get along perfectly. We talked for hours. She is 20 years old and she is Austrian. She grew up on an organic farm, I am happy to have found her. For that reason, I think I can overcome the hostel. Now with Andrea in my life, I will have more plans out of here, meeting local and interesting people.

Another important event happened yesterday: Jared. I had a magical day with him. He picked me up in the morning. The plan was to go surfing to some beaches, so we went in search of a less crowded place and drove for about an hour. We arrived at the beach but the waves looked big with very strong wind; therefore, we decided to go swimming in the river in front. We took the boards out and enjoyed quiet water. After that, he took me to a small waterfall; on the way, we stopped at a farm to buy vegetables and fruits. I was happy; with 10 dollars I bought food for the whole week. Going to the waterfall, we stopped at another river where he wanted to take pictures. He took down his skateboard and started to skate. I loved his style. We spent a lot of time in the car, happy; I love the road trip and so does he. In the waterfall, I read to him a project I made that would mix yoga with photography, showing the beauty of nature, health, and love, and we could make money. I was very nervous because when I write, I am totally honest and he could be frightened of my unconventional ideas. However, he liked it. It's amazing to feel that we're on the same frequency. We have too much in common and above all, he is naturally cool. What I have been interested in for over a year is not new to him. I loved to know that when he lived in Berlin, he was a vegetarian, his friends there were vegans, he loves vegetables, and he says he knows how to cook. Not only he is wonderful, but what is created between the two of us is very special; it's just natural and fresh. Sometimes we can be quiet without being uncomfortable. I like to stop and listen to the sound of the wind or the water running, and so does he. Again he carried me very high, I believe he was the same.

In the waterfall, he took pictures of me doing yoga and ballet poses. We had the afternoon sunlight directly towards us, absorbing the last rays of the day. After that, we went back to Byron. We had eaten bananas, peaches, fresh whole wheat bread, organic honey, and croissants during the day. I didn't bring anything to eat; it was all from him. At night we were hungry, so we ate some falafels sponsored by him, after that, I bought a bottle of wine. We met a friend of mine and went to enjoy live music on the street—had a great time. The alcohol helped us to break the distance and tension between us. Slowly we began to hug more and he gave me a couple of kisses on the cheek. I was too nervous, taking that step was something very serious for me. It meant the beginning of a love relationship, but that perfect and fluid connection between us was telling me to move on. After the music, my friend went to his house and we went to the beach, we chose to sit on some rocks and stare at the dark ocean. For at least ten minutes, he hugged me and caressed my back, while in silence I concentrated on the sound of the wind and the waves. Then I decided to turn my face and we started kissing. It was beautiful and perfect, his lips soft and smooth. With that we finally broke that barrier, now we are together. I want to see him and be with him. I think he does too; we belong to each other.

For the moment, these were the most important events of the week; leaving Sheryn's house and losing my room with Mia, meeting Andrea and having an incredible day with her, overcoming the hostel, and starting something very special with Jared. These days I am going to look for a room. I hope that I can move next week. When I find my space, I will start my yoga project.

5 November 2013

Today was an intense family day. First I talked to my sister and I explained my intentions in decreasing my internet consumption, only once a week. Later, I talked to my parents and they didn't like the idea. I was chatting with my mom and ended up rather in a discussion. I recognized that my selfish behavior is not very empathetic with my family's situation. However, I am in Australia, and I need more and more to detach myself from Mexico and concentrate on my life here, but my parents want to know about me every third day and that's not going to be possible. On Friday, I leave the hostel, later I will talk about it. When I move I want a vegan with eggs diet, I also want to spend as little as possible and live with the minimum. Every day I want to dedicate myself to my activities; yoga, surfing, meditation, eating healthy, and writing a diary by hand, with poetry and more freedom, not linear as I do now. I am also going to buy a dictionary in English and explore the language by studying regularly. The house where I'm going to move has no Internet, and at the hostel, it costs me $5 for four hours with a margin use of two days. My expenses should be minimal, nothing in alcohol, only organic and natural food; nuts, grains, seeds, vegetables, and fruits. I will not eat out ever. I will bring my food with me. For the moment, I work two days in the kitchen and with that, I pay my rent and I have some extra dollars. I want to survive with the minimum. My parents asked me to go to an Internet cafe and ask for Wi-Fi, but I do not want to spend on coffee or drinks. I will not incur expenses.

    I thought the chrysalis of my trip was over, but soon it will become a new and deeper one, many changes to come. First, I found a house with some Australian girls. One of them has a vegan diet with eggs, the other is not so intense with food. They both surf and I got along perfectly with them. I'm happy to move to a more relaxed place where I can have a good time. On Friday I move, and that's where I'm going to start with my new adventures. Another thing, I just broke my flip-flops so I'll walk barefoot all the time. This is how I will start something pretty intense. The hardest part will be food, giving up many desserts in order to lighten my body, thereby reaching higher levels of consciousness.

    On the other hand, on Saturday and Sunday, I was with Jared. I love being with him and he understands me really well. I can talk about spiritual, social, philosophical issues. I can explain my mind; we enjoy each other's company so much. This weekend he took me to a very Australian party in a town on the Gold Coast, and then we went home and listened to tasteful music in his vintage stereo. On Sunday, we had some mangoes and he cooked an omelet with spinach and delicious tomatoes.

Then we went to a huge market of second-hand items, later we went to two beaches. On the second, we ate watermelon, bananas, strawberries with organic honey, and a pear. In the evening, we went to his house to enjoy the pool, then to a restaurant of Moroccan food where we ordered two marinated tofu kebabs. Again I had a great time with him; we like to do the same, we like the same food, music, and he takes me exploring around Australia. He is lovely and treats me like a princess.

From the beginning I was right about Jared, now something is born with him. We started talking about future plans together, like going to Melbourne with his friends. Soon we are going to go to his uncle's farm. There we have a project; we are going to take his old typewriter, a canvas and some paintings, his camera and we are going to write and make art together. When I'm with him I feel an inspiration and a connection with nature as I have never felt before. That is why I want to start new writings, more poetry.

That is basically my situation at the moment. My family in Mexico is having a bad time, but I can't do too much about it, just to continue with my life here. My relationship with Jared is very good, makes me very happy, and inspires me artistically. On Friday, I will go with the girls and start my new diet.

6 November 2013

These days have been a nightmare. After my wonderful times with Jared, my situation went down. On Monday, I had a sore throat throughout the day; yesterday I started with the disease, and today I officially have one of those very strong flu. Sure, I'm being very dramatic when I say nightmare, but for the fantasy world where I live, this has been a bit heavy. The hostel is fully booked. I took my suitcase out of the room and now I am waiting for some cancellation to have a bed. This place has become impossible. The kitchen is always full and dirty by so many people. It's difficult to find a place in the refrigerator. In the television room now my friends sleep due to the full booking in the hostel, my things are spread everywhere.

They are around the pool, in the cellar, in bags, and boxes; I have an urge to move. At the same time, I like to be in this situation, so when I leave I will be really happy and satisfied.

My family situation, this flu so strong, and not having room to sleep in is enough to deal with. If I don't find a bed, I will ask my friend Andrea. On the other hand, this situation led me to something interesting. Yesterday, I felt a huge need to buy a notebook to draw and write poetry. Strongly influenced by Jared, when we are together we talk about deep subjects and he makes me feel artistic. Now a strong desire to write more freely and express myself has arisen. Never before I have enjoyed painting. I hated the aesthetics of my drawings, and I didn't have the patience for it. However, yesterday, I bought a beautiful notebook with white sheets and lined pages to write. Coming out of the store, I was heading back to the hostel when I heard a band playing in the street that caught my attention. I stopped and sat down at a table from a cafe, hoping that no one would say anything. I sat down to write and draw; first, there were some color shapes, then I drew a tree with several green leaves. I enjoyed live music by connecting with an abandoned form of expression from childhood.

I realized the importance of artistic expression; the main problem was the judgment I had about my drawings. I didn't consider them good enough, and that's why I closed myself from the world of painting. However, yesterday I learned that when we remove that prejudice and simply let ourselves go, we can find the magic in drawing, discovering our own art. I believe that creations are not beautiful or ugly—they simply *are*, they are perfect because they come from us. It's our art and it doesn't belong to anyone else. My three drawings yesterday were totally therapeutic; after them I felt much better, helping me deal with my family situation. I was fascinated to discover drawing again; in the end, I felt proud and I loved looking at them. I discovered that I like to draw shapes and colors, more abstract art. Drawing is a form of meditation too. It requires great concentration and contact with our inner creativity to express our soul.

Despite having a few complicated days, this is probably the last and biggest transformation of my trip. I am in that transitory stage and soon I will be where I have always wanted and I will free my soul. Now I began to feel, with these new needs of artistic expression, that total well-being is about to come. This book is also about to be concluded, the end could come in my next writing. For the moment I will see where I will sleep and endure these last days of discomfort and nomadism, the weekend I am going to see Jared obviously.

8 November 2013

I finally moved out of the hostel. I'm completely settled in my room. I arrived and my future roomies were going to have dinner at a bar in Byron. I decided to go with them, we came back early.

Today at the hostel I had a feeling of nostalgia. I would go back but it would not be the same, not like when I went to Sheryn's house. I felt a new beginning in my life; I saw a new chapter. The hostel had made me very happy but it was time to turn the page. I said goodbye to my friends differently. When I went to Sheryn's house, my friend Jakob took me, I left my belongings and I went back to the hostel directly. This time I took a big taxi and I put up my bike and my surfboard. I probably will return on Monday to use my weekly Internet time, though I won't remain much time there. At first, I could spend hours talking to people or just hanging out. This last week I was bored, so I started to draw, read, or did any other activities on my own.

My new home is fine. My only complaint is that it's on a busy street where I can hear the cars passing by. At some point, the brain learns to disconnect from those external noises, but for now, it's a little strange. I have a garden where I can practice yoga at any time without feeling a hostel watching me, which somehow limited me in my practice. Here I can do it however I want to. On the other hand, the beach is a walking distance from my house, then I will not need to go to the Backpackers to surf. Here I can do the activities of my pleasure without disturbance. Today I bought a dictionary in English and a notebook to write words and invent stories or phrases to learn how to use them. Besides that, I want to draw and write more poetry, not forgetting the food transition.

I'm very happy because I'll probably have another day in the kitchen in a couple of weeks. Today I earned 250 dollars because yesterday I worked eight hours and today six, with that I can pay my rent and live the week. If I get another day, I can have a quiet life without worries and without touching my money, even saving. My friend Andrea announced her next return to Austria; with these movements and the high season I'm sure my boss is going to need more help. I offered to work more. I'm happy in there. Living in Byron Bay, the beloved beach of Australia, and saving money working in a great place to travel more, sounds the best plan in the world. Maybe at some point, I'll have that. I've worked hard to earn my place in the kitchen. Bernie the owner has seen my good intentions. Let's see where it leads me.

I am delighted to be in a more local environment, working with Australians, living with three Australian girls, and going out with an Australian guy. Knowing a country requires much more than visiting it—it requires getting into the culture. I felt that at the hostel, it's amazing to meet people of many nationalities, but now I want to know more about this country and its people, a higher level of travel, more profound, and enriching. Every day I saw travellers coming and going from the hostel, despite not knowing Australia, I feel that I travel better staying in one place. I'm starting to make friends and form relationships. People in hostels have the same talk always. At first, it seemed fascinating, but at one point I didn't even talk to people, only my friends. The talks turn around 'Where are you from? How long you've been in Australia? Where you're going after here?' When you have to repeat the same thing every time, it's not so fun anymore. When you form a friendship you can look for deeper levels of talk, like with Andrea the other day. It was very interesting, now I'm going to start that stage of spending more time with local people.

Conclusions

In this book, I wanted to share through my experience how I lived this long journey with the New Age philosophies. Following these teachings has led me to find a truer path, with happiness and inner peace. I can now say that I have achieved a life in harmony with the will of my Higher Self, where I can achieve self-realization and fulfill my destiny. I believe that if individuals want to achieve this, first they need to realize and understand that being unhappy is not normal, many suffer from it but that shouldn't be so. Then comes the desire to change. To know where to go is necessary a process of internalization, meditation is crucial along with solitude; this because society corrupts our true desires and aspirations. The goal is to move away from it, its fears and pressures, to discover who we are and what we want. Once given the step to the internal search, comes the connection with the instinct or the intuition, to begin to act, of course always in peace and tranquility—there should never be stress. Here comes the most complicated stage, where fears, doubts, and obstacles happen and that is totally normal. At that stage we must be strong and move forward, trust a 100 percent, trust in God, in the Universe, have faith, and keep fighting. Our dreams are our true happiness and we must follow them.

As I write this I feel a bit confused. I had never experienced anything like this. After a long time of searching, of wanting freedom more than anything in this world, of having that internal restlessness inhibiting peace and tranquility; that has completely disappeared. On this trip I was always looking for something—a job, a place to live, a bicycle, a surfboard, a guy, hating France, and wanting to come to Australia—there was always something to achieve. Now that's over. I have absolutely everything I want and have long wanted. I followed my dreams. I came to Australia and I have found peace and total satisfaction with my life. Now I just have to enjoy myself, get up in the morning, and decide if I want to paint or go surfing if I'm going to have some fruit or oatmeal if I feel like writing a poem or doing some yoga. Besides that, I have to go to the best job possible, where I will spend incredible time cooking, listening to music, and talking about multiple topics, fun, and paid learning. I live in a house with beautiful girls. I have a garden where I can do yoga or any other activity. I go out with a super incredible guy who takes me around Australia and inspires me artistically. I live on the beach. I cannot wish for anything else in these moments.

To liberate the soul is to reach that moment of total satisfaction and fulfillment, to live the present by trusting in a perfect future, to free oneself from any worry or stress, to live in the here and now. Freeing the soul is surrendering to love; to love yourself first, then to love your life, to be *love* from morning till night. To *free the soul* is to smile from the heart, simply to be and to let it be. To free the soul is living in a healthy body, therefore in healthy relationships and healthy environments. To free the soul is simply being you.

Now begins my life as a free soul, a new chapter, a new beginning, a birth in the awakened life. I am 23 years old and everything ahead of me, this trip has taught me more than I ever imagined. From now on I fully trust in my intuition. I have left behind any stress or fear of the unknown. If my inner voice tells me to do so I go for it. The Universe will guide me through my intuition to assist me in forming my path. I blindly trust to always receive what is necessary to be well and to be happy.

Today, I am a free soul and I have the life of my dreams . . .

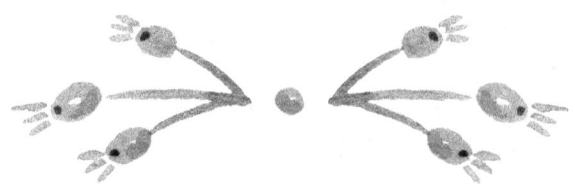

PART THREE

Becoming A Free Soul

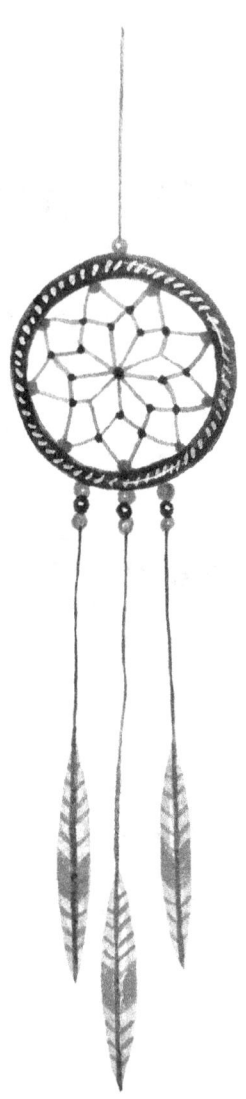

After reading the end of the last part, you might think about my title 'Becoming a free soul? But that's what you did before on the journey!' And I will answer, now the voice of 30-year-old Natalie has taken place, and let's say, that becoming a free soul needed much more than an unplanned adventure to the unknown. Much has happened since the beginning of this path, great lessons but I now believe we need to take spirituality with precaution. The objective of my book for years was to demonstrate that following the spiritual path was the ultimate way (and pretty much the only one) to acquire true happiness and peace. After the rollercoaster I put myself into, I'm not sure any more about its viability. The truth as well is that we are now in a global economic recession caused by the coronavirus pandemic, which might mark the end of an era and the beginning of a new one. So maybe this way of proceeding will make more sense in a futuristic world. The fact is that I was rebellious and opposed to the system, and the system didn't like me either. I'm now 30 years old and I never really knew how to make money, so that is one of the dangers we find navigating through this path. With this said, in the third part of my book, I want to share my experience these last years, hoping to give another perspective to this way of living. Talking about the good and bad, to stop false promises, something really characteristic of the New Age industry.

My life has become a butterfly effect, of that little idea that came to me while I was driving through the state of Jalisco. Since then, everything has been a journey that hasn't stopped. Sometimes I wake up here in Canadian wilderness with my caveman boyfriend and wonder how I got to this point. With this said, I want to share one of my favorite quotes in life, something that marked me since I was a teenager, and it's by Samuel Taylor Coleridge:

What if you slept . . .

What if you slept
And what if
In your sleep
You dreamed
And what if
In your dream
You went to heaven
And there plucked a strange and beautiful flower
And what if
When you awoke
You had that flower in your hand
Ah, what then?

The spiritual awakening of 2012

Almost eight years from this point of my life (April 2020), was when I decided to stop eating red meat, fell in love with yoga, decided to become a teacher, and learned how to meditate. I was one semester away from finishing University, and I started to feel like everything was a dream. That time I received my first message from intuition, indicating me to made to go to Australia.

Also around October, in a very spiritual way, the name of my book came to life. I was in Oaxaca City with my sister, my mother, and my grandmother. We were wandering around, exploring, and suddenly we found an art exhibition in a very abandoned construction; so old that plants grew over the bricks. I absolutely loved the place, I vibrated with it, I was so happy and enjoying every single detail, I took photos and kept exploring further. The last room had a wall full of little papers and writings from visitors. The instruction was to write about something that would make the world better. Some papers wanted a world with clean water, others the eradication of hunger and poverty, also equality in humans, and so on. I studied Political Science, and of course, I wanted to write something down. So I took the little paper and a pencil, and that's when a very strange force made me write *Viajar para Liberar el Alma* (Travel to Free the Soul). It was an idea that my mind didn't process instantly. I just knew I needed to write something, but that came out of a place that I didn't even understand. I thought I would write something related to my political ideals, like 'public policy to protect Mother Nature' or similar declarations. Instead, I wrote something so strange that I just couldn't get it.

When I read the words, I was so amazed that my body felt an intense electric field all around me; never before had I experienced anything like that. At the same time, I didn't understand at all what it meant, and I kept thinking about it all day. I loved the way it sounded, the way it rolled with the tongue, but the concept was beyond my understanding. So I let it go and moved on with my life. A few months later, I connected the dots, and I understood that I needed to write a book, and that would be the title for it.

Deciding that year to stop consuming red meat and begin meditation, was the most important step for this path. It helped me open the door to my intuition, and I began tracing my life towards what I felt right in my heart. I could've chosen to have a normal life. I could've decided to not listen to my intuition and continue the life of parties, meats, junk food, coffee, and other substances. Now I know that if I didn't choose the path of my soul, a possible life scenario would've been in Mexico City, with an office job, being extremely miserable trying to compensate my depression with money, short travels, clothes, and parties.

Now I am so grateful for the decision to be different, and pursue a life that felt right for me. Not following what they told me, and instead aim to create my own beliefs with my experiences, was the best decision I could take. So that seed in my consciousness that made me leave, was the first step for everything; for this book, for travelling the world, for finding myself.

2013: Travel, travel, and more travel

Since the first days of January 2013, I started to travel. I went to Sayulita for three months, then I came back to the city for two months, and then I started the spiritual journey to go to Australia. Doing the translation of my book was fun to go back to 23-year-old Natalie and see my qualities, mistakes, and lessons during the journey. I was very impressed to see the way I moved through life with a positive mentality and active towards my goals. I admired my courage to deal with extremely difficult situations (like being homeless at the time of my dad's accident). I was always thinking positive and trusting in the Universe. At the same time, Natalie in Byron Bay was very immature and naïve, thinking that she could invent a project in two seconds and that she could make a living straight away. I don't know at which moment I thought I could be a yoga teacher (without a title, as I didn't conclude my course) and that I would be able to pay rent and eat doing that for living. So now I go to the last months of 2013, just after I finished writing the second part of my book.

When I concluded the writings, I thought I was a free soul because of that momentary feeling of freedom I had. I was healthy, flowing incredible, in love with Jared, and concluded a dream of mine that was to be in Australia. I was feeling light, connected, and better than never before in life, but of course that didn't last for long.

I remained in that state of perfection for another two weeks, meditating before dawn, constantly living adventures. I kept working in my dream job and was doing everything right. That—until reality started to hit. I lost my job in the kitchen because the season was getting really high and we had many orders of pies. The rhythm became insane and I just couldn't deal with it. As I didn't want to get another job doing something I didn't like, I thought I could do yoga classes with donations and somehow make it work. I tried for a few weeks in the garden of a music shop. It was summer so the hot days made the classes only possible at dawn. So at six in the morning, I was teaching. My friend Andrea came a few times. I think the largest group I had was three people, many times it was only me there. That time I decided to pay for my room for one month, that until 20 December. I wanted to focus on my projects and not worry about rent. And so I did. I tried to start something called 'Yoga of the Heart' and put some ads around, opening a space of sharing, and talking about spiritual and sustainable matters in my house. But no one ever came (having a house far from town didn't help). Also, I opened a blog that still exists and you can find it, dreamingawakebyron2.tumblr.com. I was trying really hard to make my life work. One time even, I tried to sell vegan chocolates in the streets to make money. First I thought it would be the best business, but the next day I hated it and finished by giving them all away in the park.

My feet that time were far from touching the ground. My financial world was a disaster, but somehow I enjoyed living like a hippie, eating oats, and testing my luck without money. On the other side, my love life was going incredible. Jared and I were spending more and more time together, truly falling for each other. So then I decided to rent my room for a month, and go with Jared for the end of the year celebrations (including my birthday) and travel to Melbourne in January. I wanted to see if we were compatible. I felt as well that I needed to have more time with him. Our separations at the end of the weekend were starting to affect me. I struggled to be without him.

And that's how I finished an incredible year of travelling, feeling very blessed and satisfied with all the adventures I had lived.

Endings, movements, and beginnings in 2014

Jared and I went on a road trip to Melbourne, 1800 kilometers south. We stopped many times in his friends' and family's houses and had an incredible time. We realized then that we were great together. We didn't fight and everything was a perfect flow between us. For that reason, I decided to permanently leave Byron and move with him to a farm in Duranbah. He lived then in a beautiful secluded large unit in the middle of nothing; greens, cows, and a little lake surrounded us. He was working in construction every day, and I would stay alone at home. Having a lot of time, I decided that it was the perfect moment to start my book's edition. All my writings were made as I travelled by, and I didn't have much time to re-read and correct them. So I had to put everything together and work on my book. Also, I became a perfect housewife, and I spent much of my time cooking, cleaning, and organizing the place. The only thing I wanted was to receive my love and go surfing in the afternoons. As Jared was the breadwinner, I had to pay back somehow. So I took care of him, making his smoothies for the morning, and the lunch box for work. For him, I wasn't much of a financial charge—all my clothes were less than a dollar and I ate vegetarian super cheap. The rent was only 180 dollars a week, and he was making good money in his construction work.

I can't say it was easy; the solitude on the farm was very challenging. I felt trapped in many moments, and I didn't even have a good Internet connection to navigate the web freely. All the time was to be with myself, and I tried not to lose my mind. After the social times, and the freedom of being in Byron, becoming separated from the world was a big change for me. But as always, my projects kept me going and having my book gave me a good reason to be there. Also, I tried to start something called 'Trees Hangin' Out in the Sunshine' with Jared because life on the farm was highly artistic. We had a full musical set up, with a microphone, guitar, drums, and a keyboard, and we did many jams together. Also, we had an area for painting, so we really enjoyed that part of it. With this project, we wanted to share our life as an artistic couple living on a farm. That's how I managed to survive the intense solitude that lasted for three months. At the end of March, we moved to the beach.

The farm studio belonged to Jared's uncle, but when he decided to sell the property we had to leave. Jared wanted a beach shack, and with incredible cosmic luck, we got what he asked for. His friend Lucie was in India, and her place was available for rent. A very small and charming shack located in Fingal Head, 300 meters away from the beach. It was a big change to move from a large space to a 20-square-meter place. The kitchen was so small and basically everything in there. The incredible part was the proximity to the beach. Practically we just had to walk through the bush in front of us, and we would get there. It was very magical, and at night we could hear the ocean from the bed before falling asleep. Also, we had access to Lucie's car and that gave me the freedom to get out.

Jar and I had flight tickets booked to go to Nepal at the end of June, so I wanted to get a job, save as much as possible, and go on an adventure together. That's how I started to look for a job like a mad person. I went to every place in Kingscliff, spent hours on Gumtree (an Australian website), and directed my energy towards it. Nothing was popping up and I started to feel very frustrated. My book was edited, and I didn't have anything else to do. I was starting to feel bored and very lonely. I didn't have many friends and I started to miss family and friends in Mexico.

Luck came to me, and I found a job as a waitress, thanks to my friend Hayley. I would get paid 25 dollars an hour and I was really excited. But that night, I had a talk with my family, and I realized that the situation over there was pretty critical. My father was really struggling with his leg and about to have another operation. My sister and my mom couldn't focus on their personal lives because of it. So I went to the beach after the conversation. I wanted some time to put my head around the issue, that's when a strong feeling arose and indicated me to go back to Mexico.

It was really hard to tell my decision to Jared. Although our plan after Nepal and India was to go to Mexico, the change was pretty dramatic. I always talked about how amazing my country was, and all the beautiful places that I would take him to, so maybe somehow I implanted that idea in his mind. At first, he was really sad and confused. He thought I was leaving him, but then he saw the positive side of it and decided to follow me and go on an adventure to my country.

And that's how on 6 April 2014, I flew back to Mexico City. My role in the family was pretty clear since my arrival, going every day to the family business, and spending time with my dad. He needed to recover from his operations and come back to normal. This was a really good opportunity for me. He was paying me and the work was very little. I had a lot of time for myself and for my projects.

I was really excited to start Mexiro again. I tried to contact my partners and share some great ideas to generate money for the organization. Little by little, and by gathering information from different sources, I realized that my partners kicked me out of the project, took my role as President, and basically excluded me from the Board. It was really horrible to know that. I felt so betrayed and I couldn't believe that they took my baby project away from me. At some point, I thought about suing them, but my new spiritual knowledge made me accept the new reality and move on with my life.

After that, I joined another project that was called Ahó, a new label that would include Huichol art in modern clothing pieces. Four guys from my university formed it, and we started to sell some shirts. I was really excited because I knew a lot about the culture (something that I was studying in Sayulita with Leticia). I imagined a life between the city and the rural communities. It was time to build my future and that was perfect for me. I decided to invest some money in it, and I kept working until everything started to fall apart. The guys were very lazy and disorganized, and the money I invested in disappeared. It was a really bad idea I had, again, handling my heart to a spiritual/professional project and getting bitterly disappointed.

Aside from that, Jared would arrive in June, and I had to get an apartment. So I started my search and found the perfect place for us in the center of the city. I was well paid by my dad, so I had no problems with anything. We made the contracts, paid the deposit, and I started to furnish my first romantic apartment in the city. I was moving out of my house and it was a big step for me. Also, it became the perfect family gossip; for some of them, it was even outrageous that I would live with a boyfriend without being married. My parents supported me and were really excited to meet him.

Jared arrived in June and that's how we started a life together in Mexico. He joined a Spanish school and went every day. Meanwhile, I was working with my father. And because I was making decent money, I became the breadwinner of the family and enjoyed a life between travels and everyday city matters. In our apartment, we had an extra room on the last floor of the building. At first, I thought it could be a dark room for Jared's photography, but life took us to a new direction, and we transformed it into a vintage shop. Our passion for clothing and vintage findings materialized in a project that started to work pretty well. Since the beginning I loved it, our slogan was 'Be Free, Be Unique, Be Sustainable', combining my ideals into a way of dressing that didn't hurt the environment. We found bazaars in the city, and with photography, I started to model the clothes and advertise them through Instagram. At the same time, we started a travel project called '83 Pueblos Mágicos' (83 Magic Towns), the objective was to visit the magic towns of Mexico; and through my writings and Jared's beautiful photography, promote tourism in these amazing little towns that have a lot to offer. We made a beautiful website and started the countdown. We were travelling regularly, combining our time between shooting fashion photos for the JOS brand and creating material for '83 Pueblos Mágicos'. It was the perfect lifestyle, I wanted that to work out and make a sustainable living from it.

I stopped working with my dad around November that year, and by then we had many bazaars, so the JOS shop managed to pay for our bills. December was excellent for us, and for that reason, we went on a road trip at the end of the year to the south of Mexico. It was a good year, many changes and beginnings and we were financially stable, which allowed us to focus on our creative projects.

Instability, financial crises, failed political career, a really hard 2015

Jared and I started the year travelling in the southeast part of Mexico, a photographic journey where we visited five magic towns and the Mayan Riviera. Despite camping, cooking, and trying to spend as little as possible, we went over the budget we had reserved for the trip. After that we came back to the city without jobs, having the clothing business really slow. We basically ran out of resources, so Jared decided to go back home and work in construction again.

He left in March, and without him, I couldn't go to bazaars and carry all the clothes by myself. Now that I think about it, I have some sort of blank for that period. The only thing I remember doing was starting my blog and making some videos for YouTube. Of course, the family pressure started to hit, and I needed to find a job. I knew I didn't want to work in an office, at the same time I had no idea what else I could do with my life. So my plan was to sell the Magic Towns project to the government or try to get some sponsors. Back then we had a really good website, and I thought it was the only thing I could do. I needed something related to travelling or tourism. I couldn't remain in the city forever.

Once I made my cosmic intention of finding a job clear, it didn't take me long to find something. I went to the presentation of a book that one of my teachers from the university invited me to, and there I met Piero Leone, son of a famous politician in Mexico. My teacher introduced me to him. I thought he was very arrogant, but soon we started to talk. He also had a degree in Political Science from the Universidad Iberamericana, but was older so I never met him before. I told him that I was looking for a job, and after some talks, he invited me to his office located in the trendy area of the city, neighborhood Condesa. In between talks, he asked me how much money I wanted, and I said the same number that I was making with my dad; he was quite surprised with the amount, so he offered less and I accepted.

Just like that, I had a job, with one of the small political parties that never get enough votes to win anything, serving only to take money from the government, to have a bunch of people playing internal games of power. My job was without a contract, without a schedule or anything planned. The only thing I needed to do was to stick around and find my own place. Times were intense, as Piero was running for the Presidency of one of the municipalities of the city. So I took the role of social media and basically became the personal companion of Piero. I would go anywhere with him. I did the campaign with his political party for over two months. I got paid well but after that, everything started to fall.

Piero is a very intelligent person, but he is also bipolar and has many neurological problems. So after the election around June, where of course we didn't get anywhere, not even to maintain the registration of the political party, he went on a depression. My work became so strange, sometimes I would spend time in his house, sometimes we would go to different meetings, sometimes we stayed in the office, and he would get drunk talking about politics for hours. Everything was games all the time; conspiracy theories, alliances, between numbers and statistics, everything to gain power. For me, it was extremely interesting. I was living the reality of what I studied, but my work was very strange. The only times that Piero asked me to do some computer work, I wouldn't do it right, I was not going to the office unless he was there, as no one else would give me any directions. Also at least twice a week, he would stay at home in a state of depression.

The money situation was getting wore every time. After the election and with the terrible results of the Party in the city, less money would circulate in the office. Everything was strange. He would always get cash from different sources, and many times he paid people with his own salary and then remained without anything for over ten days, until the next payment. He was the big boss, everyone around him, a personal driver, an entire office for him, but he was so unstable, that everything was really impractical.

I started my own project inside. I would do the new social communication for the Party, and because Piero and his dad were very oriented to sustainability (something that I really liked since the beginning), I thought it was perfect for me. He basically forced me to do a massive document to explain my reasons and procedures. He made me put data and statistics; I had to demonstrate my role there. With that, we would go with the President of the Party and open myself a place in it.

Everything was a game, and so was the money for me—if I wanted to work there, I had to earn it. Piero kept a promise that I would get a job, so I found myself basically forcing him and doing dramas to get paid, and always at the last minute, he would give me something. Also, we had an ideological battle because he tried to lock me in the office, and reproaching the times I was not going there, but I just couldn't do it. I never stayed there, always trying to make him understand my freedom needs. The whole thing was really messed up.

When Jared arrived, after four months of separation, I was really immersed in the political game, and that caused so much trouble in the relationship. Soon he started to hate Piero, and basically hated everything related to my job. At the same time, part of my communication strategy was to use the beautiful photos of Jared, in order to get sponsored and go travelling around, doing videos, and the cool things I wanted. I thought I had a good opportunity there. I thought I could show my work to the President and make him support a trendy, new way of communicating politics. I could do what I love; travel around, and promote sustainability, with a direct impact that could go straight to Congress. This was my only chance in politics. I couldn't work in any other Party or anywhere else. I thought that through Piero, I could have the freedom I wanted, so I kept fighting for it until the end.

I spent the rest of the year on it, all the time between games, trying to get what I wanted. I lied to myself and therefore to the people around me. I wanted to have faith because I trusted that Piero was going to get me the job. And every time was worse; I was receiving less money from him and the promises were collapsing. The whole thing was toxic, at the same time Jared was struggling in the city, with basically no work, dealing with being alone on the other side of the world. He doubted about me, about being in Mexico. The whole thing was really bad.

At the end of November, I decided to finish everything with Piero. I told him I had lost faith and basically demanded him to never speak to me again. After that, he begged for a last chance. He said he would arrange a meeting with the President, and I would take the proposal with me. And so it happened, I went with him and explained my project. I showed him some videos that my friend Pato and I made in Sayulita and all the photography I could do with Jared. He seemed to like it and he asked me how much money I wanted, and without saying much, he thanked me for coming and he moved on with his presidential activities. He said he would call in a few weeks, although that would be in the middle of December, not a good moment at all.

At the same time that all this was happening, my dad wanted an investment property and put Jared in the search. That's how he found something great located in the trendy center of the city, and as a family, we decided it was a good idea to proceed with the purchase. A little building, with a commercial area for rental in the bottom, and an apartment on top. It was old and deteriorated and needed a renovation. Despite that, we decided to take the project.

And that's how I finished my 2015, feeling lost, in between jobs, a year with four months of separation with Jared, and the weirdest work relationship with Piero. Little travels, the clothing business demanding and not very fruitful. At the same time, we had the property renovation project, and we still didn't know if the purchase would take place. Everything was papers, lawyers, complicated and confusing times. I was constantly battling between fears, trying to understand why my instincts pushed me into politics. I was giving the best of me to build the profession I wanted, but everything seemed to be stuck. I finished the year very unsatisfied. I will always remember it like one of the worst and darkest moments of my life.

2+0+1+6 = year of infinite possibilities, reconstruction of the self, and a family battle for freedom

The year started with confusion. I didn't know if I would get a job in politics or if we would buy the property, so my future was uncertain. Finally, after papers and lawyers, we managed to buy the place in the street of Marsella, and we started with the renovation process. As Jared worked in construction previously, my dad offered him a permanent job there, and soon I joined using my bossy skills to organize everyone and make sure the work was done properly. And that's how we got into a very demanding and hard job, spending most of our time inside a construction site; surrounded by dust, demolished structures, and unqualified builders. I basically had to survey every single thing in there, and soon I discovered some hidden talents as an architect.

The project was good, at least we were busy and we didn't have to worry about finances. The problem that year was the ideology conflict with my family. After having some conversations with my mom, my dad decided that Jared and I could keep the top floor apartment for ourselves; he gave us 'a gift'. It was the perfect reason to keep us in the city forever. He thought that after the renovation, Jared and I would get stable jobs and be happy together. They even said a few times that the second room was going to be for the baby! I was so angry with them, but at the same time, I had to keep some diplomacy. Jared and I thought about renting the room and going somewhere else. He was tired of Mexico City and wanted to leave. Things with my dad were lies under a smiling mask. He thought I would stay in the city, become a 'grown-up', and get an office job like everyone else. In my mind, I thought about liberating myself and going away from the smog and the concrete jungle.

Around the middle of the year, Jared got in contact with his ex-boss in the construction industry that told him about the new photographic studio he decided to open and invited him to work there. That's when we saw an amazing opportunity, and we decided to go to Australia. At the same time, we started to investigate about the visa situation for me and found more about the very tedious process that it was. We had to apply for a Partnership Visa that would cost 5,000 USD plus all the papers that we needed to gather. It looked practically impossible, but I thought about selling my car and saving as much as possible during the rest of the year. Also, I kept the subject hidden from my father.

We remained working in Marsella; at the same time, we moved from my apartment and decided to live in the construction site, between my parent's house and there, everything that we needed to do in order to save more money. The situation was definitely hard. Many times I had strong confrontations with my father; the rest was just diplomacy. Things back then were toxic, but we needed to continue with the process and finish the renovation. Also, I needed to find a tenant for the area downstairs. Time passed, and we managed to rent the place to a restaurant. Then we finished the last details, and by the end of August, we decided to break free on a soul journey to California.

Jared and I wanted and really needed to go away for some time. We spent seven months locked in the construction site, so we deserved the trip. I had to lie to my dad saying that

I would only go for a month, then come back and find a job. The reality was that we left and rented the room to a friend, and used the money to travel.

We left really organized, with camping gear and some hotels that sponsored our stay with the Magic Towns project. We left for the unknown, on an adventure; we wanted to go north and then come back when the time was right. Everything went great; of course like any other adventure, we had some ups and downs, but in the end, we got what we wanted: a liberating trip, where I wrote and Jared took many photos. It was a necessary escape from the routine and the toxicity of the dusty construction site and my family situation.

We came back by the end of November, three months in total. A few days later, Jared left for Australia while I stayed in the city with friends and family for the December celebrations—always a great time to be there. I had to organize the papers for the visa, clear my room, and do everything necessary before moving to Australia.

Going away was good for family crises. They managed to understand that my soul can't live imprisoned in the city and that my need for exploration and freedom was bigger than myself. In the end, they were supportive of my decision of going. They even helped me sell my car, and they let me keep the money to pay for my visa. At the end of the year, I was very satisfied. I made myself an architect, helped my dad with his investments, I created an apartment where my sister would live, and I could make some money renting my room. I had the money for my visa, just came back from a great road trip to California, and I had a new adventure coming up: Australia Part 2.

Spirituality in the city and about my book

As you may see, with the series of events during the two and half years that I spent in the city again, my life felt like a constant fight and struggle to define myself and to know which path to take. I had my family over my shoulders; doubts and fears about my future, and basically nothing clear. I had to put things together in order to understand the whole panorama.

Working in politics made me realize that despite having a degree in Political Science, I would never work in the Mexican government or any of its parties. The corruption was something unbearable, and I decided to step away for good. As well I knew that I needed to find a job that included travelling because the routine and the city life would finish by killing me, as well I had the vintage shop and that was something really important for me. Times were hard, a lot of confusion, but I kept utilizing my spiritual knowledge to listen to my inner guidance and follow my intuition all the time.

The spiritual growth became extremely slow, I kept meditating, but the city was not a place where I felt truly alive. I knew I was stuck in there for a reason, but I needed to find the exit. And that is the difference between a spiritual journey and being a free soul. I had an amazing experience and I got to the point I wanted, to be in Australia and connected to the Universe, but my reality wasn't solid enough, I had nothing grounding me and for that reason, I came back to the beginning. Everything was a constant ideological fight, with Piero, with my dad, and also with friends. I needed to find a normal job; that was the only way I could do my life. I didn't know if I would surrender if I would have to get an office job and forget about my dreams. Maybe I was wrong, and at the same time nothing was really flowing for me, so maybe they were right!

And now about my book, in 2014 and 2015 I started to do a deeper editorial work with two teachers and an editor. I wanted to self-publish and share my experiences with the world. So I did, and in March 2016 I published *Viajar para Liberar el Alma* as an e-book through Smashwords. I shared it by changing my profile picture on Facebook, and a couple of friends bought it. My father knew about my book and started to read it, and when he got into the part of the drugs, he stopped and it became a family crisis. He said to me that my book was insulting, and he forbade me to ever talk about it with any member of the family.

So that's how my biggest pride, and everything I loved, became this *shameful* thing that I could never talk about or share with anyone. I had my blog, my photos with Jared, but it was a family secret, and I couldn't say anything. Also, I always felt like a weirdo for believing in spirituality, having a vegetarian diet, and trying to build a life of freedom where I could be happy and fulfilled. I knew as well that I wouldn't stop fighting, and despite having everyone against me, I would go my own way.

Time for a soul rebirth, the 2017 transformational journey

So life opened an opportunity for me to leave the city, and try something new. I would go to Australia by the end of January, but basically, I had no idea what I was going to do. When people asked me about my future life, I answered that I would work with Jared in the photography studio and apply for my Partnership Visa. At the time I was reading Big Magic written by Elizabeth Gilbert, everything about creativity, so that's the only clue I had—create, create, and create.

I arrived in Australia on 27 January, was received by Jared, and went to his mother's house. Since the beginning everything was fast. He had a different rhythm and started to take me everywhere with him. I was his shadow and because I had no identity or anything else to do, I let myself go with the flow. A few weeks later, we managed to get out of Lesley's house, finding a very small unit in front of the beach. And that's how we started our life back in Australia, in front of the ocean, living in paradise.

In the beginning, everything was going amazing. I was making videos every week, taking photos of the beauty around, writing a few things in my blog (still in Spanish), working with Jared in the studio, and going out with his friends. The weather was incredible and I was so happy. I started to run every sunrise, went back to surfing, I was eating really healthy and feeling inspired again. Soon an important character came into our lives, John Barret, an experienced photographer that joined the team in the studio, and we started to do meetings every Monday. Somehow, more than talking about photography matters, those meetings became life coaching and professional orientation classes. He made us talk about our goals in life, we made deep business plans, and Jared and I started to see each other as different entities with different spiritual paths, together but following our own destinies. That's when I started to see my strengths, values, and I defined where I wanted to go. I made my blog in English and understood that the center of my communication was spirituality and sustainability, and everything had to move around that. My life started to make more sense, and I embraced the path I wanted for myself; writing, blogging, and modeling.

My blog turned around health at the beginning, and soon I began to write more about spiritual things, I started to write a few deeper texts on Instagram, and my parents reacted really well to it. I couldn't believe one time they called to congratulate me for something I wrote, my mom as well encouraged me to keep writing about astrology, saying that I was doing really good with it. I had a lot of time for myself, and little by little I stepped away from Jared's photography world, to discover more about astrology and spirituality. Constantly reading, watching videos, and nourishing my head with that information. My astrology posts started to be successful, and some friends were engaging with me, something that pushed me to do it more.

I was opening myself in the digital world, but with the society, I was still hiding my real passions and beliefs. Jared and I were constantly going out with his friends, and when they asked about what I was doing, I would never talk about my writings, and when I did share about my blog and asked 'what do you blog about?', I said it was about health. I was scared to say the word spirituality because most people in the Gold Coast are really close-minded. I got along with Jared's friends, but since the beginning, everything was really shallow and the talks were not satisfying at all, it was the same sensation than in Mexico, fakes smiles, and a feeling of being lonely and not understood.

One day, on 6 May to be exact, I got invited to the baby shower of one of the girls and even having a weird sensation of not belonging, I decided to go. There I found Ella, a girl that I met the first time in Australia, and now life had brought us together again. Since the beginning we created a bond, we started to talk about spirituality and sustainability, and basically, we stepped away from all the other girls in the party. I found a high vibe soul sister, and it was great. There, the political flame turned on again, and we decided to do something together, and only a week later, I had already created COW, 'Conscious Organized World'. I was really excited about it, and I wrote a blog post called 'Finding Ella and giving birth to COW'. Ella created a moon circle, and that would be the first activity of COW. I was really excited; it felt like my life was falling into place.

A few weeks after that, I started to notice that Jared and I were not invited to social gatherings anymore, and then I had a psychic revelation, that made me go back to the post I wrote when I found Ella. I couldn't believe what I read, I basically said that those girls cared about babies and marriages, and I was interested in astrology and spirituality. I wrote this because if I am where I am, it's because I have rejected most of the societies' structures and stigmas. It has been a challenge for me to become less critical, especially if I'm writing, something that I learned over time. In the first version of my book, I criticized Mexican society in every single aspect; superficiality, education, religion, and I exposed as much as I could. That blog post wasn't the first time that my words and unconventional ideas got me in trouble, although I knew that I wanted to change it. I realized that by focusing less on the bad and highlighting the bright side, I could gain more. There was no point in criticizing for pages the Mexican society and then being excluded from my family and friends. I believe now in diplomacy, and respect to everyone's opinions. My natural criticism towards society manifested in that blog post, and it got me in painful trouble. Basically what happened, is that one of the girls did a screenshot and sent it all around the group, creating tremendous gossip. This was one of the hardest things I have ever dealt with, the exclusion felt like a dagger in my heart, especially because that mistake took friends away from Jared. That event opened the door to a dark winter, where I had to go deep within my fears, and solve some issues I had towards friendship and society.

Since autumn, I wasn't excited with the idea of winter, my Mexican blood is not very good with cold weather, so I kept asking everywhere how winter was, even going online to find answers. I didn't want to go through it, and when the colder days of autumn arrived, I felt depressed and remained on the couch almost crying (actually I did cry a few times). My sunrise runs began impossible for me, I just couldn't face the cold, and I put so much resistance to surfing with a wetsuit. I knew I was being childish, but my mood was coming down, and it wasn't much I could do.

And that's how I got into a very hard, dark and deep June and July. I decided to stop my physical activities, and because we were no longer invited anywhere, our social life disappeared as well. I was alone, in a tiny apartment, and the most difficult for me; the 5 p.m. darkness. My psyche felt it so strong, adding my astrological winter (because my Sun is in Capricorn, opposite side), and the Cancer month (emotions, and more emotions). Again, I went into chrysalis phase, I became a cocoon, and focused in my inner world as deep as I could.

I mean not everything was darkness, I was still writing, creating contents, and studying astrology, but definitely, my world was my mind, my spirit and my apartment, I barely left the house. My relationship with Ella grew stronger, and we talked every day about our feelings, fears, inner progress, and realizations, we became therapy for each other. At the same time, through a friend of Jared, I got to know Belinda

Davidson, a psychic modern mystic and started to follow her teachings. I realized that my root chakra was destroyed and I needed to work energetically, as well I opened myself to be a 'shadow hunter' (more of Belinda's teachings) and decided to go deep into my darkness.

The exclusion of Jared's group of friends was hard for me, and again, it activated wounds from the past. So one dark day, I let myself go with my writings, and this is the beginning of it (originally in Spanish) 'What would it be, this sensation of a hole in my heart, that for some reason I can't seal. Society has hurt me many times, apart from my parents and sister, I feel forgotten within my family, I have lost so many friends, and the few left I don't combine with them. And now the recent exclusion from Jared's friends was the last thing, the most recent social disappointment'. As you can see, I started with a very broken heart, and I kept going, kept expressing those feelings. When I finished saying all the sadness, I decided that it was essential to accept my solitude; I wanted to find warmth within my heart. And I kept going, kept writing, at some point I said to myself that I loved my own company, that I loved my writings and studying astrology, that being alone was a blessing. And then a vision came: 'When I see within me, it is like if I immersed myself in Wonderland, the Garden of Eden, so much life, every cell working like Oompa Loompas, beautiful colors everywhere. When I am alone, a portal opens and I can penetrate that incredible world. I can be with my Oopma Loompas, walk through my garden full of flowers, a beautiful river that gives water and life to all the species. Is the most incredible place on Earth, where I feel at home, the garden of my dreams where I can run and feel free, I laugh, I open my arms and I act as weird as I want to. . . In the middle of this magical land, there is a desk, and over it, all my astrology books, an infinite source of knowledge that I desire to bring into my consciousness, is the most perfect desk and I feel so wonderful with it, writing for hours and hours if I want to. My inner world is so magical, and every time I come out of it I feel wondered and so happy. It's my favorite place in the world, it's home'.

And this is how I transmuted my deepest fear into the most beautiful source of light. Solitude has become such a marvelous thing for me, of course, challenging at times, but mostly rewarding. Basically, my biggest accomplishments in life have involved a great amount of solitude. That winter helped me get in contact with my most intimate self, and also understand the relation between light and darkness, to know that they work for the same goal. If we want more light in our lives, we need to face darkness first and resolve the lessons it contains.

That year was one of the most transformational times of my life, resolving so many aspects of it. One of them was curing my relationship with my dad, the distance created a bond between us, and he started to read my writings and support my way of living and thinking. On father's day, I wrote a letter to him titled 'La distancia que nos une' (the distance that brings us together), and it took so many emotions out, we both cried a lot, a very special and healing moment. It was a breaking point in our relationship, where we finally left that war aside and created a relationship of love and respect to each other. Another thing that I did, was releasing forever (in the lunar eclipse of 7 August) any shame I had towards showing myself as I am. There was no need to hide my interests and topics of my writings. I had assumed my role as a modern witch, and I felt proud of it.

2017 was the year that astrology came into my life, I took a course with Lee Coleman from Straight Woo called 'Very Luminary, Living la Vida Lunar' that started on the total solar eclipse in Leo (21 August), something that marked the following years. In October I went back to Mexico for a month, had an incredible time with friends and family, healed my heart from wounds, made new social connections with the same spiritual interests, and felt loved and accepted once again. My mother gave me books, a computer program and all the tools to undertake my astrologer profession. I started my first

YouTube videos and came back to Australia fully equipped. Astrology felt like a strange force that pushed me towards it, somehow inertia was taking me to that direction.

That year felt like a complete rebirth, the isolated winter made me travel so deep within myself, that I cured traumas and past wounds. Astrology was the light in my darkness, the only thing that kept me sane and going. I was so alone, so hurt, dealing with so many internal issues, that the only thing that helped me was the hope that the planets would get better, that a new moon cycle would change the current energy. I wanted to find an explanation and a guide in the process. I thought the answer was in the stars and for that reason, I spent so much time studying it. Winter that year was one of the hardest periods of my life, and at the same time, it was so beautiful because astrology was born. Because a seed can only germinate in the dark, right?

2018 - Living the millennial dream

My year began on a road trip to the north of Australia like a hippie again, camping everywhere and using as little money as possible. We had a great time, and both Jared and I agreed of pursuing the millennial dream of monetizing while travelling. We had to always do everything possible towards making that our reality. Coming back to the Gold Coast was a trauma for me, the idea of work was really painful, but the rent of 380 dollars per week needed a greater contribution from my part. The year before I began to look, but I could only find a temporary job selling Christmas trees that lasted for three weeks. I was happy to not be attached to something, that way I could go on a trip with Jared for New Years. Again "normal life" was something that caused a lot of rejection, but we needed money, and my Instagram posts about the stars were of course not brining much coin. So I moved energies like I've always done, and found a job in a furniture shop two times per week. It was a great gift, a beautiful shop with almost no clients where I could bring my computer and continue my astrology matters.

My life at that moment was better than many other times. I was enjoying summer and the beautiful beach in front of my apartment. I had a job, I was going to publish my book with the editorial Xlibris and I was becoming the millennial girl I always wanted to be. I was making videos on Youtube about lunar cycles, I was posting content on my blog and two

Instagram accounts, also I created a group called "The Age of Aquarius Lunar Group". Every new and full moon, a group of like-minded people would come together in a crystal shop called Sparrow and Fox where I would teach astrology, guide a meditation, and do a ritual together. My students loved it and so did I. Also I had met a girl in an extras job I got through Sass Management (a modeling agency I enrolled the year before), her name is Megan. We became best friends and had beautiful times together. So yeah I can say that the beginning of that year has been one of my best times. Complete, never bored, I felt a strong spiritual purpose and was passionate about everything I did.

Things didn't last long like that. At the beginning of April, two important things happened. Jared had a video assignment for his University (doing a master's degree) and decided to shoot it on his uncle's farm. Because we were going to have a crew, we needed a place to stay, and Tim the uncle proposed an abandoned house of his neighbor and friend. A weekend before the shooting we visited the place, and very quickly I felt a strong connection to it. I wanted to stay there but we needed to do a lot of cleaning, it had been inhabited for at least 5 years and was deteriorated, dirty and full of spider webs. On the weekend of 14 April 2018, we did the shooting there, and before that an intense cleaning. The house was incredible; it was built on mud-brick, it ran on solar systems and collected its own water from rain. It had two rooms, a kitchen, a living room, and a studio. The design was inspired by an eagle with extended wings, and it had windows everywhere. It was surrounded by green heals, underneath Doughboy mountain. A 200 acres property thirty minutes away from the closest town; Uki. I fell in love with the house like never before in my life, and I cried so much when we had to leave. As soon as we left, Jared and I thought of ways to come back for a longer period of time.

The same month another event happened which changed some things; I lost my job in the furniture shop due to the Commonwealth Games, that instead of uplifting the economy brought loss to many businesses. The shop wasn't doing very well and couldn't pay for my salary anymore. That took me down a lot, finally, I was happy to have a normal and stable life, I wanted that job to go for longer and give me a satiability that I hadn't felt before. I was upset with the Universe for having me in such a rollercoaster, where I could never be a little bit normal. At the same time the event combined with the strong infatuation for the mud-brick house, made us think about other possibilities. I was becoming tired of the Gold Coast and the conservative society, apart from Megan I didn't have friends, and maybe it was time for a move. It took us basically one afternoon and two phone calls to make the decision. First, we needed to see if we could have the Internet, and after browsing we realized that satellite was an option. So we called Tim, who then called his neighbor and got back to us. We could live there, no rent was needed (because of how deteriorated it was) but we had to work on the property to make it better. The owner had the place as an investment property, lived in Melbourne, and basically didn't care at all about it. And that's how an incredible opportunity opened for us; to go live in the middle of nowhere.

The main problem we had was to get rid of the lease contract with our apartment in Kirra. It was due for August but we didn't want to wait until then. It felt like a fight to the system; forms to fill, appointments with different people, and some lies about family getting sick in Mexico. I felt so much hate towards the Real Estate and wanted so hard to liberate myself from it, but until they had another person renting the place, we would still pay 380 dollars a week. I tried to be positive about it (like always) but we ended up paying until the end of the contract because rents during winter and after the Commonwealth Games' little recession, were low in demand. Nevertheless, our decision was made. Move to the mud-brick house as soon as possible, and two weeks later we were there.

At the same time that this was happening, I received the first printed copy of my book. It was one of the happiest moments of my life, such an incredible feeling to hold the baby project in my hands. Five years of work coming into fruition. I was also feeling really nervous about it, opening my whole world like that, ready for being judged by anyone who wanted to. A couple of weeks later the first copies arrived, and I gave some away. I needed to have some comments from my first readers. Another thing I want to confess with you all is that I truly believed that my five-year plan was going to manifest. In 2013 I wrote in a notebook where I wanted to be at 28. I visualized myself as a world leader, international best selling author, and in the 30 under 30 lists. For years I thought of myself as a "chosen one" and I had a strong sense of being someone who would change the world. I thought that year I was going to become that person. That writing all my wishes in new Moon was going to help in the process of manifestation. I would prove that magic works and pretty much conquer the world. My life had been an experiment on spirituality, and I wanted to show how it did wonders for my life and guide others to do the same.

    Now back to the events. One of my problems that I think others can relate, is thinking than moving somewhere else is going to solve our problems and we'll finally find happiness. With my experience, I can say it's true, but it takes time to adjust to a place and sometimes several moves. The mountain brought me joy but also gave me a lot of new times of loneliness. Jared was working all day and I had to figure out my life again. Some moments I adored being in the house, surrounded in green and infinity time to study astrology, write and do what I loved. Some other moments I was tired of that solitude. So one day I had a talk with one of my friends in Mexico and she asked me if I was going to my friend Xavier's wedding, I told her I was in Australia and it was almost impossible, but she insisted. Then I had a strong sense inside of me that I needed to go to Mexico. So I was forced to ask my father for sponsorship to make my way there, he agreed. I decided to leave for six weeks and escape Australian winter during June and July. Jared wasn't very happy about it, but I needed that break.

I was happy to be back in Mexico with friends and family, but I needed nature again so I decided to visit my friend Leticia in Puerto Escondido. She had recently moved there and was working in hostel Selina. I thought I would go there for 5 days, but I ended up staying almost for two weeks. I was having all the social times I didn't have for months, becoming friends with Leticia's co-workers and other travellers in Selina. It was so much fun, and of course, I didn't want to leave. On my last day the manager Fernanda offered me a place there, she loved all my astrological stuff and wanted me to teach workshops, classes, and moon rituals. It was heartbreaking to receive the invitation in that moment of my life, because I couldn't leave Jared in Australia and just decide not to go back. I had fallen in love with Mexico again, I missed the warmth of the people and my quality social times. But I had to do the right thing and go back to Australia.

Before leaving, in Mexico City, I had dinner with a friend from the University and CEO of an important digital platform called Cultura Colectiva. I gave him my book and had a really good talk. I also wanted to take that opportunity and offer collaboration with me. I knew they needed more original digital content, and all I wanted was to travel. So I could send them photos, articles, and video footage for their website in order to extend the audience. He was really interested and I was very happy to have formed that connection. Now I was going back to Australia, but with a new plan in mind: Mexico vol. 2.

Coming back was another trauma; of course, I didn't want to be in my reality again. And a few days later, on the longest lunar eclipse of the century in Aquarius (27 July) I had a major crisis. I had fallen deep into sadness, I couldn't find sense to my life anymore. My book was pretty much forgotten, I had only received two good comments about it and made very little sales. I was far from being that person I visualized five years from then, I was very unhappy about everything. I had an intense conversation with Jared and told him about my new plans. Mexico seemed like the right place to be, we had my money from the rent of the apartment, and two good opportunities on the horizon. We were now free from the Real Estate and could pursue our nomad digital dreams. It didn't take long to convince Jared, then we decided to go back in November.

I spent my last three months in Australia studying an Astrology degree, writing a lot, and doing digital content. I was loving the mountain in some ways, others were really hard. During winter the house was very cold, at night we wouldn't separate from the fireplace. All those windows gave no insulation and the temperature was the same as outside. Our bedroom at night was not higher than 8°C. I cursed the cold, making life really uncomfortable. The only thing I had was the idea of spring getting close, I only needed to survive August and then better weather would come. Some other moments I loved the place so much; beautiful birds and kangaroos were coming to visit, the kookaburras sang every sunset, we rescued an exotic bird trapped in the fence, I saw eagles, black cockatoos, I heard a dingo howl to the eclipsing moon and a koala roar. We also received several visits from a large reptile named goanna. I was living in wild Australia and I loved it. My soul that time felt really connected and in peace, nature wondered me and I could spend hours just contemplating it.

Another thing that made me upset, was all the housework I needed to do. I grew up my whole life with housemaids, so that's a work I never had to worry about. That time I was really tired of all the chores I needed to do. I thought of myself as an important person who had much more relevant things to do than cooking and cleaning. I was that rebellious feminist that wanted to focus entirely on her career and stay away from house duties. I was feeling a strong rejection of that part, but at the same time, I wasn't making any money so you can imagine poor Jared, cooking, and paying the bills.

Apart from my rejection of housework and struggle with cold, I was pretty focused on my Astrology degree and my digital activities. I knew it was a temporary thing, and that soon I would be back in Mexico. Again, always living in the future, thinking of the next place, which would cure all my problems.

With that, I enjoyed my last months in Australia, the beautiful spring weather, the beaches, my best friend Megan, and my last moon circles. It was the end of a cycle and the beginning of a new chapter in my love story with Jared: Mexico vol. 2.

We arrived in Mexico early November, and then we left on a holiday trip with my family to Egypt sponsored by my father. It was definitely a nice welcome to Jupiter in Sagittarius, but after that, we needed to focus on our next place to live. We decided to take my parent's Ford van and go on a road trip to Oaxaca. We wanted to scout different places and figure out some options. I wanted to be back in Puerto Escondido and see if that opportunity of teaching in Selina was still available, also to be in the city of Oaxaca that is one of my favorites in Mexico. The trip was very fun, but in the end, I couldn't see myself living in any of those places. In Selina, they had changed the manager and they didn't find much interest in my proposal. My friends were partying too much and I couldn't connect in the environment anymore. Also, that humid heat made life more complicated; it became hard to study, write, and concentrate. Because of that, we realized that being on the coast was not an option for us. The city of Oaxaca is full of culture and really beautiful. Being there we imagined our possible life, so we asked around about some rentals. In the end, I thought that the lack of nature was a big thing for me, I couldn't be in a concrete place anymore. We came back to Mexico City knowing that the south coast was not the place for us, so we decided to try Valle de Bravo. Two hours away from the city, it has been my second home. My grandparents have a house there, and I've been going since I was a baby. A little town in the woods, with a lake, green and beautiful. The plan was to spend New Year's with my family, then stay at my grandmother's house until we found our new home.

It was a crazy year, lots of travel and movements. Still on the verge of becoming something; trying hard to build a career as a digital entrepreneur, wanting to be able to work from my laptop anywhere (which I did, not really making money). At the same time it was hard being such a gypsy, with nowhere to call home, looking for something but at the same time running away from the system, from reality. I wanted so hard to make my dreams come true; to manifest that life I always wanted for myself, with lots of travel and doing what I loved. Somehow I made it true, but at the same time, it wasn't sustainable at all. Of course, we exceeded the budget of the trip and spent double of what we thought, realizing how expensive travelling is, and understanding that my monthly rental wouldn't be enough. My friend from Cultura Colectiva pretty much forgot all we talked about and he stopped answering me, so we didn't have a plan or opportunity to make it work. At that time I was just enjoying December in Mexico, with parties, my birthday, and family time. And when people asked me what I wanted to do with my life, I responded that I wanted a two-year trip to Ushuaia (the southern city in America, located in Argentina). My dream was the same; to travel and be paid for it.

Time to confront reality, assume adulthood and face Saturn return. A 2019 that changed all directions.

The year began in Valle de Bravo with family, then they left, and Jared and I stayed in the house. It was nice to be there, but again, so much time in isolation. We spent all day focusing on our activities, and I had a new project going on. I was invited to write weekly about astrology in a small digital magazine. So my time was spent writing, studying, walking my dog Cosmo in the afternoon, and being with Jared. We didn't have any friends there; we only had our companies, which became quite boring eventually. We couldn't stay in my grandmother's for too long, so we moved energies and began seeking for our perfect place. It didn't take long to find the right one, a beautiful two bedroom small house overlooking the lake. Then we organized the move, this time we needed pieces of furniture, kitchen appliances, and pretty much start again. I borrowed a lot of things from my grandmother and my mother. I didn't want to invest too much on it, as I preferred to keep a minimal life. Our goal was to be able to pack the van and move to the next place, and being those digital nomads we wanted, changing location regularly.

We signed a six months contract in the house, we would use that time to study, Jared on doing his masters, and keep building our careers. The fantasy didn't last for long, because when we finished furnishing the place and having it perfectly ready, I realized I was completely miserable. I had a day where I couldn't get out of bed; I was so depressed, bored, and tired of my situation. The house had a great view but there was nothing to do, we only went out to get food and then back to lockdown. We didn't see anyone except our faces, and we were getting tired of each other. We arrived on a road with no exit, there was nowhere else to go, I didn't have the next place that will cure all our problems. We were there, in that house, thinking we were free because we could focus on our things but feeling so trapped. The money I had from the rent was barely sufficient to survive, we couldn't travel, I didn't have another money income and neither had Jared. It was a really painful reality hit, we could see that after five years of pursuing the digital nomad dream we had nothing and we were far from it. My career as a writer was a failure and astrology wasn't paying my bills. We had been working for years, dreaming, using all possible tools in the spiritual realm to manifest that reality but we couldn't see it. We realized that Jared was 30 and I was about to have that age too, we couldn't continue like that. It was time to take life seriously and trace a different direction. It was really painful, but I decided to break up the relationship, and Jared agreed. Something about our combination wasn't working because life didn't seem to cooperate. Since the beginning, we were seeking that perfect job where we could express our full potential and be happy. Our relationship was always based on that futuristic idea, the utopia, an exotic couple travelling the world being really successful. I imagined my life with Jared childfree, as an international influencer and writer, an empowered woman leading the world. And that's one of the lessons that I want to share with you; expectations lead to disappointment. And what a huge disappointment mine was, being in Valle de Bravo, so far from where I thought I would be.

Friends and family were in total shock about my break-up. After five years of being together, it felt like my life partner for eternity. Valle had done its work, and I knew it was the right thing to do. It was so hard to accept it, but more than my relationship failure, it was my life failure that hit me the most. I wasn't able to manifest what I wanted. In a matter of weeks all my ideals, how I thought the world worked, all my spiritual philosophies, everything collapsed. I was alone, in Mexico again, with no plans, back to the beginning but being 29 years old.

We broke up the day after Valentine's Day, you could only imagine how romantic that day was, having no money in the account and unable to go out on a date. After that, we needed to undo the contract (again) and confront the consequences. The owner understood the reason, we told her we broke up and that we never thought that would happen. So I paid for an extra month and left my security deposit with her. Now we had to undo the house, sell some things, give all back to my mother and grandmother, and get Jared's flight to Australia. We didn't last one month in that house; I couldn't believe how ridiculous my life was becoming. For years I thought of myself as a leader, that I understood how the world truly worked, that the system was obsolete and I had many answers. That moment I was back to being an insignificant human, a spoiled girl unable to understand and accept reality.

We unpacked the house, went back to the city, and said goodbye in a lovely way. Jared and I were really grateful about our encounter, our journey together was a true adventure and we had done things we would've never done alone. We were partners in crime for five years, working together in everything. Our trips, the experiences, my opportunity to live in Australia, and for him to be in Mexico, learn Spanish, and know our culture. We had given each other so much, and for that, we were so grateful. We weren't sad about the break-up, because we could only celebrate what we had lived. It was an amazing ride, but we had to let each other go and conclude our cycle together. All my spiritual practices really helped with my break-up process. Quickly I erased photos from my phone, computer, and I stored material memories I had of him. I did lunar rituals to let go and release, saying thank you, I love you and sending light to everything. I knew I didn't want to attach myself to him, and people were really surprised by how I was dealing with my breakup. I just understood life as a cyclical thing and accepted with grace what had happened to me. Jared left on 20 March, it was really sad to say goodbye, but that was the last day I cried for my loss.

I was back in my parents' house, jobless but with new project ideas. In Valle, I had done an online course for Crystal Healing, and a few weeks back I went to a city named Jalapa to do a course on astrological talismans with my Spanish teacher Elias de Molins. I wanted to combine the realms of crystals, astrology, and magic to do talismans to attract what we wanted in life. One day my mother and I went to the center of the city to get our stones for us to build our astrological talismans, and that day an event, which would change my course, happened. My old friend Sebastian wrote to me on Instagram asking if I was in Valle de Bravo because he had a family gathering there for the weekend. I was happy to hear from him, but I would remain in the city because I had my friend Chloe's barbecue. That time I was turning my single radars on again, a fun surprise from the Universe that I never thought I would live again. I was already chatting with some guys, and going out a lot. So when Sebastian asked me out, I was pretty happy because I always liked him. Now the story about our friendship.

Sebastian and I met in 2009 when we were both 19 years old. I was in Valle de Bravo in my grandparents' house, when I saw some guys in the neighbor's house. I invited them to play volleyball and later decided to go to a party together. It was three guys and myself, drinking on the terrace and listening to some good music. Then we went to an electronic party in town, and I was behaving exactly how I did then; drunk, dancing like crazy and flirting with the cute guy I found there. That was Sebastian that night, my flirt and party hook-up. Our night concluded in the streets outside our neighbor houses, kissing and playing around. After that drunken night, Sebastian and I continued to talk through digital platforms, I really liked him as a friend and we started to hang out. I invited him often to my parents' house to play pool and then go to parties together. It was that time of my life where I loved going out and wanted no commitment with anybody. I didn't know it then, but Sebastian was always attracted to me, although he was too sweet for that period of my life and I gave him no chance.

One of the nights we went out together, I found a guy I used to like and pretty much abandoned Sebastian to spend the party kissing him. For what he told me now, he was really upset and for revenge he hooked up with a really good friend of mine. That girl was pretty crazy and trapped him easily, making Sebastian her boyfriend. Then I became Cupid for those two and was friends with the couple. And now let's talk a little bit about Sebastian's story.

He is a cute brunette guy two months younger than me. He comes from the same type of family, the rich society of Mexico City. He had a troubled childhood because he was terrible at school since young; he went to at least 6 different institutions to have his high school degree. Since 14 he started to rock-climb and wasn't interested in anything else, that explained his beautiful wide back I felt always attracted to. He was very rebellious and skipped school really often to go climbing, of course, he loved parties and that became a bond between the two. After high school, he was forced by his father to attend University and he chose a Psychology degree in Universidad Iberoamericana, so we used to see each other there too. That didn't last long, because Sebastian decided to abandon school, take his car and leave for the United States. My friend was really sad about his decision and the break-up, but she understood his need to leave. Sebastian lived in his car for several months like a gypsy and then started a course with NOLS to become a mountain guide. After that, he left for Canada and very soon found his paradise. He was based in Squamish and started to do all outdoor sports he wanted; climbing, biking, skiing, ice-climbing, and more. He started to paint houses and later began working in the medical marihuana industry. Since then his life has been stable and focused: work, earn money, and progress towards having the life he always wanted. To be in the mountains and able to do everything he loves.

Sebastian and I remained in contact and saw each other twice since he left for Canada. And for that reason, he wrote to me again that day I was working on my talismans. Then we continued to talk through Whatsapp and he invited me out. We had our first date on April first; we had dinner in a Japanese restaurant and then we went to a couple of bars. My objective was to get us drunk and flirt with him, I was happy to be single again and have some fun. Although, since the beginning, I had a strong attraction to him, and the day after our date, I told my mother I had a feeling that I was having dinner with my future husband and father of my kids. It was really intense; I couldn't believe how that was happening to me so fast. It had been 10 days since Jared left, I wanted to be single and have fun! That night with Sebastian was like old friends, he was still shy and didn't even try to kiss me. We had fun and we would see each other again before his departure to Canada.

Since that moment everything started with him and I fell in love straight away. At the same time, I was terrified because I knew he would take me out of all of my comfort zones. I wondered how a super sporty mountain guy would be with someone like me? A city girl that loves nature but doesn't exercise much with it. He invited me to Canada, he wanted to try us out and know fast without wasting time. He seemed like a woman with a biological clock ticking; on a phone conversation we had, he told me he didn't want to waist another couple of years with someone and then back to nothing. He was seeking a lifetime partner, and apparently, I was a good candidate for him. He didn't seem to care about my useless skills for the outdoor realm and proceeded to his invitation to be with him in the mountain.

I had chosen a very crazy guy to fall in love with and I knew it, but why not? As usual, I followed my intuition and enjoyed the ride. After two dates in April, Sebastian went back to Canada to continue his busy life. He too had broken a relationship in February and needed to move out from his old house and get the new place ready; where I would go in a couple of months. That time in Mexico City I was partying a lot, attending yoga with my mother, teaching astrology online, and continuing with my digital duties. At the same time, my father started to be pretty annoyed at me back in the house, doing very little so he assigned me some boring extra work he had. I believe it wasn't fun for him to see his daughter being 29, single, jobless, and back to his house. I didn't like it either, but that was my situation, I needed to figure out my life again. That time I took a holiday to Guatemala with my sister and organized my next move; India 2019. I had always dreamed to go there, and I knew it was the time to do it. Now I had my money from the rental and I didn't have to pay any expenses, so I bought my plane ticket to Rishikesh, the new Promised Land. Before that, I would do a stop in Paris and be with Victoria for her 30th birthday. So that's how I had my year traced; Canada in summer with an open ticket to see if my relationship worked, then Europe with my girlfriends, then a new adventure to India.

It was good to be separated from Sebastian those months and have some time to be with myself and heal. Psychically I was pretty destroyed and I was back in therapy. My whole world, ideas, and philosophies collapsed. Adding to that, I was now traumatized at Sebastian's intentions of having a family with me. I had for years been a feminist, defendant of a childfree life and I always saw myself as a busy woman with no time for home duties. That made me question everything, I was definitely doing something wrong. I saw myself as a big failure, and all my beliefs didn't make sense anymore. I was in my parents' house in Mexico City, I had no idea how to make money, and which direction to choose next. I stopped finding peace to study and write, so I kept myself busy with social plans because I didn't want to overthink. Times where I was alone I started to miss Sebastian like crazy and felt really bad. Also, a few days before leaving for Canada I got into a huge fight with my father and left the house; he told me he would cut my money from the rent, that I needed to stop behaving like a child. My life was a total mess, and I spent 10 days sleeping in different houses, homeless.

That period opened a huge phase where I questioned all spiritual theories that I blindly decided to follow. I realized I was that millennial girl unable to commit to anything, rebellious, stubborn, and pretty much useless for the material pragmatic world. I started to blame the authors I once I admired. Since the beginning I did what they told us; I followed my intuition, I made visualization boards and lists, I meditated, I sought my passion and tried to make it a career. Seven years since my 'spiritual awakening' and back in parents' house with nothing. That period of my life was a collapse, and for the first time ever, I decided I needed a break from my creative pursuits. My talismans project became an Instagram account with 50 followers and no clients, the magazine articles lasted for one month and then the owner kicked me for unexplained reasons. I realized I had tried at least 30 projects and nothing really worked, so I needed to stop. Therapy helped me gain a new state of my mind when my therapist made me question "should I go seek for my destiny, or should I wait for destiny to come to get me?". I was really tired of being in a constant warrior search, fighting for the next thing to happen. I was exhausted, so I decided to be in a more receptive state, and wait for destiny knocking on my door.

I kept teaching Astrology only because I was committed to it, four months one class a week until the end of August. Apart from that I slowly started to lose interest in my studies and digital platforms. As I said, I didn't have a peaceful set of mind to concentrate anymore. The talismans project was my last one, creating something new and seeing its failure would've been too painful, so I stopped. Then I left for Canada with my new sweetheart and started Mountain Living vol.3

(after one attempt in Australia 2013, then 2018). I didn't even tell my father about my new relationship; he was pretty traumatized after my break-up and was too soon to talk about a new lover. Then I left and my mother told him I was going with a friend and I would work with him in construction. Now I had no financial support from him, so I needed to find an opportunity over there.

    I arrived in Canada on 5 July; Sebastian picked me up from Vancouver and took me to his house, three hours north in a place called Darcy. Our closest town? Pemberton, half an hour away. It was a piece of land with a tiny home he recently bought, with no electricity and no water. It was a construction site. First impressions? I didn't like it much, a very small house over mud. After the beautiful mansion I used to live in Australia, it wasn't great. But because I was really in love with Sebastian, all problems just faded away. So instead of complaining, I enjoyed my adventure of pooping in the woods, showering in Sebastian's job, and doing dishes in the river. At the same time, I couldn't believe I was back in the middle of nowhere after I complained a lot about being in the mountain in Australia. The mission of my time there was to figure out if Sebastian and I were compatible, and if our relationship could become something serious for the future. That felt sometimes like a burden, I was pretty confused about my life and had no idea what I wanted anymore. But I let things flow and enjoyed the ride. In the end, I liked it, I got involved in the construction matters, went swimming to different lakes, made friends with some cool people around, and felt the peace that only nature can give me. Sebastian and I were really in love, passionate, and connected as we've never been in other relationships. Everything was flowing amazing but we still weren't sure about our combination for outdoor activities. Sebastian was a pro mountain person, and I was pretty bad at it. I didn't like long hikes, didn't rock-climb or biked, and camping wasn't my favorite. I wanted to know about his world but I was a beginner, and I knew he would get tired of it. Our first camping experience was good until I saw the size of his tent and was forced to sleep in a sleeping bag, I had a terrible night but I didn't hate the experience. I know he had a confrontation of reality, dreaming romantically about us, doing what he loved together, then being in front of a city girl complaining about the size of the tent. I know that night he wanted to send me back to Mexico. It was a fight, but we overcame it.

I felt a strong pressure to change and become something I didn't know I was capable to be. I was interested in doing those things but I was also terrified. By then my beloved arrived with a gift that put me in a state of shock; a brand new mountain bike. My skills on those wheels were limited to a couple of laps in the city, but he now pretended I would take that vehicle in the bush. My first attempt was a disaster, so we decided it was best for me to take some lessons. I had four of them, once a week. I was liking it but on my last class, I hurt my knee with a sprain. So after two months together, Sebastian and I knew we loved each other like crazy, but we still weren't sure about compatibility on those matters. We needed to live winter and that scared me the most. I hated the cold and that seemed like the worst nightmare, but we needed to find out.

I came back to Mexico at the end of August and got ready for my upcoming adventure. Fortunately, I had some savings and in Canada, I didn't spend anything because Sebastian took care of me. So with that money and what I received from a gold coin (Christmas gift from my grandmother), I threw myself to the world again. I arrived in Paris on 6 September to Victoria's house, Manoella was already there and the three of us would share her tiny apartment. We had a great time together, but I was more excited about my future encounter with Sebastian. He was in Lisbon working with an upcoming medical marihuana company and came to visit me in Paris. We had two nights of intense passion and love, honoring the city for what it's famous for. It was awful to say goodbye, we had been apart for two weeks and we wouldn't see each other until India. Since Canada, I had convinced Sebastian to come to India with me and have a cultural trip. Being a mountain climber, all his trips have always been about that, so he was hard to convince. In the end, he agreed, so I would be in India alone for a month, and he would join me later.

My time in Paris was all about girlfriends and my love for a couple of days. At the same time, everyone was asking me about India and my plans there, I told them I had no idea. They were really scared for me. As usual, I didn't care, trusted my intuition, I knew I had a calling there. One day before leaving, my friend Manuela sent me a link about a yoga teacher's training that would take place a couple of days after my arrival. It seemed like a good plan, but I didn't have enough money. I decided to let things flow, so I booked a place in Rishikesh (known to be the capital of yoga in India) for a couple of nights. I would figure out my destiny being there.

I arrived in India on 18 September, it was pretty much traumatizing. Since landing Delhi and figuring out my next plane to Dehradun was a drama, I needed to transfer airports and no one seemed to help. In the end, I decided to jump in a taxi with a man I felt a little bit comfortable with and paid a lot of money. I was feeling really insecure and all the guys stared at me. Then I arrived at Dehradun and took another cab to Rishikseh, this time shared with a Chinese man. The place I booked wasn't where the address had shown, and that took another hour to figure out, doing phone calls with different hotels. At the end a guy picked me up and took me to my place. I paid 30 euros per night, and it was awful. Horrible bed, a brown-stained carpet, and a tragic bathroom. My first hours I was hating it; everything looked horrible, dirty, noisy and men with penetrating eyes frightened me. If I imagined myself being in Rishikesh for a month hipping around like in Mexican places, it seemed impossible now. I had to find another location or do something; I couldn't remain like that for long. Then I decided to move energies around, and in a very magical way I ended up joining a yoga teachers' training that would start in two days. Another thing dangerous about India is that everyone told me it was really cheap, so I thought I could survive with little money. What I had was far from enough, and I had to ask Sebastian to pay for my yoga course. So another lesson here; don't dare to go to India on a low budget. The place is so challenging, that you need a good hotel to recharge and step away from chaos.

I only had one full day left before starting my course, and that was really enjoyable. I stopped feeling scared and walked around the town, which I found so interesting and colorful. Then, on Friday 20 September I joined other students and left to the Sattva Yoga Academy retreat center to start our 200 hours teachers' training program. I won't go further in detail because this year's section is already long, but I want to say that in general, it was a great experience. The school was beautiful, next to a clean river where we bathed; I made great friends and enjoyed the spiritual teachings of our guru Anand Mehrotra. Classes at times were challenging because days were filled with demanding activities, but the hardest was my separation with Sebastian. The love we felt for each other was so intense, we talked every day and cried on the phone. I missed him as I had never missed anyone. The separation was so painful we decided to move his flight and make him come sooner. Everyday I dreamed about the moment I was going to be back with him.

The course was a transformation place for everyone there, and it did an important shift within me. One day I woke up in a state of depression and decided to skip classes and lock myself in my room. I was crying for no apparent reason. I knew I had to start writing and the source of my problem would arise eventually. I spent at least fours writing non-stop, and the conclusion was something I wasn't expecting at all. What I now wanted for my life was everything I was rejected for years; to have a family, and live a housewife life in the mountains. It was so painful to accept and embrace that new reality because the persona I invented for myself was not that traditional woman raising kids. I think I was the only person in that course with a lesson like that. People were there to shift their lives and begin the spiritual path, others to have that paper and become teachers. For me, it felt like the end of my spiritual seeking. I was so tired of it, of my uncertainty, of moving around to all those locations and at the end feeling the same emptiness. I thought at the beginning of the course that having a prestigious yoga diploma from India is what I needed to be a legitimate guru. That I would be ready to be that spiritual master I always wanted to become. To be an astrologer, an influencer, to help people in the pursuit of happiness. Then I realized my path had been so hard and complicated, that I didn't want other people to attempt the same. I didn't want to teach at all. I was a student again; I didn't know anything any more.

Realizations in my yoga course were deep and transforming. At the same time, it helped me release the old Natalie and leave her behind. One day my best friend Mateus and I did a baptism ritual in the river, where we let go of the past and rebirthed in the Himalayan sacred land. That time I unlinked my blog from my Instagram account and started a new Facebook profile. All I wanted was to be a normal human being and to stop preaching things around. I said bye for now to astrology, to my upcoming failed projects and my book, which was a great source of my deception. I tried to be someone important and change the world, but it was time to change my world that was a complete mess.

The year so far was all about the collapse of my own structures, and that time was rock bottom. From that moment I released my old self and birthed new Natalie with Mateus on the river. Submerging myself into the chaotic void of a shapeless form; humble and receptive. Ready for another chapter in this never-ending school of life. I was so grateful to India, to my amazing friends who listened and helped me heal. A place which I thought would make me a teacher, but instead showed me how much I still needed to learn. So thank you Sattva for this gift, the place where my biggest death and re-birth process took place.

Sebastian arrived in Rishikesh on 15 October. We were living our passionate relationship just like in movies. Giving so much love to each other, crying in ecstasy as the only channel where that intense energy could flow. We had suffered so much in the separation, but we knew we wouldn't let each other go anymore. Our time together was magical on the love side but intense on the India side. Travelling in that country is challenging but we survived, enriching ourselves with its incredible culture, temples, and historical sites. That trip contributed to the release of my intense needs for travelling. I was so tired of living in my suitcase, eating horrible unhealthy food and moving around constantly. I started to feel sorry for people that needed to travel a lot, an excruciating task that got me fed up. I was ready to plant my roots and felt excited to do it with Sebastian in the wilderness.

At the beginning of November, we went back to Canada, then to Los Cabos for a week, where we introduced his parents to my family. It was a lovely family trip, where my father could see some hope for my future having a good boyfriend like Sebastian. Then we returned to Canada and began the next challenge; winter. Temperatures started to drop and Whistler Mountain opened with some man-made snow. It was the beginning of ski season and my goal was to learn the sport. My first time with Sebastian was an absolute disaster, so I had to take some lessons. I was so terrified, but I wanted to push through. I spent two weeks going to ski regularly but progressing really slow, green runs were extremely challenging and I hated how bad I was at it.

After my hard skiing experiences, I returned to Mexico City for holidays. I wanted to see the family, celebrate my 30th birthday and go to Valle de Bravo for New Years'. And that's how the craziest year of my life ended; breaking up a relationship and starting a new one, visiting 4 different counties, and killing my old self who wanted so bad to be a digital nomad and spiritual guru.

Reshaping Natalie in the mountains. A 2020 of global lockdown and change of paradigm.

My year started in Mexico City and really tired of the city life. I had booked my flight until 15 January and I was again missing Sebastian like crazy, we hadn't seen each other since he left the city on 20 December and it was becoming long. It had now been three years since I formally lived in the Mexican capital and I was disconnecting every time more. I lost track of so many people, and my social plans became scarce. I felt depressed being in my parents' house. Now I didn't have any digital things to do as I released everything the year before. I wasn't interested neither in astrology nor creating content for my platforms. I also felt the crisis of being 30; with no money in my bank account, jobless, and what I thought my passion and career was, didn't make much sense anymore. I felt hopeless, I only wanted to leave and start over.

My year in Canada began with one objective in mind: learning how to ski. It has been an incredibly difficult ride, testing me both mentally and physically. So challenging that it took me 20 ski days to learn how to do my turns properly. The mountain confronted me every time, but I was willing to overcome it. I wanted to feel that freedom of being able to take different trails and enjoy the sport. My year hasn't been very spiritual, as I wanted. I stopped meditating and following astrology. I wanted to concentrate on my house duties, help Sebastian on construction work, and learn skiing. It was time to focus on the material, physical plane that I was so long-running away from. I knew I needed to have a better balance between everyday reality and my spiritual, creative side. So I decided to forget that part of myself (which I felt deceived by) and remain as busy as possible. With darkness arriving at 4 in the afternoon, I had my lover with me for a longer time. He would go to work, some days I would help him, other ones I would go to Whistler, enjoying a normal life trying to be a normal person.

The results of the first time in years of disconnecting myself to the spiritual realm? I was so happy. Including a sport plus some asanas at home, made me feel incredible. I was returning home being tired, so I could now enjoy my time there. Opposed to my life in Australia, where I didn't have a space to exercise and release that energy. This time, I've only had one project to do which was important; finish writing my book and publish it for the third time. In reality, I was working little on it and enjoying my life a lot. I began liking the cold; the snow and its beautiful white landscapes, skiing and snowmobiling, our nights in the Jacuzzi looking at the stars, and a warm house perfectly insulated. With that, I could overcome the fear I had for winter, something really important in my relationship.

Sebastian, unlike me, is a person that has focused on navigating the system and making the most of it. Now he has beautiful land with a tiny home, and multiple toys to enjoy around. We have a Jacuzzi, a sauna, two motorcycles, two mountain bikes, and two snowmobiles. Also a variety of skis and equipment for different occasions. Adding to this, he is building an all-terrain Toyota campervan, which we would use to travel around. My challenge in this is to learn the art of mountain living and become a sporty woman. So far, it has been difficult but I'm progressing towards it, and Sebastian is starting to have more fun with me. We had been more than five times out with the snowmobiles, and I've learned powder skiing. After doubting for months about our compatibility in that realm, we could see that I love the activities and I'm getting better each time.

As you all know, this year has been an incredible challenge for the world, because the coronavirus pandemic has hit hard. For every person it's been different, and here is what it did to me. On 12 March I had my last day skiing, which was an amazing progress and I'm now able to do blue runs. Three days later they closed Whistler Mountain and I was pretty upset. I had a day where I was crying rejecting the change; I didn't want to be locked in the house again. Going to Whistler was an amazing distraction and activity for me. I didn't want to be with myself again, in solitude and reflection mode. For years my life had been a quarantine without the label, and I didn't want to repeat it again. For the first time, I was having a practical life and I loved it; being busy, not overthinking, keeping it simple. Apart from that, Sebastian and I had to leave for Portugal on 20 April for a couple of months, but it became impossible.

For me the confrontation has been about forcing me to stay in one place, to establish myself in the mountain, to stop fleeing to the next location. Spring is now with us and I'm so in love with it. While everyone is experiencing a challenging lockdown in different cities in the world, we have nature as our backyard. We can still take the snowmobiles and go skiing, take the mountain bikes or the motorcycles and go for a spin. I can go hiking or to the lake, and write for hours in my deck overlooking the mountains. More than ever I feel an immense gratitude to be in this place, far away from the craziness, in a place where they can't take away our freedom. This time has given me the opportunity to reconcile with my spiritual path because all those teachings and the journey I took, made it possible for me to be here right now. I have the most beautiful life, with my love and endless activities to do. Social distancing hasn't hit much because this place is really spacious. Now I'll be learning about gardening and growing my first vegetables. I feel connected to the land; also I have included sports, which makes me feel amazing. I love where I am and I wouldn't imagine myself elsewhere. I have seen the world, I've travelled so much, but this place is my favorite. I'm living a countryside life, slow, calm, in a beautiful house that I love. For the first time since I started this journey, I feel like I want to stay.

So the question now is, have I freed my soul? The purpose since the beginning of this book. First of all, I want to say, that I believe there are many ways to define freedom, and each one of us has to find their own. Some can do it in sports, others through creative expressions, travelling, or many more. But what it's important to understand is that a pursuit of freedom as an escapism from reality can be counterproductive. What I ran away from was a life of work. I thought if I found a passion I wouldn't have to work anymore, it would naturally flow and I would easily make money. I have now understood that living is constant work; cooking, cleaning, organizing, and especially having your own business. It was hard for me to see this, and that caused a lot of pain. I thought that being a free soul, was to be able to travel around with little responsibilities. Those Instagram influencers, just like many other millennials, became our role models. We wanted to become someone, achieve fame, and enjoy a luxurious life where money would never be an impediment. I had an inflated ego, I thought I was important and I had a mission in the world. Then life hit me with tough lessons, making me destroy my ideological structures, and release the wanna be influencer Natalie in the Himalayan river. So Canada this year has been about being a normal woman, focusing on a normal life. I shifted from being a public figure to a private one and it's the best thing I've done.

So am I a free soul? I don't want to label myself so I'll leave it to you to decide. My state right now feels very similar to what I lived at the end of my spiritual journey to Australia, but this time I am more stable, with a beautiful house and a committed relationship. I do what I love every day, I have found joy in house duties and the little things. I feel healthy and strong in my body, I am in love with nature and looking forward to developing my garden and grow vegetables. Even though I miss my family, I'm eternally happy to be away from Mexico City that always caused me stress and discomfort. So I'm incredibly grateful to the Universe for taking me in this direction because, after almost 8 years since the beginning of all this, I feel found. I'm in peace with myself, solid, with a house, and plans to build a dream life with Sebastian. So thank you Universe for all these challenges and lessons, it has been an amazing ride.

Reflections about spirituality, would I recommend it?

The New Age movement is a multi-billionaire industry that includes philosophies and practices, to help humans have a better life. Its authors seem to have discovered the universal truths and are here to guide us in our journeys. Since I'm 17 years old, I started with "The Secret", quantum physics and later got involved with all mystical knowledge I could find. I decided to believe blindly in those books and use my life as an experiment. I thought I would be able to manifest everything I wanted, and this book would be a living proof of it. With almost 8 years of experimenting with it, I can say that much of it doesn't work, and we need to be very careful with what they're selling to us. So many charlatans out there, financed by people hungry for guidance and answers to their problems.

Now I would like to break down a couple of concepts I used for my journey all these years.

Enlightenment

This path since the beginning made me pursue one goal. I wanted so hard to be a free soul, always aspiring that perfect state, but that made me not fully appreciate my present moment. Something really dangerous in spirituality; achieving enlightenment, right? Not being good enough, not being spiritual enough, always needing more. If spirituality is about finding happiness, the first concept we would have to eradicate is this one. Because its pursuit is a painful ride. I believe enlightenment can be felt momentarily but not as a permanent state because the cyclical nature of life will always take us in death and rebirth journeys. Something intense that opens our Pandora boxes and releases inner demons. Revealing another problem in the spiritual field; they say we should always be light, be love, and think positively. Yeah well, what about all that intense work we need to do with our darkness in order to transmute it into the light?

Intuition

If you are ready for a life of chaos and financial instability, follow your intuition. After so many years of blindly following those gut feelings, I can see I made some stupid decisions. The spiritual realm and the economic system have never been friends (ask India, the country where all this predominates). So unless your plan is to end up in a monastery having prana for breakfast, lunch, and dinner, I suggest following a rational mind with a good financial plan, something I never did.

Find your passion and you'll never have to work another day in your life

The biggest lie of them all, and the main one I decided to pursue. My unstable life never told me how to have a routine and long working hours, so when I found a passion (astrology) and saw the amount of work it became, I started to hate it. It doesn't matter what we decide to do, we can't escape the responsibility and hard work it'll need in order to become something functional. This is something millennials struggle with, and those ideas are really dangerous. Work will always be tedious and annoying, let's accept it.

Manifestation

In the spiritual field, they make us believe we are true creators of our lives and destinies, and we can manifest everything we want. We can use some tools like visualization, rituals, lists, vision boards, amulets, talismans and other objects around. Then magic would take care of the rest and what we want will appear. This is not a universal law and we need to be very careful with it. With my experience these 7 years, as you can see, I never got what I wanted (being a digital nomad and creative entrepreneur). Instead, the Universe gave what I never wanted for my life; to be a housewife. So does it work? It depends a lot on the ambition of what we are trying to manifest. And much of it won't depend on us, but life itself and the lessons we'll need to learn.

Unattachment

This concept helps a lot when we are unable to accept change in a situation. We understand the cyclical nature of things, and we let go of people, things, or events that cause us harm. A problem with it is when we are focusing on living in the sublime state of the being, and we decide to be unattached from the material life. Too much spirituality can be escapism, so we always need to find a balance between both realms. A great danger is to find ourselves in an unstable financial reality, which is really dramatic.

Freedom

The toughest concept for me, because since the beginning I always wanted to liberate myself from something. Now I realize it's only an illusion because life has endless responsibilities that keep us tied one way or another. True freedom will be achieved the day we die, otherwise, we should conform ourselves with momentary sensations of freedom and go back to our demanding lives. Everything that makes us feel free, such as travels, sports, creative expression, or any other, require money somehow, and that needs work. We can't escape from it. Eight years for me to understand this, wow.

Self-love

Definitely the best tool and teaching in the spiritual realm. With self-love, we stop aiming for concepts or ideas, which is a state that doesn't want anything or anyone. It's the purest philosophy and we can't go wrong with it. If I did something right in this journey, it was to focus on loving myself and having a life I loved. And I did that well. So the spiritual path we should embrace is the one of love. Where we stop asking things to the Universe and accept what we already have. Maybe my book should be *Travel to Love the Soul,* where I had a journey of resolving my inner dramas and find a state of peace, where I don't have anything more to achieve. A state where I only need to enjoy and appreciate life in all its aspects.

Conclusions

In my humble opinion, I want to say, that spirituality should be used as a complementary tool in our lives. To assist us in the excruciating task of working with our fragile, hurt, and traumatized selves. To believe blindly in the New Age philosophies is dangerous, so we need to proceed with precaution. Freedom can never be achieved with a precarious financial situation, so our lives should be oriented as well, in resolving our fundamental needs at the same time we develop in other areas we want.

So be wise and choose a life of love over a lifetime of achievement.
Be here, and enjoy the ride.

With love and light,
Natalie

Gallery

September 2010; some activities for my NGO Mexiro. Reforestation and recycling event.

Australia 2013. Photo on 35mm by Jared O'Sullivan.

Working on the first edition of the book. Australia 2014, photo by Jared O'Sullivan.

My vintage shop in 2014/2015 and my travels around Mexico modelling the clothes.

The three months of a gypsy road trip to northern California, more awesome photos on the @traveltofreethesoul Instagram, taken by Jared O'Sullivan.

Australia 2017.

My moon group in Australia from February to November 2018.

My astrology diploma completed in the mud brick house where I lived in 2018.

See more of the incredible photos I used to make with Jared O'Sullivan on my website www.natalieollivier.com

Incorporating outdoor sports into my life. Canada 2019.

Encounter in Paris with Sebastian, September 2019.

Graduation day for the 200 hours yoga teacher's training in Sattva Yoga Academy, Rishikesh India, October 2019.

My current home in Canadian wilderness, 2020.

Acknowledgements

The first acknowledgment goes to my father Felipe Ollivier. Again, I am so grateful for everything he gave to me, and his unconditional love and support. He has become the most incredible man, and I am so proud of him. The second person I want to acknowledge is my mother Carmen Cuétara, who has always been the best person to talk to, and she has always supported me and my sister to think differently and pursue the career we wanted. The third person is my partner Sebastian de la Rosa. I'm eternally grateful to him and all the outdoor activities he has shown me. Living in the mountains has been incredible, and I look forward to our new adventures together and that dream life we want to create. The fourth person is my sister Mariel Ollivier, she was the person that was tough on me, saying the cold hatred truths that no one else could tell me. She played a very important role in shaping the person that I am now. She is also my best friend, and the times we spend together are incredible and so much fun.

This book wouldn't be possible with the help of my teachers Carlos Sirvent and Héctor Hernández García de Leon; their opinions when they read it were really important. Also, my first editor María Luisa Álos, with whom I restructured my book into a better form. I also want to thank my teacher Mariano Gutiérrez, who told me at the end of our semester: 'Never doubt your ability to write'—something that marked my life forever.

In my family, I want to acknowledge my grandmothers Simone Ollivier and Carmen Canale, and my grandfather Jean Ollivier; they all took such good care of me, and I'm so grateful to have them in my life. My uncles and cousins played a really important role in my development, and I will always be grateful for those beautiful family moments we spent together. Someone that I consider a very important part of my life, almost like family, is my nanny Gela, a playful young woman that made my childhood a dream.

I also want to thank my incredible friends; Manoella, Chloé, Victoria, Manuela, Leticia, Andrea, Lily, Hayley, Megan, Valentina, Lucía, Nicky, Chori, Mauri, Jorge, Megan, and Santiago. You have a very important place in my heart, and you will always have. I also want to thank all the beautiful people that have crossed my path because they all mean something to me.

In general, I'm so grateful for my life and everyone that has made all this possible. Thank you to everyone.

Namaste.